The Maltese Falcon to *Body of Lies*

RECENCIES

Recencies Series: Research and Recovery in Twentieth-Century
   American Poetics
Matthew Hofer, Series Editor

This series stands at the intersection of critical investigation, historical docu-
mentation, and the preservation of cultural heritage. The series exists to illu-
minate the innovative poetics achievements of the recent past that remain
relevant to the present. In addition to publishing monographs and edited vol-
umes, it is also a venue for previously unpublished manuscripts, expanded
reprints, and collections of major essays, letters, and interviews.

ALSO AVAILABLE IN THE RECENCIES SERIES:

How Long Is the Present: Selected Talk Poems of David Antin edited by Stephen
   Fredman
Loose Cannons: Selected Prose by Christopher Middleton
Amiri Baraka and Edward Dorn: The Collected Letters edited by Claudia-
   Moreno Pisano
The Shoshoneans: The People of the Basin-Plateau, Expanded Edition by
   Edward Dorn and Leroy Lucas

The Maltese Falcon
to *Body of Lies*

Spies, Noirs, and Trust

ROBERT VON HALLBERG

University of New Mexico Press   Albuquerque

Library of Congress Cataloging-in-Publication Data

von Hallberg, Robert, 1946–
  The Maltese Falcon to Body of Lies : spies, noirs, and trust /
  Robert von Hallberg.
      pages cm — (Recencies Series: Research and Recovery in
      Twentieth-Century American Poetics)
  Includes bibliographical references and index.
  ISBN 978-0-8263-5136-4 (pbk. : alk. paper) —
  ISBN 978-0-8263-5162-3 (electronic)
  1. Film noir—United States—History and criticism.
  2. Spy films—United States—History and criticism. I. Title.
  PN1995.9.F54V66 2015
  791.43'655—dc23
                                    2015006092

Cover illustrations: (top) The Third Man (1949);
(bottom) The Night of the Hunter (1955)
Designed by Felicia Cedillos
Composed in Trump Mediaeval LT Std
Display fonts are Rockwell Std and Grotesque MT Std

For Isaac Burgess von Hallberg

Take with you someone you can trust.
—*ODD MAN OUT* (1947)

You know, I don't think you can trust anybody.
—*OUT OF THE PAST* (1947)

Lie not one to another.
—COLOSSIANS 3:9

CONTENTS

ACKNOWLEDGMENTS

I am a newcomer to film criticism; my intellectual debts feel fresh and bright. I had not even thought to write about film until my former wife, Danielle Allen, pointed out that the films I keep watching are all about trust. The conversations I have had with colleagues at the University of Chicago and at Claremont McKenna College have given me a great deal. At Chicago I discussed nearly all the films that now appear in part one of this text with Kelly Austin and benefited deeply from her acumen. Robert B. Pippin and Jim Conant were also generous in talk about particular films. However, Pippin's lectures on Westerns (later published as *Hollywood Westerns and American Myth*) really awakened me to the resources of thematic film analysis. At CMC Jennifer Taw spoke with me about agents on the ground, and this was especially instructive concerning *Body of Lies*. John Farrell read a draft of this book and showed me the cost of my terseness. Robert Faggin repeatedly made possible collaboration at the Gould Center for the Humanities, and two enabling deans at CMC, Greg Hess and Nick Warner, have also generously supported my research. Oliver Conrad in the information technology office at CMC helped me to get the scene-captures in shape for readers. I thank Cal Bedient (of UCLA) for his interest in this project; some pages from part one, I'm happy to say, were published in his journal, *Lana Turner*. Marjorie Perloff and Ken Fields (of Stanford), like Cal Bedient, are constant conversation partners—and teachers. They too helped me find a way into film criticism.

Grauman's Chinese Theatre

INTRODUCTION

The architecture of old movie palaces like Grauman's Chinese promises audiences something remarkable, but not convincingly there. Ah, yes, escapism, one says. Yet many mainstream films are fables, more didactic than dreamy. Whatever else goes on in movie palaces, certain genres—such as noirs and spy films—are more or less committed to social instruction. One says that, when the lights go out, viewers enter their own distinctive imaginations, and that surely happens. But notice that theaters are built for crowds: the Chinese happens to have 1,492 seats. The film industry has long had the means to address the nation collectively. George Tenet's director of public affairs at the CIA observed that "the vast majority of the American public forms its impression of the intelligence community from TV and movies."[1] In 1996, one year before Tenet took over, the agency appointed its first entertainment liaison officer in order to promote positive representations of the agency. Even in a democratic republic, the state has an interest in the representation of its activities.

Viewers engage images, stories, and claims about civic and personal matters, and they do so together, in the dark but in public. Film directors recognize the didactic potential of the medium, and some conceive their work in terms of political policy or even theory. For instance, in 1976 Sydney Pollack, who directed *Three Days of the Condor* (1975), said, "I tried to deal . . . with trust and suspicion, paranoia, which I think is happening in this country, when every institution I grew up believing was sacrosanct is now beginning to crumble. It's destroying . . . a certain kind of trust that is essential to have in a working society. . . . I don't think we should abolish the CIA. What we have to do is find some way of making a check and balance [sic] system work that, conceivably, hasn't been working before. The CIA has grown autonomous in a way that's horrific."[2] New films are discussed among friends who, within a few weeks, get to more or less those theater seats too. Some films are engaged in intellectual projects, practical, timely ones that concern many people. If not immediately, then in time, the visions asserted by these films emerge into the light of public awareness. Sydney Pollack spoke of corrupt institutions, lost trust, and getting on with the work of the republic. His film made a difference in 1975, but his constellation of issues had come together nearly four decades earlier in *The Maltese Falcon* (1941) and the noirs that followed in a remarkable period of film production that ended in the mid-1950s.

The term *film noir* is especially indefinite, even by comparison to literary critical terms.[3] William Park's recent *What Is Film Noir?* is devoted entirely to definition. Scholars want stable terminology, but this term has to fit hundreds of films already produced and an indefinite number yet to be made under the influence of those predecessors. "The most compelling proof that film noir is a bona fide genre," Park argues, "is its reemergence in the 1970s in what the critics have dubbed 'neo-noir.'"[4] Filmmakers continue to develop the resources of the genre despite concern among critics about the viability of the term. Some critics refer to noir in terms of its conspicuous stylistic features: high-contrast lighting juxtaposed with chiaroscuro, key lighting, depth of focus, low and oblique camera angles. Other critics stress its narrative features: elaborate, obscure plots, most obviously. One should remember that, as Park says, "No group of films, not even a single film encompasses *all* the characteristics of film noir."[5] The first film noir, *The Maltese Falcon*, for instance, shows few of these stylistic features. Park says more particularly that "noir consists of a fallible protagonist, a crime, an investigation, and a contemporary setting."[6] The protagonist he has in mind "has taken a false step, attempted a cover up, become an accomplice, or in some way fallen into crime."[7] The themes this sort of narrative engages are temptation, duplicity, betrayal. "The dominant world view expressed in film noir," according to Janey Place, "is paranoid, claustrophobic, hopeless, doomed, predetermined by the past, without clear moral or personal identity."[8]

My argument is that many noirs approach this darkness with an ethical value, and that they explicitly name this value *trust*. Characters repeatedly implore one another, "Trust me!" This trust is rarely realized in its fullest form, but it is often a horizon of hope; these films are not desperate works of art. In setting up his analysis of fatalism in film noir, Robert B. Pippin distinguishes between "what we actually think about some issue, collectively and at a time, and what we think we think."[9] The noirs, as Pippin proposes, are correctives to collective thinking; by engaging viewers in exception-taking narratives they show that audiences actually see the point of complications, qualifications, and negations of what we think we think. This is an aesthetic with a distinguished recent history. T. S. Eliot quoted Mallarmé in speaking of poets as purifying the dialect of the tribe, and Ezra Pound developed the idea by noting that without clear terms one cannot legislate or litigate justly. (One may object to Pound's account on the ground that modernist poems do not circulate sufficiently widely to influence the language as he imagines, but that objection cannot hold in the case of popular films.) Some art—in particular that of the noirs—corrects what is commonly termed *agency*, Pippin's concern, or trust, my own. In order for this art to succeed, audiences need to understand just what is under examination: its subjects must be named. This is why so many characters in the films I analyze explicitly seek the trust of others. The art of the noirs and the spies engages directly with familiar, not exotic concepts. Some artists seek to provide terms for experiences or subjects that elude familiar concepts. Paul Celan, for instance, constellates words so that they may stand in place of particular concepts: these words and only these in this arrangement configure his subject; a poem may be the only suitable name of its subject. But the films discussed in this book engage recognizable subjects with familiar names, though the films seek to clarify what is actually thinkable, by popular audiences, as trust.

A large number of films are gathered in the following pages in order to set out what audiences may generally understand about the representations of trust and commitment that noirs and spies propose. I analyze scenes of many different films in order to render visible this general account of trust. A critic with different aims attends more closely to the "density of stimulus," as Stanley Cavell puts it, in a small number of films, revealing their exceptionality or focusing less on their narrative and more on their formal and aesthetic features.[10] My claim is that the noirs develop a subtle and coherent account of deep trust between two individuals. Most of part one is devoted to an explication of just this. One would like to be able to cite the speeches of characters about trust. Sam Spade has a memorable one at the end of *The Maltese Falcon*. But sustained speeches are rare, exactly because the noirs observe a code of male taciturnity. I have constructed a synthetic account of trust largely by interpreting the films as parables of cooperation. The account of deep trust that interests me is a collaborative effort, not just in the sense that filmmaking is always a collaborative effort, but in the sense that many films contribute to this account. This claim about a collective discourse concerning trust has the surprising consequence that the significance of some apparently modest films—*The Narrow Margin* (1952), for instance, or (a much lesser film) *Where Danger Lives* (1950)—is enhanced when one recognizes that they were understood originally as responses to intellectual issues already in play. The spy films I discuss in part two are unlike the noirs in that they are obviously topical: the United States has sharply escalated its covert operations since 2001. Presidents Bush and Obama have overseen particularly punitive and deadly operations abroad. Several of these films, the noirs and the spies, are more meaningful in relation to the collaborative thematic I describe than they are in isolation.

I long ago spent many hours in theaters that I should have spent in school (I was a dropout). I like to think of theatres as a little like lecture halls: one interrupts ordinary activities in order to think about something there, and to do it with other people. One leaves one theater reminded of something heard in another, but carrying something away that will affect how one understands another film in another theater next week. As one passes from one theater or hall to another, one's judgment is not exactly formed but it is directed along some paths more than others, and these paths tend to cross over or coincide with one another. I stress the ways in which films collaborate with one another to present patterns of understanding that constitute a network of significance. Although noirs cohere thematically, my notion is not that directors sought to speak with one another about trust and commitment, but rather that diverse filmic conventions led to an intellectual coherence that audiences sense as they pass from one screening to another.

About trust and commitment, filmmakers and philosophers can speak to one another, and filmmakers more than hold their own in the dialogue. Philosophers conceive of trust as a consequence of rational inference and a means to a definite objective. The noirs propose an analysis of trust that can be reduced to two claims: first, that deep trust is neither rational nor definite in its objectives; second, that it is constructed by two electing and consenting agents. From these ideas much follows, but this is the heart of the analysis in part one. The filmic analysis rests, I admit, as much on instances of failed as on successful trust relationships. Nonetheless the films present durable ideals and fine-grained analysis of practical difficulties. One does not expect more. As a literary critic, I am accustomed to paraphrasing a text concerning a particular topic like trust. Because I am convinced that the noirs present an elaborate but coherent and in some ways attractive set of judgments, I reconstruct, in chapters two through five, the trust constraints of the noir regime by pushing the films' implications toward explicit general propositions. Professional interpreters prefer to engage meaning through constant mediation of a text, whose significance is understood to derive from a particular place and time. Most of my statements about trust are illustrated or supported by particular passages in the films under discussion, but that is not the only reason to talk about trust. In truth, this book is as much about commitment as about noirs and spies.

Has trust gone the way of fedoras? No. The noirs successfully bequeathed this theme to later filmmakers in other genres. Many recent films continue to explore the construction of trust between two individuals. Noir inquirers seek to build trust relationships when people and circumstances around them warrant suspicion. They work against the grain of daily experience. Trust is exceptional, in no sense normal. Where they succeed, the powers of imagination and perseverance are proved. Where they fail, ordinary life is to blame. Inquirers know to expect little assistance from social institutions and civic agents. When now and then a benign servant of the state offers help—a Bernie Ohls, say, in *The Big Sleep* (1946)—the resistant character of individuals is demonstrated. Particular people surprise one—a hopeful sign—even if large communities are not to be turned around. In the first film discussed, *Kiss Me Deadly* (1955), the last of the true noirs, individual trust and initiative are subordinated to trust in the state.

That was the crucial historical development of the theme: the state has come to overshadow individual relationships. In part two I shift to a set of films that begin by setting aside the construction of such trust between two people in order to give one's all to state service. Think of the enormous success of the Bourne films (2002–2007), but of many others too in which individual characters struggle with their need to trust a state that is said to "know better" than individuals. Also spies are masters of misperception who earn a living by exploiting the trust of others. A half century after the noirs, the thematics of trust have been radically altered. Talk of trust is common now in a wide range of films, but trust itself, aside from talk, is central to spy films: the issue is no longer how one may construct trust, but rather how mistrust pervades state activity and thinking about the state. The construction of trust between two people is merely vestigial in contemporary spy films. What if, instead of thinking about the regrettable obstacles to the construction of trust between people who know one another well, one were to make oneself trust a representation of the interests of a large number of strangers? CIA agents do not expect to build trust relationships. Their trust in the state is instead chosen and avowed, not constructed. One signs on to state service, as to a contract. "You said you wanted to save American lives," Dr. Hirsch repeatedly reminds Jason. This abstract, innocuous claim was David Webb's way of honorably retreating from his own personhood in a manner that looked like an advance: he became Jason Bourne, or one who acts decisively, effectively, and of course impersonally. A quest for public trust—trust in the state in particular—mutilates the spirit.

Why compare 1940s mysteries with thrillers of the new century? The thrillers do not match the artistic achievement of noir. They are thesis films that, when they excel, engage topical issues with some intellectual independence, as the underrated *Traitor* (2008) does. They show that there is an economy of trust in American society: when the desire to trust one's intimates meets with systematic frustration, as in the noirs, that desire does not simply go away to sulk. It resurfaces in another form. A half century after noir lost its great vitality, that desire is replaced by a willed resolve to trust impersonally, to lay aside the issues that provoked failures of personal trust in order to participate effectively in the political life of a nation under threat. Through the 1940s, well into the 1950s, and again in the last decade, successful films have been made from an engagement with trust and commitment. Success matters: audiences continue to take interest in noir configurations of trust and in the problems of commitment examined by spy films. This is to say that these particular structures of thought and feeling have been drawn into public discourse. The contrast of the noirs and the spies says something about the imaginative terrain crossed in the last half century, as filmmakers know.

In 1965 Martin Ritt and Oswald Morris, his director of photography, shot *The Spy Who Came in from the Cold* as a retro noir in black and white. They wanted audiences to see the bond between these genres. Both sets of films reveal ways that audiences wish to think about trust and commitment. Noir inquirers and spies too display the effects of crafty interaction with others. They all seek to move adroitly through perilous circumstances in order to disarm or elude wicked adversaries, though they have different techniques for achieving these ends. Noir inquirers think their way through the minefields of others' needs and desires. Spies do more punching. All the thrusts, parries, and car crashes render obvious now what has been lost in moving from noirs to spies. These later films suggest that noir was a resource of a now-lost moment. Public esteem for effective agency has endured, but esteem for independent practical judgment has been eroded. Spies generally consent to be instruments of others' judgment. They are willing, as noir protagonists are not, to be used. Spy films ask how long special agents can sustain indifference to the ends to which their labors are put. Filmmakers have had the courage to reject consequentialism as a final means of justifying dubious service to the state; by so doing, they have dissented from the dominant views of contemporary political philosophers. The noirs and the spies propose ideals of behavior, concepts of motivation that bear on the thinking lives of general audiences.

My first job was at the Chinese. I was hired as an usher at minimum wage, then promoted to doorman, also at minimum wage (in 1961: $1.25 hourly). The expression was that one "worked the door." I had the day shift. Weekday afternoons hardly anyone goes to the movies. My work was killing time. I stood for hours, and occasionally tore a ticket in two, maybe forty of those on a weekday. The Chinese is a tourist attraction kept open during the day for the sake of appearance. This seemed reasonable, because all the enterprises on Hollywood Boulevard were there for the sake of appearances. A tour guide, Larry, about fifty, constantly smoking, hawked motor tours of the movie stars' homes—former homes, in fact, though that was not mentioned. Al, a sixty-year-old thick-set Caucasian wearing a Chinese-style jacket and peaked straw hat, but also a pencil moustache like William Powell's, offered Polaroid photos of the tourists with their hands in the prints of their favorite stars—one dollar. And Wild Bill, about seventy, dressed after photos of James Butler Hickok (1837–1876), wore a long moustache and a silky white goatee, like a little horsetail, and made a show of birdcalls for the tourists' children. It was attention, not money, that he wanted. I watched the tourists, the street, and its regulars for hours—more or less the same scene every day. Strange always, but without consequence.

Fifty years later, far more tourists arrive every day, and more entrepreneurs improvise the same sort of living there. The commodities are the same: maps, tours, photos, costumes—traces of merely imagined presence. It is more apparent now than it was then that what is on sale is fakery. I knew in 1961, as I put on my Chinese uniform, that the whole enterprise amounted to a sham. Everyone who worked there felt that. What I did not realize then is that the tourists somehow felt it too, and that no one minded the fact that there were no movie stars at the theater, only their footprints, and that the stars did not in fact live in the houses to which Larry drove the tourists. No one complained of fakery. No one was fooled by the pretenses of the scene. The theater was no more Chinese than the Egyptian theater Grauman built down the street was Egyptian. Tourists came to Hollywood Boulevard then (and yesterday too) as to a studio back lot, where all is façade. That is the real point of the Boulevard, and of the film industry: no one is gulled by these façades.

In 1961 there were three banks at the adjacent intersection of Hollywood and Highland. Two of them were in the massive architectural styles meant to inspire confidence among depositors. On the fourth corner was a drugstore. None of the banks has survived. The massive buildings are there still: one houses Ripley's Believe-It-or-Not museum; the other Madame Tussaud's Wax Museum. The drugstore remains too, but as a bazaar for Hollywood memorabilia. All that appeared solid fifty years ago has been transformed into faux curiosities. Do people *want* the banks? No, they want to put their feet in the concrete impressions made by John Wayne, Clark Gable, Marilyn Monroe, and Michael Jackson. For that, they are ready to pay with cash. The real economy—that which endures and grows in time—is not sustained by banks or the stones used to suggest permanence. But *real* is the wrong word. It derives from the Latin *res*, signifying things, matter. My introduction to the working world had nothing to do with making things and everything to do with the manipulation of illusions. Hollywood Boulevard has come to resemble a movie set; the Kodak Theater next door to Grauman's, and built for the Academy Awards, looks not like a Mesopotamian palace, but like a studio imitation of such a palace. This is the structure that replaced the third bank. No one is meant to be fooled by this palace entry. Sham itself is the attraction. The actual model was D. W. Griffith's set of the Great Wall of Babylon for *Intolerance* (1916), then the most expensive movie set constructed. (The film enjoyed high attendance, but Griffith could not recover the production costs.) This bizarre economy of open fakery, not duplicity, had staying power and greater growth potential than anyone then realized. In what should one trust, when appearances are obviously false?

I started work just after a great era of American film had come to an end. Of the films under discussion here, only the neo-noir *Charade* (1963) played the Chinese during my time. I first watched film noir on late-night television with my mother; that was the art of her time. She is long gone now, but the noirs are still on television. The cities they depict have utterly changed; the crimes that fill the jails, changed too. Why have the films, compelling still, not lost the force of art? In the 1940s and 1950s, one says, there were great directors, actors, well-staffed studios, and two vital native

Kodak Theatre, Hollywood and Highland

genres for that talent: Westerns and noirs.[11] In an obvious sense, the noirs treat ethical issues and the Westerns, political ones. Noirs focus sharply on single characters, but they seem to begin from a point at which politics has already proved disappointing—in particular, fraudulent.[12] The noirs, I think, speak to us because they depict a still recognizable, even familiar, social and political context—one of pretense, dubious labor, extraordinary complication, and misadministration.

And noirs speak altogether acutely of the kernel of human relations, trust itself. My object here is to clarify what they say about trust relationships. Of course the Hollywood film industry excelled in its treatment of this particular theme because its resources in showmanship, or fakery, are unrivaled. Understand, though, that the noir focus on trust among friends implies that to trust in political institutions no longer makes sense. My argument is not only that the films reveal the nature of trust, though they do. The writers, directors, and actors who made these films contributed to an archive of ethical and even political theory on this theme. What is the trust at issue, and how is it distinguishable from practical cooperation? When can skepticism reasonably end and trust begin? Does trust facilitate agency? In what circumstances do such generic questions make sense? The personnel of one film collaborated with those of many other films and doubtless did so without an agenda to advance this particular project. The fact is, though, that the noirs had a collective philosophical project—from which anyone can learn. And a half-century after the end of the noir era filmmakers have returned to that project in a hotly topical context.

Many of these are famously great films: *The Maltese Falcon*, *The Big Sleep*, *The Third Man* (1949), *Double Indemnity* (1944), *The Postman Always Rings Twice* (1946), *Notorious* (1946). The other noirs I discuss are wonderful too, but of the second order: *Out of the Past* (1947), *Gilda* (1946), *The Narrow Margin*, *Criss Cross* (1949), *In a Lonely Place* (1950). And the spy thrillers, yes, are lesser still. My concern, though, is not with the art of filmmaking, and only incidentally with distinctive filmic properties. I want to know how noir constructions of trust affected the generation born just before the First World War. Mine is a sharp thematic focus. Noir is a forceful imaginative regime, and my parents were among its many subjects. The representations one loves, as Plato says, determine one's thinking, feeling, and future. What would one know of trust if one knew only noirs? A great deal, is the proper answer, particularly about give-and-take, maybe more than one might learn from philosophers or even poets.

One can also speak of a noir viewpoint in social terms. These characters *presume* the incompetence of the state; they desire commitment to one person. The spies, a half century later, desire the opposite: some consequence in the public sphere. Prosperity and the elaboration of an economic empire during the intervening years have directed attention away from the state's incompetence and toward its duplicity. That *is* a discovery for the characters of recent films. Jason Bourne and his near-contemporaries recoil from civic mendacity and surrender hope of a meaningful life grounded in state service. They are appalled by duplicity, as the noir characters (and the tourists at the Chinese) are not. The spies end where the noirs begin: in hope of a private life. But the spies are more narrowly conservative insofar as they imagine privacy as a conventionally settled subject: a reproductive family. And that is a serious intellectual limit. As a critic, I do not do justice to all the films I examine, but I have written a mercifully short book about a large number of engaging films. May my readers bear with me for the sake of a compelling subject.

PART I

Noirs

CHAPTER 1

Work

The ostensible purpose of a noir plot is the production of knowledge; that is the detective's industry (though many of the noirs I discuss are not detective stories). Noirs require an inquirer to work through the entire film to see things, in the dark, as they truly are. He starts off seeing little or wrongly. Knowledge is shadowed, covered, several times over. The private eye, though, is the right inquirer because he is paid to look where others maintain darkness, at least surrounding their common privacy, if not also their illicit activity. He looks where the state is constrained from looking or where it is just unwelcome. Many of the noirs that I love begin conventionally with a detective or inquirer (Jake Gittes in *Chinatown* [1973], Philip Marlowe in *Lady in the Lake* [1947], or Holly Martins in *The Third Man*) who needs work and wants to be paid. A woman may walk into the office, as if out of a dream, and propose a snow job. The inquirer knows that she isn't telling or doesn't know the real story. Jake tells Ida Sessions, who he erroneously thinks is Evelyn Mullwray, to ignore her supposed husband's apparent infidelity and move on, confident that her husband loves her. His counsel is given with cynical glances at his coworkers who have heard it many times. He thinks in this scene that he knows better than "Mrs. Mullwray." However, she refuses to live with illusions. Jake takes the case, and he begins to track the phantom of Hollis Mullwray's infidelity—money for traces of imagined presence. From the opening scene, Jake's work is all wrong.

What is proper work? Very often one cannot see plainly, as Jake cannot, the consequences of one's labor. Is one in fact working for what one thinks one is working? Most workers trust a process of collaboration and institutionalization to allow them to affirm their labor. The inquirers, however, are self-employed, locked into a small economic unit; they cannot grow their businesses, or generalize their efforts, exactly because they trust no one very far—even their business partners. Often, like Jake or Phillip Marlowe (in *The Big Sleep* or *Murder, My Sweet* [1944]), they have already failed to work successfully as part of a staff—Marlowe at the district attorney's office, Jake in Chinatown. However, Marlowe, Sam Spade, Mike Hammer, and others cannot work alone. They maintain instead a strictly hierarchical structure in their offices; the other men are subordinates, and the chief female assistants are often vaguely involved with the detective in some sort of nonprofessional intimacy. At the outset of *The Maltese Falcon*, Sam Spade's partner is killed by a new client, Brigid O'Shaughnessy. Sam and Miles Archer did not really trust each other: Sam was actually sleeping with Miles's wife. The internal operations of a detective's business will not bear critical scrutiny. In the opening sequence, Sam tells Miles that he has brains, whereas toward the end he mentions that Miles was not very sharp. The theme of trust has far-reaching and quite general economic significance. Social scientists like Francis Fukuyama have compared national patterns of trust in mercantile and corporate activities. Economies capable of establishing large networks of trust have advantages over others that remain locked into familial organizations.[1] A detective's skepticism, however, is always breaking groups down into smaller units. And with each such division the economic future dims.

I began by recalling my "work" in Hollywood, because the vague, dubious services of noir inquirers are an explicit theme of many noirs, and because the dullness and fakery too of my first job are recognizable qualities of many other jobs in the postwar era. *Lady in the Lake* begins with Marlowe (Robert Montgomery) at his desk, derisive about the modesty of his earnings and the insignificance of his labors; he tries the crime-writing business as an alternative to detective work, but he cannot get away from the latter. His editor (Audrey Totter) needs a detective more than she does another fiction writer. She has lots of bogus product to promote. Adverse conditions of labor are a point of departure for so many noirs. Joe Gillis (William Holden) in *Sunset Boulevard* (1950) is nearly destitute: "Things were tough at the moment. I hadn't worked at the studio for a long time." He pulls off the street into Norma Desmond's garage in order to elude auto repossessors, and he tries to make an ambiguous living where public and private spheres overlap. Like a writer, a private detective is not an entirely private person; both are professionally engaged in inquiring into privacy, which they observe from a professional remove.

The boundary between public and private spheres is the usual corrupted site of a detective, and it reappears in one film after another. The wealthy class protects its privacy with diligence. Marlowe must pass through three doors and a butler to speak with General Sternwood in *The Big Sleep*. People of fewer means do worse with their boundaries: Joe Brody and Eddie Mars are gunned down at thresholds. Detectives may easily be insulted or even punished with impunity for their category errors, as when Roman Polanski slits Jake's nose in *Chinatown*. A detective is no man of property. His insulation against state interference derives from personal relations with state agents; his access to legal redress is minimal. Noah Cross (John Huston), on the contrary, is a man of property whose political authority and insulation are far greater than Jake's. Lou Escobar is willing to let Jake go home, at the end, but that is about all. Noah Cross has his way because he owns so much. Mike Hammer, in *Kiss Me Deadly*, drives a nice new Jaguar, but a car is not real property. He lives in a handsome, modern—but rented—apartment on Wilshire Boulevard at Beverly Glen. These inquirers live on sufferance. Their licenses can be revoked, as Marlowe is reminded in *The Big Sleep* and Sam is in *The Maltese Falcon*, or they can be handed a plane ticket out of the country, as Holly Martins is repeatedly told. Mike Vargas (Charlton Heston) in *Touch of Evil* (1958) is only tolerated north of the border, where he is a private inquirer, whereas Hank Quinlan (Orson Welles), the state's agent, has jurisdiction, if not property. An inquirer is a private citizen laboring at a public task; his situation, essentially unstable. He is a terrier on a leash.

Noirs are set in proximity to a foggy zone where public and private concerns shift shape with one another. At the outset of *On Dangerous Ground* (1952), Jim Wilson (Robert Ryan) is all cop, no private life. Paradoxically, he has become a menace to his department: his exclusive focus on his work leads him to brutality. His commanding officer rusticates him to a village where a murderer is being sought largely by vigilantes. There, everything is personal, and Jim tries to secure some lawfulness. His own disturbed character is healed by intimacy with Mary Malden (Ida Lupino), a vulnerable blind woman who is sheltering her brother, a murderer. Jim learns from her and from Walter Brent (Ward Bond), the aggrieved father of a dead girl, that only a temperate mix of lawfulness and tact permits social life to proceed. Evelyn Mullwray knew this all along, as did General Sternwood, and many other clients of private detectives, who are hired exactly because public authorities cannot perform such a task adequately, and private citizens who can afford to pay know that they themselves are ill-suited to pursue their own justice. Marlowe is a shapeshifter whose guises enable him to complete advantageously the tasks for which he is paid. Sam Spade earned $900 finding Miles Archer's murderer, and that might have been his own personal project—or of course the state's. Noirs display repeatedly the ways in which private resources can be used effectively to resolve public problems. In so doing, they reverse the course of distinctively US legal prosecution. The concept of a *public* prosecutor, to whom citizens entrust responsibility for bringing causes of justice to litigation, is a modern invention. Prior to the eighteenth century in Europe only private citizens brought causes to the court; however, a public prosecutor was used in the American colonies and later institutionalized in the founding of the United States.[2] Noirs are deeply retro in their suspicion of the efficacy of a public-driven system of justice.[3]

The police are agents of the state; their office is to safeguard public welfare. The public is asked to trust them to deal with tense situations, even to grant them the benefit of doubt when they are accused of using undue force. The logic of this exchange rests on a calculus that the public interest is greater than any particular private interest. A private detective, though, is another matter altogether. He might claim to be doing the same work that the police do, to be similarly entitled to the benefit of the doubt, and so on. But the political significance of noir depends on him not to say such a thing. A private detective should acknowledge that his interests are personal and professional, even selfish: he wants to be paid. Or when his interest is better characterized as simply professional, he is in pursuit of other individuals' private interests. The success of a private detective, then, casts doubt on authoritative notions of public good and reasons of state. When a private agent better accomplishes the tasks assigned to state agents, the efficacy and value of state institutions come into question. Marlowe's success, like that of other private detectives, makes one wonder whether justice is well served by advocates of the pre-eminence of public safety and the rule of law. The rivalry of private interests may more accurately account for the status quo and even for lawful behavior. In which case, the modern state, like so much else, rests on illusion.

Kiss Me Deadly begins in the characteristic conviction that anything worth doing will not be done by the state—libertarian noir. Mike Hammer (Ralph Meeker), every bit a "rugged individual," as we say, refuses to cooperate with his friend Lieutenant Pat Murphy (Wesley Addy), a local police detective, but more importantly with federal detectives investigating, it turns out, a missing cache of radioactive fuel. When Mike is interrogated by the feds, near the outset of the film, he disregards their

Kiss Me Deadly (1955)

authority and stares blankly at a wall as they bait him with ugly innuen-
dos that turn out to be just observations. Although they have ample material resources—five of them to interrogate this one subject—they are
unable to proceed because he withholds conventional respect for federal
authority. Without that, they can do little but snipe at him. In most noirs
the questing detective comes up against government detectives at various
points in an investigation; one might reasonably expect another interrogation later in the film. Here there is no further contact with the feds. The
point of this scene is exactly the weakness of the state in negotiating with
a recalcitrant civilian. When they fail to penetrate his disdain, they are
effectively out of the story altogether, because the real authority of the
state derives from an idea—certainly not from a monopoly on violence.
He says to his friend the police detective: "It'll be a long time before those
characters find out who killed her," dismissing the federal investigators
as incompetent. They regard him as a sleazy detective who panders Velda
(Maxine Cooper), his secretary-girlfriend, in order to corrupt husbands
into infidelity. And they are right: his practice is based on entrapment.
"Too many people like you have contempt for anything that has to do
with the law," Pat says to Mike, in defense of the feds. "You'd like to take
it into your own hands. But when you do that, you might as well be living
in a jungle." In earlier noirs, detectives and many other citizens do alright
without governmental assistance. But by the mid-1950s Pat's sense of the

jungle as the only alternative to enforced social conformity was being made to seem increasingly plausible to audiences.[4]

The political significance of *Kiss Me Deadly* becomes more visible when one notices how Mike collaborates with others, how his personal agency might be generalized in a society. Has he a place in civil society where, as Michael Walzer says, "in principle, at least, coercion is used only to keep the peace and all associations are equal under the law"?[5] Mike does indeed collaborate with others in his quest for information about Christina Bailey (Cloris Leachman). He (quite happily) relies upon force and intimidation to get cooperation from others, as when he breaks a valuable phonograph record to compel Carmen Trivago (Fortunio Bonanova) to provide information, or when he crushes the coroner's (Percy Helton) hand to get the key Christina swallowed. More still, he depends upon his subordinate to do what he says, not because it is in her interest to do so, but simply because he tells her to do so. Her motive is the standard one: she is in love with him, and he is hard to get. However handsome Mike appears, the structure of authority in his vicinity makes any version of the federal government look good. Samuel Johnson observed that "they who most loudly clamour for liberty do not most liberally grant it."[6] The film suggests that libertarians depend on authoritarian methods to get their daily work done.

Much of what Mike does requires assistance from others who do not act entirely in their own interest. His reliance on coercion and sexual manipulation sets him at odds with civil society. With his peer Pat Murphy, he does not cooperate until the very end, when he realizes that he is in over his head. He does, however, collaborate in a fashion with single men who perform undesirable physical labor. Nick, the grease-stained mechanic (Nick Dennis), is one instance (though Mike leaves him in the dark), but the Italian immigrant porter at Gabrielle's former Bunker Hill hotel is a more revealing one. Without fuss or any comment, Mike lightens the load of the old man carrying a trunk. At the end of the scene, the porter whispers to Mike Gabrielle's new address. The porter did not ask for help, and Mike did not have to ask him directly for Gabrielle's address. This is modest interaction between men too proud to request assistance. And it is limited, because Mike does not give information to others; he means only to receive it. Nonetheless, he does seek cooperation, and he is willing to give something; but his male collaborators must cooperate freely and intuitively—with a kind of trust. No explicit protocols. The consequence of this approach to cooperation is that little things become very significant. Mike collaborates only with those whom he *trusts*, and that is a way of placing a high bar before interaction that might otherwise be routine.

Kiss Me Deadly (1955)

A nation-state offers no such collaboration. The interrogators for the Interstate Crime Commission know exactly why Christina's death is important, and they could say so to Mike. But instead they leave him, as he left Nick, in the dark. They rely upon indefinite state authority to compel cooperation or inspire deference. When they get neither from Mike, they are out of business. An exchange of information is not a possibility. Even Pat Murphy, who no doubt all along knows about the missing fuel, says nothing of it to his friend Mike. In other noirs, the investigating police collaborate to some extent with private detectives, but not here. The postwar state, the film suggests, must refuse to enlighten citizens, presumably because the stakes have risen with the proliferation of American economic interests and the introduction of nuclear weaponry. Private citizens, it seems, keep each other in the dark too. In the opening scene Christina is unwilling to tell Mike about the fuel because of the old adage (utterly mistaken, as the film shows) that Mike recognizes: what you don't know can't hurt you. Yet without full knowledge one cannot collaborate with others on equal footing. No matter: collaboration and equal footing are irrelevant norms anyway. In a society in which information is a prized commodity, citizens are constantly interacting with one another without adequate knowledge of the stakes of their interaction. Inequality is built into an information society, a feature of civil society that Mike and all noir detectives understand perfectly.

The noirs were gradually transformed from social resistance to political conservativism; they were made to advocate admiration for the capacities of the state. Most of the films in this conservative mode are not worth reviewing—no surprise. But there are exceptions, *Kiss Me Deadly* and *Charade* among them. The former does not propose, as others do, that a technocratic state is artfully protecting the nation's resources. Instead it asserts that in some areas of the economy and society only a nation-state can effectively manage responsibility. The threat of rogue merchants of nuclear fuel, and of radioactive contamination—this is the limit-case the film considers. Lay individuals know too little to manage even a small cache of such fuel. Ignorance is made to seem the general situation of post-war US citizens, and it severely constrains in this case. Individuals simply have insufficient resources to compete with the state now. The private detective is out of a job.

That ignorance is dangerous, no one disputes. The film is more exact, though, in showing that libertarian individualism is especially dangerous in a state of ignorance, and ignorance is newly pervasive. Mike's ignorance is conspicuous and profound. He doesn't know why he and Christina, at the beginning of the plot, were pushed over a cliff; she would not say then what her worries were, and later she could not. Viewers watch him proceed through nearly the entire film without the faintest idea why this mystery matters. He is motivated not by free-ranging curiosity but by self-interest (the lowest common denominator). His ignorance renders the inquiry, for

Kiss Me Deadly (1955)

Kiss Me Deadly (1955)

him and for audiences, extraordinarily abstract: he wants to know what a total stranger declined to tell him, because he imagines that information itself to have, of all things, a cash value.[7] She gave him a recondite literary clue: an allusion to a sonnet by Christina Rossetti. "Remember Me" turns out to mean, incredibly, that she swallowed a key to a storage locker: remember, that is, to look in my corpse. Pat advises him to tell the authorities what he knows and then leave them to do their work. Mike replies, "What's in it for me?" Similarly a coworker advises Nick to ask himself, in his dealings with Mike, what's in it for Nick. Material self-interest and base egotism are explicitly associated with Mike. When Pat says, "Manhattan Project, Los Alamos, Trinity," Mike is finally made to understand that he's been pursuing nuclear fuel. He then gives the cop the key to the locker with the fuel and says, "I didn't know." Pat responds derisively, "You didn't know. Do you think that you'd have done anything differently if you had known?"

After 92 minutes of a 106-minute film, Mike, altogether dispirited, capitulates: his quest has come to a surrender to the state. The truth is that the state, as the film shows, is incapable of maintaining mastery of the knowledge that produced nuclear technology. Organized crime is similarly inefficacious. No social sector and no enterprising individual can hold this Pandora's box closed. Human curiosity and greed are too strong. That quest began with a barely covered woman on a highway near the state mental hospital, presumably at Camarillo. I said that Mike is motivated by a desire for money, but this is only partly true. Another perspective derives from the stunning opening and credits sequence that ends with Christina leering rearward from Mike's roadster. She comes on screen with a memorable soundtrack: panting from her run on the road and whimpering too in terror of her pursuers. This soundtrack continues long after she enters Mike's car; it suggests a passionate union of these two characters. On a symbolic level—rendered explicit by a filling station attendant's lurid innuendo—Mike and Christina have formed a deep bond, and for the remainder of the film he pursues not only financial gain but also the meaning of their conjunction.[8]

Noirs were originally anti-statist, as I've said, and suspicious of all government. When Jeff Bailey (Robert Mitchum), in *Out of the Past*, referring to a tax liability Whit Sterling (Kirk Douglas) hopes to elude, asks Whit, "Why don't you just pay it?" Whit replies, "That would be against my nature." And this is true. Not his individual nature, so far as the film lets on, but his generic nature as a noir crook. For Whit to pay taxes to the state makes no sense at all. Crooks and private detectives alike are libertarians. Whit doesn't need to argue the point; once said, it is clear to Jeff. But by 1963 the US state was larger, stronger, and more determined than ever to assert itself. *Charade*, a handsomely colored noir plot, set in tourists' Paris, addresses quite abstract questions about political theory: Whose is the wealth of the postwar United States? And who should serve

Kiss Me Deadly (1955)

Charade (1963)

as custodian of that wealth? The film is clear: the US government claims the wealth, and Peter Joshua (Cary Grant) is its proper custodian. The kernel of the plot is a rogue act of duplicity by five OSS officers who betrayed—of all people—the French Resistance by stealing $250,000 in gold and blaming, of course, the Germans. By the end of the film all five are dead; their faithless conniving should have no postwar future. The one who gets the "money" in the form of rare postage stamps—originally government-issued commodities themselves—is Peter Joshua, a charming, Odysseus-like prevaricator who lies for the US Treasury Department. The rogues have been persistently hunted down by this clever, witty, zany, resourceful, but finally honest Treasury agent.

Charade proposes a faith in the postwar state that the weaker noirs and the police procedurals had also advocated, ultimately on television serials like *Dragnet*. It matters that the Treasury, not the CIA, is tracking government funds so assiduously and effectively. The postwar nation-state is represented not as a site of deliberation and controversy, or even as a combatant in the Cold War, but as an instrument of far-flung administration.[9] What is suggested is that the postwar regime is dogged and honest, willing to lie when it is useful to do so, but finally humane, even selfless—not what one wants from the CIA. Remember the OSS was the predecessor of the CIA; the dead rogues were CIA types *avant les lettres*. The point is that this government controls wealth especially well—and, for that, most households might be grateful, because they count themselves shareholders of the nation-state. The contest with communism is irrelevant and kept out of the plot entirely. Insofar as one cares about wealth maintenance, this is the government one wants, according to the film.

Mrs. Charles Lambert, or Reggie (Audrey Hepburn), is an interpreter, French to English, at the diplomatic level. At the beginning of the film she is ready to divorce her husband because (she rightly senses) he is deceiving her. "Why do people have to tell lies?" she asks Peter Joshua. It turns out, once she is interrogated by the Paris police, that all she knows of Lambert is his name—and she has that wrong. It's Vrozz not Lambert. Misrepresentation, like the weather, is all around us. Peter Joshua, the apparent successor to Mr. Lambert in her life, also lies repeatedly, particularly about his name. A career of administration seems to require duplicity in regard to naming, from good guys and bad, and that of course leaves a translator and all citizen-readers at a crushing disadvantage. She is thoroughly confused by her life and her world. Peter Joshua urges her, "I beg you, just trust me once more." She replies with exasperation, "Why *should* I?" He wins her assent by answering, "I can't think of a reason in the world." Ingrid Bergmann, in *Notorious*, also playing opposite Grant, was offered patriotic reasons for trust; Audrey Hepburn is offered only charm. She must simply find that trust in her own capacity for faith. The film sharply dissociates trust from reasoned judgment. She must take a leap, as others must too. That is the metaphysical challenge of trust. After all rational assessments, the sorting of evidence pro and con, trust is something more than that. The film makes the test easy, though, in that it's Cary Grant toward whom she must leap.

Charade (1963)

His particularity is especially significant because he is an officer of the postwar US government in the most cosmopolitan, culturally legitimate metropolis of the world. He is an aggressive custodian of what the United States *owns,* one who truly wants the money that Charles Lambert stole from the French Resistance, though he does not want it for himself. The inquirer—heir to the shady Marlowe, Sam Spade, and Mike Hammer—is now a government agent of an imperial state. Reggie Lambert wishes he were less aggressive, less determined to get the money—more determined to get her. But his intense though impersonal determination is his qualification for his post. The special feature of this determination is that it is only apparently and not truly self-interested. He is in fact a stranger to the greed that drives the scoundrels who must all be killed. He has only the motive of wishing to succeed at his job, and for that success he will lie repeatedly or jump from balcony to balcony across the face of a tall building. He will do almost everything that enterprising thieves, or private detectives, might do. He only *seems* to be a crook. That's his charade, at which he is very good. The regime for which he labors must similarly seem as wicked and greedy as its rivals, but in fact it too should proceed by rules that can be stated and avowed in public. He has a dull office and a plain secretary; his agency alters its procedures in response to interoffice memos. This is a regime of administrators.

I have indicated that *Charade* is propagandistic, though Cold War ideology is not directly relevant to its concerns. The film dissociates economic from political authority, and that is a large part of its political significance. The US government is characterized as an economic institution dedicated to *collective,* not individual, wealth maintenance. The assertion of the state's ownership of the stolen money entails a concept of collective property—not what a capitalist regime customarily boasts. This concept has everything to do with global US hegemony, which is why the film is properly set in Paris. Economic empire is given a fair face here. The US government is an instrument not of capitalist greed, according to the film, but of collective ownership. The US participated in the French anti-occupation effort, on this view, by transferring gold bullion to the Resistance. Once the transfer went bad, the US economic regime had a claim on the lost assets of the French Resistance—a claim that would be persistently pursued for two decades. That the French government, then presided over by Charles de Gaulle, might rather advance such a claim is not considered. The United States (never mind its allies) defeated the Nazis; the Resistance fought the Nazis. Therefore the US government is a lineal descendant of the Resistance. The wealth of the West is vigilantly guarded by selfless state agents

Out of the Past (1947)

on behalf of a nation of impersonal shareholders. Yes, the United States is an empire in 1963, but it is an *economic*, not a political, one, and its wealth belongs to us all, the film suggests.

Peter Joshua, on the job, is a reassuringly dashing figure—just the reverse of Jeff Markham (Robert Mitchum). *Out of the Past* begins well outside the land of Noir, and far from Paris too, at a dull, ordinary country gas station that has, for Jeff, replaced a detective agency. He has left behind the pursuit of action, wealth, difficulty. The film refers to three sites of his labor. At the outset of his story he is a smart-but-honest private detective in New York, like Sam Spade in *The Maltese Falcon*, in business for the money, with a partner he describes as "stupid, oily." Later, in flight from his nemesis Whit Sterling (Kirk Douglas), he opens a small office in San Francisco and takes on doubtful assignments to get by. Finally, the gas station, with his alias on the sign, though his mechanical labor is never shown on screen. The work there only identifies a concept: detective-turned-worker. He actually left dubious detective work behind him.

The question that begins the film: Can a shadow man survive in the light of legitimacy? Others, like the bail bondsman Max Cherry (Robert

Forster) in *Jackie Brown* (1997), talk about leaving the shadow zone, but Jeff did it, to live among lakes and trees. However, despite a spectacular landscape, this new life is figured paradoxically in terms of sensory and social deprivation: his young assistant (Dickie Moore) is a lip-reading deaf mute who understands what he sees quite exactly and is fiercely devoted to Jeff, but his participation in the shared life of language is minimal. He is an icon of upstanding, permanent taciturnity. Jeff explains his work to Whit, the client he had earlier betrayed: "I sell gas and make a small profit so that others can make their small profits; it is called earning a living." The modesty of the straight life is figured as collective deprivation.

There is vagueness in Jeff's character, even at times confusion. He has strength, courage, boldness, but less competence than he thinks, and little vision. He is easily outwitted by Kathie Moffat (Jane Greer), repeatedly, and he gives up as Sam Spade never would. He tells Whit that he has learned to trust no one. Then the next day he tells Meta (Rhonda Fleming), "People trust me. Whit trusted me twice." Actually, only once; Jeff does not yet realize that he is being gulled. When he asks, she responds that she trusts him just as far as she must. Jeff is altogether confused about what trust can secure. Robert B. Pippin identifies Jeff's "lack of clarity"—or incoherence—about his feeling for Kathie.[10] His idea of a good life is a woman who believes all that he says, and agrees with him too. Add to that a remote spot in the country, and one is done with his avowed values. These ideals seem a remainder after some prolonged subtraction. They characterize the life he seems to want to retain, when the film begins, but his effort to work his way free of past transgressions draws him into the shadow zone again, and he dies trying to get out.

Jeff's motivation is puzzling, abstract. He imagines that the past, present, and future are linked one to the next in a causal chain, from which he tried to slip free, first in Acapulco, when he fled with Kathie, then again when, under the name of Bailey, he took up village life at the lake. But almost no persuasion is needed to convince him that his past cannot be tied up and left behind. Germans speak of *Vergangenheitsbewältigung*, or a coming-to-terms with the past; they have a single term for this concept, because they recognize for themselves a need that English-speakers feel only at the distance indicated by periphrasis. He tells Ann Miller (Virginia Huston) that he must visit Whit because he wonders what Whit knows; in particular he worries that Whit knows that Jeff was an accomplice to the murder of Jack Fisher (Steve Brodie), Jeff's former partner. Fisher, it should be remembered, had a just claim on Jeff, who had promised his partner half of the $5,000 he received from Whit, but Jeff paid him nothing. Fisher wanted to be paid that and much more by the time he caught up with Jeff and Kathie. Jeff then learned from Fisher that old misdeeds return; those are the terms in which he narrates to Ann (who naïvely thinks that the past has passed away) the encounter with his partner that led to Kathie shooting Fisher while Jeff beat him. That complicity is Jeff's one legal liability, and it took all that to put him off Kathie.

When Kathie shoots Fisher and flees, a staple of noir plots is fulfilled: the private eye is made to appear an accessory to murder. In the usual plot, he treads the shadows to solve the crime and reveals a more extensive series of crimes as well. He then calls the police to make arrests and returns to his office. Jeff instead flees the shadows, adopts a new name, posted on a big sign, as if to boast of self-transformation. But because he is an honest worker, as Whit observes, he feels the mark of Cain on him— shame. At the end of *The Maltese Falcon*, Sam acknowledges a modicum of professional obligation to "detectives everywhere." Jeff blew off two professional obligations: one to his client, the other to his partner. He cannot bring himself to settle firmly in his country retreat; he has become too timid even to meet his girlfriend's parents. His self-loathing chagrin over the straight life and his ambition too lead him to change clothes and imprudently return to the shadow zone to see what Whit has for him.

Noirs begin almost always in the middle or at the end. They presume a past to clarify the status quo. Jake Gittes in *Chinatown* has some history with Lou Escobar, but what that amounts to is obscure. Jake tells Evelyn Mullwray (Faye Dunaway) that he was trying to protect a woman in Chinatown, though he only helped her to get hurt. That backstory is never told, but its magnetic pull is constantly present. (The backstory of *The Lady from Shanghai* [1947] is left to lie still on the Crazy House floor.) The one-time romance of Gilda (Rita Hayworth) and Johnny Farrell (Glenn Ford) in *Gilda* is never told, but it nonetheless drives the entire plot. The backstory in *Cape Fear* (1962) *is* told; Max Cady (Robert Mitchum) and Sam Bowden (Gregory Peck) even try to establish its cash value. That doesn't work. The value of the past is evidently immeasurable. A backstory stipulates deep feeling among the characters. In *Chinatown* this device is only abstractly useful or significant—as a concept more than a dramatic fact. The relevant concept is explicability: a backstory promises to resolve a present enigma. So much so that some noirs, like *Vertigo* (1957), *Out of the Past*, and *Chinatown*, promote the view that the backstory *determines* all that follows.[11] Characters meet in a context where individual autonomy is reduced, not so much by rival individuals as by some large system or force—maybe the past itself, or maybe the state.

One needs to trust some others because so much is organized against one's independence. Noir inquirers are not enemies of fraud, nor even advocates of candor. They accept, as they must, the fraud all around them. "We all have to swim in the same water," Jake Gittes reminds Noah Cross. They rather try to get by well—by whatever means necessary—and construct honesty among a very few friends—one, or maybe two. This is the context in which noir examines trust, at least as plausible now as in 1950, when these films peaked. On the face of things there is little reason to trust anyone, but people are nonetheless drawn again and again away from comprehensive cynicism and toward some effort to make trust work.

Three different screenwriters worked on the script of *Out of the Past*, and they did not work together; it was revised and then revised again. Tracking the plot is difficult. There are two distinct segments of the film, and they comprise its first and second halves. That rift keeps this strong film from achieving satisfying formality, or greatness. (Few critics, I should note, agree.) Forty-seven minutes into this 97-minute film, Jeff poses against a panoramic scene of San Francisco Bay; he is about to enter Meta Carson's apartment and set in motion the second or main plot. This is to say that the film begins all over again, this time with a new femme fatale, a new villain, and two new supporting characters—Leonard Eels and Jeff's old cabbie buddy. This plot focuses on the framing of Jeff for two murders: of Whit's tax accountant Eels and of Jeff's former partner Fisher. The first plot, about Jeff's romance with Kathie, is mere background to this sequence, yet the first is more affecting and its cinematography more ambitious. The first plot also proceeds at a more leisurely, humane pace than the second. Jeff liked life in Mexico and then in Bridgeport too. He moves slowly, even drowsily, with a sense of fatality about him. In Bridgeport he says he has been to one too many places, as though his life were already determined. Kathie's last words to him are a curse, at the end of the film, but moments before she says, "Hurry, Jeff," as they get in the car to take their death drive. As usual, he is in no hurry, not even to start the car. She reaches down to pull out the choke as the engine turns over without effect. She repeatedly pushes ahead, speeds up the plot, and Jeff lumbers along toward the edge. His tardiness is fatal: he gets to Eels too late to displace the frame, and to Whit too late to close the deal for his freedom from the law.

Tempo counts for a great deal in noirs. Over time, characters attempt to construct trust, but they also anticipate betrayal, and they do so with pleasure.[12] This is a great dramatic resource. The second half of *Out of the Past* represents Jeff's failure to anticipate betrayal quickly and effectively. He leaves Bridgeport for Tahoe ostensibly because he suspects that Kathie may have betrayed him to Whit. At every moment after he reencounters this reunited couple, Jeff is trying to catch up with their effort to betray him. He recognizes that they are setting him up, but he reacts too slowly. One realizes that he is pleased and satisfied to recognize their betrayal, when he quips about his bookmaker cousin in conversation with Leonard Eels. Jeff wrongly, vainly, thinks that he has time to return later to develop a counterscheme with Eels. But the schemes of Whit and, more fatal, of Kathie outpace him. He sees the problem clearly: "My timing is a few minutes off," he tells the cabbie. But he still cannot catch up. Once Kathie has killed Whit, events have passed by Jeff. His life is over. Think of Sam Spade in the *Maltese Falcon*. He too with pleasure anticipates betrayal; his edginess about this heightens the drama of scenes with Brigid and his secretary. Betrayal itself should not surprise noir inquirers. "You lied to us about your sister, but that doesn't matter. We knew that," he tells Brigid. About timing, though, Sam cannot be so genial. He races to stay ahead of events. He talks fast and prudently picks his moments to talk. First he calls the police, then he submits Brigid to her final interrogation. She is made to feel the pressure of his impending betrayal of her. Jeff instead gives Eels time to puzzle over some enigmatic remarks; he gives Baylord an hour to think how to cross him, as he says. He gives Whit several hours to respond to a costly ultimatum. Jeff is as cynical as Sam; they both proudly anticipate betrayal. But Jeff lacks the sense of urgency that protects Sam. Pleasure taken in anticipation of betrayal—this is an odd feature of noir, but it is meaningful. So long as inquirers can anticipate betrayals, they enjoy their cynicism. Jeff has this pride stripped from him by Kathie, a quick, responsive adversary. Betrayal, he sees, is not manageable.

Although Jeff seems intellectual in believing that the past does in fact return, his particular engagement with it is rudimentary: he means only to protect himself from legal prosecution; he has no will to understand the past any more deeply than he already does. Why does he accede to Joe's request to see Whit? Jeff rightly feels that Whit and Bridgeport are worlds not miles apart; the road sign arouses just this observation. Why not refuse the very proposition of a meeting with Whit? Joe tells him cleverly, "You can't." Jeff may fear that Fisher, just before he disappeared, told Whit that he located Jeff and Kathie. That could connect Jeff to Fisher's disappearance. (But Jeff has no reason to fear what is actually the case: that Kathie has provided testimony of Jeff's involvement in the murder.) In Mexico Jeff told Kathie that he is no slave to his fears. His narrative for Ann shows that he has repeatedly been indifferent to prudence. And he stubbornly refused to make a deal with Fisher to elude Whit. In Bridgeport he may have discovered some prudence, though that appears offset by an appetite for something more than small-town life. As soon as Joe proposes that Jeff talk to Whit, Jeff is off to Tahoe. He shows up before dawn at Ann's, ready for the seventy-eight-mile drive to Whit's place. He has already abandoned rustic wear for a tie, trench coat, and fedora, apparently eager to resume the game. As he opens the gate to Whit's Tahoe home, he returns to his old job as private eye. Whit claims to want help in misrepresenting his actual income to the Internal Revenue Service. In the shadow economy, all is misrepresentation: Whit is playing Jeff, as is Kathie; Meta Carson is playing Leonard Eels; Jeff plays Meta and tries to play Kathie, and so on. The fabric of deceit in the second half of the film is dense, taut, which is why scenes follow one another so quickly. Jeff tries unsuccessfully to make a way around those who misrepresent for pay. He recognizes that his "stinking life" yields no way out of the shadow economy. His change of clothes back in Bridgeport is a sign not only of the incompatibility of the two economies—that of a rural gas station, that of high-stakes gambling—but also of his awareness that he has to return to the shadows. The audience understands, from the opening sequence, as Joe's car speeds menacingly to Jeff's gas station, that Joe speaks for a blunt, cruel, invasive force. Whit only looks good; he is nothing nice. Kathie warns Jeff of Whit's particular force: "You don't know Whit: he won't forget." Jeff had reason to know better than to drive to Tahoe, but he is not so smart after all. He is eager when he should be skeptical, slow when he should be quick.[13] Behind his new-found prudence is an undescribed, unacknowledged counterforce (comprised of ambition, shame, and simple surrender).

There are a number of scenes of self-sacrifice in the noirs, and some are puzzling, none more so than Jeff's suicidal surrender to Kathie's control at the end of the film. Why does he acquiesce in, or even provoke, his own death? Why does Swede (Burt Lancaster) lie in bed, apparently indifferent to the approach of assassins, in *The Killers* (1946)? Why does Edmond (Louis Jouvet), in *Hotel du Nord* (1938), give a pistol to his assassin? Cora, in *The Postman Always Rings Twice*, believes that she can determine truth by disregarding her own safety in her last night swim with Frank Chambers (John Garfield). And Frank goes peacefully to his execution for a murder he did not commit, because he did commit another murder for

Out of the Past (1947)

which he was not convicted. Self-abnegation has particular significance for the noirs: willed destruction is a means of rising above the rule of self-interest that otherwise dominates life in these films. All of these characters are disgusted by self-interest—their own and that of others who have hurt them. These conclusive self-sacrifices express a desire to transcend just that which drives the events of the films. These characters all come to see the inanity of a world ruled by self-interest alone.

The true conflict of *Out of the Past* is between Kathie and Jeff, not Whit and Jeff. Kathie is cunning, ruthless, capable. Jeff is self-sacrificing, slow, conscience-stricken. Whit, as he says, actually likes Jeff, and to the eye they resemble one another. The first version of the conflict concerns contractual obligations from the past. Jeff thought he could simply flee from his contracts with Whit and Fisher; Kathie knew better. The second version concerns the means of rectifying violations. Kathie consistently kills those who press claims against her, and she does so with dispatch. Jeff means instead to negotiate the legal system: he calls for the police to intercept his apparent "escape" with Kathie—and Kathie shoots him. They are both equally dead: neither approach works in the long run. Only mendacity works. Ann asks the kid at the end for a judgment: whether Jeff was running off with Kathie when he died. The kid knew Jeff better than she did, she says. He ponders the question, then nods that, yes, Jeff was running off with Kathie, which he knows or suspects to be false. Ann then gets in a State of California vehicle with Lawful Jim (Richard Webb), and she sets out on her new life. Had she thought that Jeff had kept faith with her, she too would have been a prisoner of her past. The kid sets her free with a lie and then salutes Jeff's remaining alias on the gas station, as though to acknowledge an obligation dispatched. The film indicates that the very idea of coming to terms with the past is folly. A better idea is to stay mum, as the kid does; get in the car, and drive away, as Ann does. "In acting and speaking," Hannah Arendt wrote, "men show who they are, reveal actively their unique personal identities and thus make their appearance in the human world."[14] *Out of the Past* begins and ends with a deaf mute. The entire project of self-revelation—so admired by mid-twentieth-century intellectuals—is soundly rejected by the film. Silence and prevarication actually enable others to live happily.

"It's honest work," one says, ordinarily meaning *legal*, but more than that too; *dishonest* and *illegal* are near but not exact synonyms. Honest work signifies some plainness or lack of duplicity. Jeff Bailey has honest

Out of the Past (1947)

work at his gas station. But before that he was a detective who deceived his client, breached contracts. He felt shame at his duplicity and wished to set straight his crooked past. That is what brought him to a miserable end. Mike Hammer works by entrapment; this much is established at the outset of *Kiss Me Deadly*. Peter Joshua lies like mad, but he is an honest agent of the state because he does not profit from deception. He and Mike Hammer are postwar characters, the audience's contemporaries. They live in a distinct present, at peace with pragmatic duplicity. Jeff is an older guy, handicapped by his attachment to a bygone era: a simple life by the lake. This is what it means to speak of his timing being off. He is late in a large, inexorable sense. The conditions of work have shifted. Honest work is hard to sustain. My working life began in 1961 with a dragon embroidered on my back; I was instructed to turn my back, should I ever see a theater-patron slip and fall. "Never confirm an allegation against the theater." That economy of pretense is now far grander. John T. Irwin has argued acutely that the noirs are largely about working for yourself, or honest and autonomous work in an economy of massive duplicity. This is a true and far from obvious observation. These films analyze a conflict between honor and making a living. They are studies in shame. This is one reason they continue to live.

CHAPTER 2

Trust

Film noir is certainly a variety of realistic narrative: one recognizes particular cities, neighborhoods, and automobiles. Audiences are drawn to its characters and narratives, but its object is abstract and idealistic. The films are governed more by ideas than by action. *Night of the Hunter* (1955) draws this dimension of noir to the screen's surface by punctuating the action with a series of tableaux. Schematic coherence of theme and character prevails in even the grittiest noirs. Not surprising, because to ask for trust, as noir characters repeatedly do, is to solicit metaphysics: "Just trust me." A truster holds to an interpretation of a trustee in the absence of confirming evidence, or even in the presence of countervailing evidence. "I know it looks bad for me," Steve Christopher (Elliott Reed) says to Jill Lynn (Jeanne Crain) in *Vicki* (1953), "but I just have to ask you to trust me." The practice of trust is problematic, often apparent folly, because of this constant absence. But if conclusive or even probable evidence of trustworthiness were present, there would be no need, or little point, to trust. The absence of confirmation or the appearance of invalidation increases the difficulty but also the value of trust—to a certain point. For blind trust is unimpressive where it is indistinguishable from intransigence.

"You've got to trust me, Mr. Spade"—women often directly ask for trust in noirs (as Brigid O'Shaughnessy [Mary Astor] famously does in *Maltese Falcon*); but only rarely is it the trust common to lovers. Noir women are lovers, but the trust they solicit goes well beyond romance. A lady asks a detective to trust less her sexual fidelity than her good word and benign intention. A detective measures a call for trust against signs of mere self-interest, because everyone is out for him- or herself: Noir is a Hobbesian land. The extent of self-interest is sufficiently great to render most ethical and legal issues merely practical, instrumental considerations; characters

35

The Night of the Hunter (1955)

move right past even the most widely avowed ethical constraints. Some characters, like Harry Lime in *The Third Man* and Ed Prentiss in *Thieves' Highway* (1949), are admittedly larcenous and satisfied to dwell in what others count as shame. Corruption goes far in this art, as elsewhere (I never met a theater manager who lived on salary alone). A detective sees beyond material self-interest, though he always begins exactly there—often with an explicit assertion of his rate of pay. Truster and trustee are at the edge of material social life, building a relationship to stand *against* self-interest. They begin in self-interest, but seek an alternative to the fakery and greed around them. I spoke of Jeff Bailey's distaste for a world governed by self-interest; Sam Spade concurs but with no illusion of an alternative. A libertarian republic in particular runs on self-interest, the limits of which render doubtful the adequacy of a libertarian account of desire. Dark as these films are, the characters desire something exceptional and immaterial—deep trust.

What I understand as trust is to some extent familiar, but still different from that concept used by political theorists. Russell Hardin helpfully sorts out theories of trust in terms of the origins of the concept of trustworthiness, which may derive from character, conformity to moral

The Maltese Falcon (1941)

precept, or what he calls "encapsulated interest."[1] According to the last model, a trustee becomes trustworthy when a trustee's actions take the truster's interests into account. My own understanding is that a truster is motivated to trust not only out of a desire to realize some particular end of his or her own, even so general an end as "social cooperativeness."[2] A truster may be moved instead by something less rational, by a need for an exceptional relationship that is not dependent on self-interest, as most other relationships admittedly are. Noir trust usually bears an explicit sense of exceptionality about it. Philosophers note that discussions of trust as a relationship between two people are misleading in that there is a third term: a truster trusts a trustee with regard to a particular end.[3] While the triadic model covers many situations, the most important tests of trust entail indefiniteness with regard to ends. This is why trust is inevitably mysterious. One trusts a trustee in regard to situations that cannot be stipulated in advance. Deep trust is open-ended. Hardin's encapsulated interest model asks a trustee only to take into account the interests of the truster; his truster is looking for a win-win situation. Hardin imagines trust to be cognitive: one knows a trustee to be worthy or not. The definition of trust that engages me goes further. A truster trusts that a trustee will not knowingly compromise the truster's autonomy, that the trustee will in fact constrain him- or herself in order to safeguard not just the truster's interest, as understood by the trustee, but the truster's autonomy as understood by the truster. The extension of trust, on this account, entails a decision to risk loss for an indefinite good.

There is a special generality about deep trust: the premise is that a trustee would not willingly compromise a truster's interest; the trustee is instead expected to be not only benignly inclined toward the truster but vigilant about supporting the truster's interest. One is often disappointed in such general trust, usually by an inadvertent failure of vigilance. Everyone gets several opportunities to be told what comforts only the speaker: "I would never deliberately do anything to harm you." And rarely *does* a trustee deliberately work against a truster's interest in order to gain something definite for him- or herself. This is why Matty Walker (Kathleen Turner) in *Body Heat* (1981), Phyllis Dietrichson (Barbara Stanwyck) in *Double Indemnity*, and Dusty Chandler (Lizabeth Scott) in *Dead Reckoning* (1947) are so memorable: all three, one learns gradually, are proficient betrayers—the Iagos of noir. Their malevolence is masterful. This is the severity of noir. Its drive toward strenuous moral judgment produced characters to validate a misogynistic claim that trust is undermined by ambitious, evil women. Or these characters show that the generality of trust is not so trivial as it may seem; that the unapparent nature of some people does in fact block them from a benign orientation toward anyone. Trusters need to consider not only the practical limits of their trustees' vigilance but also the fact that some trustees *would* deliberately harm those naïve enough to trust them, and Matty makes even the most negligent trustees look good.

The indefiniteness of deep trust provides this theme with its wide currency. In one film after another, characters explicitly beseech each other for trust, or complain of its impracticality. Talk of trust is everywhere—for good reason. To seek indefinite trust is to refuse to test *all* one's life for reasonable conformity to observable phenomena. Lenin said that "trust is good, but control better." His calculus of outcome is directly rejected by those who trust. They set out instead on a metaphysical inquiry: to establish a way to live by something grander than historical experience. The relevant question is not the nature of truth or reality, but the basis of conduct and feeling—which sounds ethical rather than metaphysical, but trusters neither appeal to justice nor proselytize others. Instead they express, by example, how they *want* to live. Trust derives from desire, a

Body Heat (1981)

reservoir of hope withdrawn from the wastes of bygone failures. Shadows fall on everyone—no impunity—but one by one people nonetheless call out for trust.

The noirs I analyze are frames for considering how trust and autonomy can be practically configured, even in nonintimate social contexts. One wants to rely on civic institutions to function effectively and directly, but the police routinely display incompetence, in noirs and elsewhere. Yet inquirers nonetheless regularly *rely* on the police, or at least on their friends on the force, to provide information or to cut them slack to solve a criminal case the police themselves should solve. This is an effective collaboration: the state shows forbearance and patience, and an inquirer moves ahead until uniformed officers can come in to make an arrest. An enterprising semiprivate individual makes a living by competently supplementing the state's activities. But these films show that, aside from institutions, one can rarely rely on individuals either, though once one ceases to rely on institutions one must rapidly find individuals to trust. To rely on an agency or an individual to do something definite is obviously a lesser thing than to trust another person. One needs some individuals with whom to deal honestly and openly more than just occasionally, and some to approach one with special care in circumstances that cannot be stipulated in advance. Trust, as distinct from reliance, has this indefinite sense. One trusts another to do well by one especially in unforeseen circumstances. One's inability to rely on others with general confidence is exactly what leads one to look with urgency for those few who can be deeply trusted; one never knows when one will be unable to rely on all those who should respond predictably and satisfyingly to one's needs. This is the chief point at which noirs should be understood as utopian; they try to identify a ground of trust in a dark social terrain.

This concept of trust is indefinite insofar as it stands *against* self-interest or material social life. One is *building* trust, but self-interest and fakery are well established all around one. The distinctions that render social life comprehensible and discussable are in place, recognized intuitively by citizens of the material order. The distinctive feature of trust is that it resists boundaries, categories. The line between private love interests and professional obligations, for instance, is the focus of several great noirs—*The Maltese Falcon* and *The Big Sleep*, but also *Notorious*. T. R. Devlin (Cary Grant) is stymied in his courtship of Alicia Hubermann (Ingrid Bergman) by the work he has recruited her to do for the US government: deception, the last thing a lover should encourage in a beloved. The greater her self-consciousness about her deception, the greater the risk that she might fail to produce an illusion of trustworthiness. Spies' slips cost lives. Dev is taciturn but charming at first; they fall for each other quickly. He soon sees that he is caught in a contradiction between romantic desire and professional obligation. However, rather than take direct responsibility for this conflict that he brought to her door, he becomes petulant and speaks derisively to her of her virtue, as if she were a notorious tart and he had no ground for trusting her in the first place, nor any reason to regret her involvement with Alex Sebastian (Claude Rains), the target of her espionage.

The film offers scant evidence, however, for the judgment that she is a woman of easy virtue, except that she more or less acquiesces to this mistreatment. Rather than slap him when he speaks this way, she pleads with him to trust her. "Why won't you believe in me, Dev? Just a little. Why won't you?" she asks plaintively. Dev (not Alicia) is the film's central character, and he is a site of confusion and incoherence. He might better sustain his category-blur if he had faith or trust in Alicia, but that trust has not yet formed; he careens from one collision of categories to the next. At base is the mistaken notion that trust is a private matter that should be suppressed in order to pursue professional objectives with a clear head; for all his repression, Dev's head is anything but clear. This is the thematic crux of the film.

Trust is a value in itself in most noirs. Is it properly regarded as an inherent good of the first order, one may wonder, or as a quality of relationship that permits other, higher goods to be realized? The film asks whether trust can reasonably be subordinated to higher considerations—specifically, matters of state. Dev originally recruits German-born Alicia in the name of American patriotism; that is the higher motive he proposes to drive her to prey on the trust of others, as he knows spies must do. She says not that she is incapable of betraying others, but that she does not value patriotism; he then plays a surveillance recording of a conversation with her father to show that she is patriotic and idealistic where she avows cynicism. Her later cultivation (i.e., deception) of Alex does indeed, the film indicates, aid her adopted country. She is an effective spy. However, she is eventually discovered (because of Dev's clumsy error in the wine cellar) and then poisoned, slowly. The spectacle of her suffering is grotesque, exactly because she has otherwise been a picture of natural health and beauty, not of dissoluteness. Her suffering, in the film's economy of feeling, is an unacceptable cost incurred by her nation's project in Brazil.[4] Moreover her seduction of Alex effectively poisoned her personal relationship with Dev. Even an ironic, confident spymaster, it turns out, cannot repress the need for a straightforwardly trustworthy partner. However useful trust may be, it refuses instrumentalization.

This film is oddly fissured: the dominant thematic problem is viewed by

Notorious (1946)

the lead character in a fashion that does not conform to the scenes on the screen. Dev is inexplicably obsessed by Alicia's prior sexual activity, and even abusive in attributing to her the promiscuity of a courtesan. He says sharp, hurtful things to her, as if sarcastic speech somehow legitimated his reluctance to enter into intimacy. He knows that he's in business to prey on the trust of others, and he draws her into this work as she asks him to believe in her. He tries to construct a cynical relation to her that might allow her to do her work and him to have an intimate life with her nonetheless. She does not go along with that at first. She too might have spoken ironically and dismissively of her own virtue, rather than plead with him for his trust. But she didn't. Eventually, though, she tells him that he can add Alex Sebastian to her "list of playmates," as if sexuality were a game.

This is just the dynamic that Dev has been asking for: two jaundiced lovers toying with corruption, but loving romantically all the same. Yet he has much more trouble with it than he anticipated. One is all the more skeptical of his judgment because Ingrid Bergman appears gorgeous without much makeup, quite unlike stereotypes of women with many conquests behind them. She was thirty-one when the film was released, but looked even younger; she had refused David O. Selznick's request that she

Notorious (1946)

Notorious (1946)

cap her teeth and shape her eyebrows. Her beauty is distinctive, and she looks trustworthy, in terms of the semiotics of Hollywood films. Why does Dev charge her with promiscuity, and why does she receive the charge with abjection rather than outrage? This issue colors the whole film and makes Dev seem a dark, opaque character running on his own energy, yet still very much at her cost.

Hitchcock stressed just this feature of the character in planning his shots of Dev. The first is a portrait-refused, and many others like it follow in various scenes. A number of close-ups of Alicia show the back of Dev's head. The camera angles seem to ask what he has in the back of his mind. He is visually presented as a character repressing some counterthoughts. In his first scene with Alicia, he establishes himself as the strong, silent type: enigmatic, imperturbable, slow to speech and action. Nothing fazes him—not her drunk guests, nor her drunk driving. He hides his affection and backs into intimacy with her—from the audience's perspective. When he walks through her apartment in Rio, the air seems thick and resistant for him, even though he knows that he fell for her right away in Miami. In the presence of other intelligence officers, he is fiercely loyal to her—so long as she is absent. Captain Prescott (Louis Calhern), the head of this intelligence operation, also trusts her entirely in regard to her political loyalty. She shows extraordinary courage in her espionage work, as Prescott and Dev recognize. Dev appears to be shamed by her intimacy with Alex Sebastian. He is more deeply shamed, though, because he solicited her for this task, and she executes it with a firmness of conviction that reflects poorly on his own ambivalence. He denies even his professional loyalty to her when she asks him how he speaks of her to his colleagues. He reports that he has been silent on the matter, and this—the audience knows—is untrue.

Why does Dev lie to her? One infers that he means to protect her from the burden of his own esteem; that he wishes to say nothing that could compromise her ability to perform her work effectively (and thereby protect herself). Another way to put this is to say that he insists on a radical and rigid sense of her autonomy. She must assent to her professional duties as a spy entirely on her own, even in ignorance of her lover's feelings. Dev understands that his professional obligations override in every instance his personal needs and desires. Captain Prescott, usually a charming, avuncular character, imposes his military authority on Dev in the scene immediately preceding Dev's lie to Alicia. Dev is angry because he is caught in a contradiction. He speaks sharply not only to Alicia but to a fellow FBI officer, Walter Beardsley (Moroni Olsen), as well. Prescott, however, is not reproved when he says: "Oh, come now. What experience do you think she lacks?" Dev restrains himself only with his boss. He is unable to maintain civility in his workplace generally; he can only yield to authority there. The champagne bottle left behind in Prescott's office stands for the strict subordination of personal relationships to institutional roles. Dev is a recruiting sergeant in an intelligence agency. Captain Prescott is a commanding officer. Alicia is not informed that she has joined an army. She means to redeem herself, particularly in Dev's eyes, by collaborating with him in work of international consequence.

In May 1945 the Breen Office objected to the film's acceptance "in stride" of a "grossly immoral woman" and withheld approval of the film.[5] In response to this prerelease censorship, an establishing scene (prior to the bungalow party in Miami after Alicia's father's sentencing) about Alicia's relationship with Ernest, an older man who kept her in the bungalow, was cut out entirely. In this scene Ernest ended their liaison and left, rather than travel with her to Havana. The thematic fissure that renders Dev's character so obviously mysterious and does something similar for Alicia's is the direct consequence of an excised scene. *Notorious* without Ernest makes Dev seem obsessive about her imagined sexual character. Hitchcock may have felt that its present form actually gets right the irrational and absolute sense in which some lovers want to imagine their entry into a beloved's history—as the first. Dev knew he could trust her political loyalty and her courage in dangerous situations. He never feared that she might really fall for Alex. That is, he trusted her in important ways. But he needed greater confidence in her sexual fidelity, even though he had no reason to think that she had betrayed him in spirit. That she had slept with other men made her impossible to trust; his imagination of her sexual experience disables him. For this film, trust is a first-order value on its own, not a facilitating virtue. Whatever else it becomes, it requires sexual exclusivity in order to withstand onslaughts of suspicion driven by fear of commitment. The film insists that trustworthiness is not open to pragmatic redefinition.

A word about uranium. Selznick thought the espionage plot dicey because the military significance of uranium was obscure. And the love plot has a related vulnerability: Alicia must be an attractive character in order to be a convincing love-interest for Devlin, yet she sleeps with a mature, short, rich man in order to get information. Devlin's retort that the wife of an FBI agent who plays bridge with other ladies in Washington is less admirable than Alicia may seem an adequate response to denigration of Alicia's character, but that leaves Alicia nonetheless a whore for America. That is a problem with state service—and not only for women: how are dishonorable acts in the name of the state to constitute evidence of noble character? Uranium is the film's answer. Hitchcock and Ben Hecht began work on the script in 1944, and they consulted Selznick as they proceeded for a year; but the producer lacked confidence in the project and so sold it to RKO. His judgment was made before the bombing of Hiroshima; thereafter everyone understood the stakes for which Alicia was playing. "Something big," as a regrettable lapse in the dialogue has it. Her espionage prevented a group of die-hard Nazis from getting an atomic weapon. Hitchcock claimed that he and Hecht consulted the physicist Robert Milliken at Cal Tech, who did all he could in 1944 to put them off a plot about uranium. For three months after this visit, Hitchcock said, he was under FBI surveillance.[6] In 1955 nuclear energy was proposed as a cause for submission to state authority in *Kiss Me Deadly*; in 1946 it was meant to justify prostitution in service to a democratic republic. "By whatever means necessary," one says, when it comes to Nazis and atom bombs. This is the corrupting force of a notion of higher ends. Nuclear energy, both films assert, has thoroughly altered civil order. After 1945 the state had ready means to dismiss even the most personal prerogatives of individuals.

Critics have been hard on the character of Devlin. Tania Modleski says that "*Notorious* encourages us to condemn Devlin in his role as with-drawn, judgmental spectator. . . . Devlin appears to be the quintessential sadist—stern, remote, and punishing, always in command of himself and the woman who nearly dies for love of him."[7] That this sadism is driven by a prior masochism, as she shows, does not mitigate her condemnation. Hitchcock's elimination of the Ernest sequence accentuates the incoher-ence of Dev's character. Dev compulsively insults his beloved by imputing to her gross promiscuity. His sudden first kiss appears to overcome for a moment his obsession with her sexual past. "I've always been scared of women," he later tells her so implausibly that it sounds like a line from some other film. Modleski is right to say that he generally seems in com-mand of himself, not particularly afraid of anyone. With one exception: he fears Alicia's past. He is certainly a worried character, and his worries begin on the flight from Miami to Rio. At Alicia's bungalow he is adroit, elegant, clever. Sobriety, however, is costly: the playful dialogue of the party scene dissolves forever when the party ends. His worries begin once he has recruited her into state service. Thereafter he cannot dwell in his own words. He repeatedly resorts to rude sarcasm—and not only to Alicia. She asks for "a little bird-call from my dream-man," and he stonily refuses to coo. He insists that she decide for herself, without any guidance from him, whether to prostitute herself for the state. He himself is not a whole character, neither sadist nor masochist: rather, riven by military profes-sionalism, romance, and sexual anxiety. His taciturnity is a cold, ugly expression of a lover's commitment to the autonomy of the beloved. One week earlier Marlowe appeared far more artful at this in *The Big Sleep*.

Many political theorists think of the formation of trust as a reasoned response to particular experience, a sum of logical inference from reliable information. This is the contractual model whereby one trusts someone in regard to a definite activity—not, for me, especially interesting or illumi-nating. One might better think of trust as a refusal to allow an absence of experience and information, or just suspicion, to undermine belief. Some individuals, it is true, seem to nearly everyone particularly trustworthy; in that sense trustworthiness appears to inhere in some extraordinary trustees. This phenomenon too, I acknowledge, seems uninstructive to me. The more surprising and common thing is that trust is *given* by a truster, and once given is expected to endure; that is, trust resists contex-tualization. In *The Strange Love of Martha Ivers* (1946), Martha's (Barbara

Stanwyck) trust of Sam Masterson (Van Heflin) is timeless. One knew already, before the amazing last sequence of the film, that she had sustained complete confidence in him ever since they were children, though he is a very different person as an adult, with little more than a swagger to show for his rebellious youth. Her bond to the boy held firm for eighteen years. She believes instantly, upon their reencounter, that he is as loyal as ever. However tough and calculating she has been as a business woman, she is ready to share her fortune with him simply because he is Sam. She has no fear of his blackmail scheme (though Walter [Kirk Douglas] does) and rightly ignores it entirely. She has simple faith in him and wants nothing more than that he reciprocate that faith. Even at the very end of the film, after Sam has walked away from their wealth, she tells Walter that Sam will never reveal their lies about the death of her aunt eighteen years earlier: Martha caned her aunt on a flight of stairs, and her aunt then took a long, fatal fall. Martha knows her boy and trusts in particular that he would never harm her. She doesn't say it, but his pride would not allow him to accuse her. She can count on his loyalty, as he can on hers. There is no such thing as temporary loyalty.

Any story of trust is a romance, and therefore backward- rather than

The Strange Love of Martha Ivers (1946)

forward-looking, even though trust is oriented on future fulfillment. Dev looks back into what he imagines as Alicia's past and finds his own sexual anxiety. The backward glance is a searching one: Where is the bedrock on which trust can rest? Its formation is understood in terms of some moment of origin. Martha lives even more irretrievably in her past than she knows. Love may fade with the passage of years, but years seem only to fortify trust, which, as with Sam and Martha, eventually becomes a fixed point of loyalty—no longer only a judgment concerning the trustee but instead a proud point of the truster's character. When Walter informs Sam that Martha has been a faithless wife with a string of petty paramours over the years, she begins to fear that Sam might be unable to trust her, if he were made to doubt how special he is to her. The concept of equivalence or substitution (of one intimate for another, say) threatens the practice of trust, as she knows, because a trustee is always understood to be exceptional, not easily replaced by another. She tells Walter, after Sam has left, that henceforth *he*, not Sam, will be special to her. She knows herself well enough to acknowledge that she needs to trust and be trusted; it may be Sam or Walter, she erroneously assumes. This is why she rushes to reconciliation with Walter. Trust, she miscalculates, is hers to give or withhold. Walter knows better now. The deep trust she seeks requires a reciprocal choice to extend faith. He declines his place in the equation and puts a pistol to her ribs, just as two years earlier Walter Neff had done in *Double Indemnity*. And she assents; together they pull the trigger. With her dying breath, she is still the girl Martha Smith who refused to be known as an Ivers. Trust is essentially a resistant, retentive element of character. A truster insists that a past moment will not be lost.

Why can't Martha reassign her faith from Sam to Walter? She has a long past with them both. Contracts can be reassigned, but not trust, which is agent- and sometimes object- though not time-specific, and it requires some measure of reciprocity. Annette C. Baier observes that not all trust is willed—hence the concept of "automatic and unconscious trust, and of unchosen but mutual trust."[8] However, she notes, "when we are trusted, we are relied upon to realize *what* it [trust] is for [those for] whose care we have some discretionary responsibility."[9] That is, a trustee accedes to awareness, at least, of a truster's expectation—that much reciprocity is expected. Walter will not give even that. He is truly present as a separate, autonomous person, and that puts a stranglehold on Martha's egotism. In *Sunset Boulevard* Joe Gillis (William Holden) tells the narcissist Norma Desmond (Gloria Swanson) that her massive script of Salomé needs the

The Strange Love of Martha Ivers (1946)

attention of an editor. Quite reasonably she says, "I'd have to have some-one I could trust." Then she whimsically settles the difficult question of whom to trust. "When were you born?" she asks Gillis. "I mean which sign of the Zodiac?" "December 21." "I like Sagittarians. You can trust them." For a narcissist, other people are all more or less the same, in that they are other; selecting one to trust is not difficult, because trust is a mere reliance on someone to get something done, an extension of will. Deep trust, however, requires reciprocal recognition between, in some sense, equals. What is reciprocated? A risk of loss. Trust and egotism are ulti-mately incompatible, because an egotist risks too little. Norma is thor-oughly indifferent to the consequences of her actions for others. Martha has for decades been indifferent to the consequences of her actions for Walter. The narcissism of these characters puts trust outside the reach of their otherwise potent wills.

I have spoken of *general* trust of a person, as distinct from reliance on someone to do something definite. This sense of trust may mean that a truster generally believes that a trustee will arrive at a sound judgment of something or other. But it is a challenge to trust someone to come to sound

The Strange Love of Martha Ivers (1946)

judgment by his or her own methods, at his or her own tempo. One may expect a trustee to recognize and, once it presents itself, be satisfied with a sound judgment but doubt whether, left to him- or herself, that person will get to that judgment—ever or expeditiously. Martha believes that she trusts Sam deeply (in relation to him, she is an awestruck girl, not a narcissistic woman), but she worries that Walter might undermine Sam's trust of her. She wishes to control what Sam is permitted to know. She does not in fact trust him to come on his own to a sound judgment of their future options. Her egotism interferes with the practice of trust when she asserts control over not only the ends of a collaboration but the *means* as well. Means are crucial to trust. *Where the Sidewalk Ends* (1950) focuses on the bad faith of a well-meaning person, rather than a narcissist. The film analyzes the practice of trust without the distraction of narcissism.

During an interrogation, police detective Mark Dixon (Dana Andrews) inadvertently kills Ken Paine (Craig Stevens), a murder suspect who is thought to be innocent, in fact. In fear that he will be prosecuted for excessive violence, Dixon conceals his misdeed and investigates the crime in bad faith. Although he knows that the local gangster, whom he accuses,

did not in fact kill Paine—because he himself killed Paine—he nonetheless
seeks to build a case against a loathsome but, in this particular matter,
innocent man, Tommy Scalise (Gary Merrill). *Bad faith* generally refers to
the knowing exploitation of another's trust in order to misrepresent oneself as more earnestly engaged in a trust-dependent collaboration than in
fact obtains. This is the vice of those whose confidence in their own management skill is greater than their trust in the autonomy of others. Dev,
Norma, and Martha are all managers. Dixon too is trying to manage, first,
a murder investigation and, second, a cover-up.

Dixon's abrogation of professional responsibility causes him little ethical difficulty. He knows that the gangster more or less deserves imprisonment, and that the city will be better off without Scalise on the street. He
feels painfully duplicitous only when he falls in love with Paine's widow,
Morgan Taylor (Gene Tierney), whose innocent father, Jiggs Taylor (Tom
Tully), is mistakenly held responsible for the killing. Dixon tries to com-
pensate for the very personal consequences of his duplicity by paying for a
costly attorney to defend Jiggs, but he sees that this mechanism for undo-
ing the mess he has made will not do, when the attorney refuses to take
the case. Eventually he confesses his duplicity, but not first to his beloved;
first he confesses to his commanding officer, Detective Lieutenant Thomas
(Karl Malden). He seeks to set straight his professional misdeed even before
acknowledging the personal bad faith he showed to his beloved. The strain
between the two lovers is the major dramatic force of the film: the audience knows in several scenes that one lover is misleading the other, and
this is painful to watch.[10]

Misprision of police responsibility is unremarkable, but the betrayal of
friends and intimates makes for drama and shame. What Dixon cannot
understand in general terms, he is made to feel in personal terms. Acts of
bad faith or knowing untrustworthiness not incidentally affect both professional and personal lives. These acts, like other lies, are not so discrete
as one wants them. The critical question is not whether one acts mostly,
often, or in some areas in good faith, but rather whether one's good faith is
constant. Dixon's efforts to limit the effects of his misdeed fail. Which is
only to say that one lie leads to another. The trust that lovers need in order
to proceed together is comparable in one regard to that needed by the
police: neither admits of exceptions. Detectives and lovers both must act
steadily in good faith. One breach, and everything comes into question.
Dixon comes to consciousness of his ethical failure only because of his
love life; public and private are reciprocally productive. Private relations

between partners don't fit compartments. Dishonesty as a police officer in this case entails a lover's dishonesty too. The idea of boundaries between diverse ethical obligations is illusory, as Dixon comes to see only because of his love for Morgan. Private obligations can make one feel the true weight of professional obligations. Rationalizations for professional missteps are abundant because so many others have already led the way; whereas no one may have already betrayed a particular beloved, and one takes one's beloveds one at a time. Each beloved holds a lover responsible for every single act. Love tunes one to particularities.

Dixon, a taciturn tough guy, eventually and with difficulty learns to represent his commitments in language as well as in deeds, and this is one of the protocols for the construction of trust. His original misdeed was a failure to pick up the phone to report his action to his superiors. The bond between Morgan and Dixon is almost entirely tacit. He mistrusts communication, as other noir heroes mistrust all record-keepers and seek to "take care of things" themselves. Dixon demonstrates his bond to Morgan and his shame at placing her father in danger of prosecution by drawing on his personal relationship with his coworker, when he asks Paul for cash to pay an attorney. Morgan, however, is less impeded by mistrust: she is the one character who directly espouses her trust of him. In the end, he grows into responsibility by recording on paper his responsibility for the death of his prisoner. He was unable to imagine facing this responsibility, so he left a letter to be opened upon his death. But he ultimately summons the courage to face the matter squarely and gives the letter to his commanding officer, and then to Morgan. Avowal is necessary to the maintenance of trust. A truster wants to express his or her trust, and a trustee struggles to answer courageously for the meaning of his or her actions in relation to that trust.

Speech and trust seem to noir characters to be rivals. For men in particular, the film suggests, what is said fails to correspond closely to trust felt. Paul Klein (Bert Freed), Mark Dixon's partner, has a strong scene with his wife, when they discuss his tortuous desire to give his partner $300 toward a lawyer for Jiggs. His wife (Eda Reiss Merin) is marvelous in this scene. She reminds Paul of all that he has said against his partner that very day, one in which the two detectives quarreled. Quarrels notwithstanding, Paul knows, he has to be loyal to his partner, for his own stability, and he needs to do so without further discussion. He does not debate the matter at all with his male partner; only to his wife, and with great pain, does he express his difficulty. Similarly Dixon never looks Morgan in the eye to admit that

Where the Sidewalk Ends (1950)

he committed the crime for which her trusting father was incarcerated. Instead, with his back turned to her, he tells his commanding officer to hand her his letter of confession to read. He matures to the point of standing up, in writing, for his own actions, but he cannot describe his actions in speech. From a male point of view, represented here by two tough detectives, trust is given, not requested, and it is given silently, as it is too in *Kiss Me Deadly*. Speech and trust are at odds because language is a medium insufficiently clean and reliable for these men, who hear lies all day long, and, to criminals and to each other, tell their share too. Detectives are masters of an instrumental language that they use against their adversaries. But the result is that they have faint confidence in affirmative language—expressions of faith in particular—and cannot muster the courage to use it. To the protocols of trust they prefer tacit understanding among strong characters who, in themselves, recognize ethical imperatives without discussion, certainly without negotiation. Nor can these men be easily reproached, because they never actually say what they will and will not do. The gods of irony cannot humiliate them. Silence conveniently helps them preserve a steady autonomy.

Where the Sidewalk Ends (1950)

Notorious, The Strange Love of Martha Ivers, and *Where the Side-walk Ends* expose characters who strenuously attempt to manage trust relations. A trustee chooses at some level to behave in a trustworthy manner, even though his or her motive may not be to conform closely to the trust given by the truster. Managers withhold trust because they think they can more assuredly achieve their ends by substituting one character for another (Walter for Sam, say) or one explanation for another (Scalise convicted of this rather than that crime). They deal not with the particularities of a lover's experience, but with general equivalences determined by abstract needs. Management is indistinguishable from manipulation, where the maintenance of trust is at issue, because trust requires one to defer to the agency of the trustee. Management and trust are incompatible.

One commonly speaks of "learning to trust" someone, of information or experience fitting into place, providing footing for a leap of faith. What about learning to mistrust? Where does trust begin to fray? Learning to dismiss or reject someone altogether may be a simple matter. But how does one *judiciously* implement doubt? Is it important to bring knowledge to bear on trust, to qualify mistaken trust in light of unwelcome knowledge about a trustee? Or is that a corruption of one's faith? To look for a way back after a leap of faith seems preposterous, but one does it nonetheless. Two characters in *The Third Man* have given their trust to Harry Lime (Orson Welles) before the film begins. Anna (Alida Valli) is driven by love and devotion. She will not modify her trust in any way, no matter what she learns from Inspector Calloway (Trevor Howard) about Harry's criminality. She stays loyal to the end. That is the way one wants to be trusted, absolutely, but it is often not the wisest way to trust. Harry's old buddy Holly Martins (Joseph Cotten) is a different sort of character entirely, though he feels fully the appeal of Anna's passionate trust. At first he too refuses to hear ill of Harry; he even takes a drunken punch at Calloway, when the inspector expresses contempt for Harry. Holly is Harry's loyal friend, and he means to keep faith with what he knew of Harry years ago. The film tracks the unraveling of that faith.

It opens with an amused and skeptical voice-over concerning the efforts of the four allied powers to reestablish civil order in postwar Vienna, though the stock footage on screen of military forces, black marketeering, and a corpse floating in dark water is not amusing. This particular political context is kept in constant view during the film, partly by virtue of the military uniforms worn by much of the cast. Inspector Calloway is a cool but honorable representative of the British occupying force who means to prosecute malefactors like Harry for the deadly consequences of their connivances. While several characters are caught up in the black market, he and his assistant are clean and attractive, particularly by contrast to his cynical and unctuous Soviet counterpart. The story of Harry's hold on his friends is held in tension with the efforts to found a responsible postwar regime in Vienna. Surely the wickedness of Harry, Popescu, Kurtz, and Winkel must be ended: Calloway is right about that. Left to their own devices, individuals produce corruption. Holly is an American citizen in war-ravaged Europe who repeatedly and thoughtlessly resists the authority of the occupying forces. The film, however, makes a cogent case for a firmly institutionalized civil order. But on what economic base should that be founded? Socialist officials are represented as officious and duplicitous, even complicitous with the black market: Harry is under protection in the Soviet zone. The film examines the obligations of citizens in a democratic republic, even though Austria is not yet that; it would take a full decade of occupation before a new Austria would be founded. Holly, an innocent abroad, learns from Calloway where the limits of private autonomy lie, where the public authority of a state legitimately overrules that autonomy.

It makes sense, in considering the revision of trust, to reflect on loyalty, a subcategory of trust that derives from an earlier moment, one not represented by this film.[11] Loyalty is a lesser thing than trust; one can give loyalty while withholding trust (as does Dev). A relationship of trust is repeatedly replenished by acts of renewal. Loyalty, on the other hand, requires no replenishment; it is a settled conviction, like Martha's assessment of Sam. The point of loyalty is that it is not momentary. One either *remains* loyal or one is not loyal. Yet, however virtuous it is not to waver, loyalty may be misplaced. A person may behave so odiously that he or she forfeits loyalty formerly deserved. Harry, remember, does not beseech Holly and Anna for their loyalty. Holly needs no reminder that he owes Harry loyalty because Harry is Holly's chosen friend. One person alone—Holly or Anna—can be loyal, exactly because loyalty requires no replenishment, whereas ongoing actions of two are required for a trust relationship.

Calloway's task is to show Holly that loyalty to Harry is misplaced.[12] This entails convincing Holly that the values that guide Harry's behavior

The Third Man (1949)

are incompatible with those for which Holly wishes to stand. Calloway has to take Holly from commitment to a particular person to consideration of general values. To enjoy the trust of another entails a responsibility to the truster, as Annette C. Baier argued, but to enjoy another's loyalty is a different matter. No reciprocal obligation is entailed; one just remains loyal to a particular person or group. Loyalty is tribal. Calloway challenges Holly to understand that for the sake of the city it is necessary to keep in view a more general good. This is the importance of the visit to the hospital. Calloway knows that Holly is a sentimentalist, which is why he shows him dying babies and a teddy bear; he makes the problem simple for Holly. When Holly realizes that Harry's work entails the deaths not only of anonymous "dots" on the ground below the Ferris wheel, as Harry explains, but of innocent babies, Holly acknowledges the incompatibility of his values and Harry's. He then understands that personal loyalty is not an ultimate value, that one's affirmation of general values needs to extend beyond elective affiliations. He sees that he must abandon his personal loyalty to Harry in the name of a more general good that includes the survival of sick children who need penicillin. He had already argued that the porter, like other citizens, is obligated to give lawful testimony to the police, but he himself later has difficulty practicing this civic virtue.

By means of a slide show (a very *slow* movie), Holly is made aware that Calloway has correctly characterized Harry as a predator who, for the sake of others, should be stopped. At first Holly decides simply to leave Vienna, as if withdrawal of his admiration for Harry were sufficient, as if knowledge of Harry's viciousness entailed no responsibility to stop him. Holly says that at least Harry won't be arrested with the assistance of his old friend: "I won't have helped," he tells Calloway. Calloway responds meaningfully that that is a dubious boast. His view is that, once Holly realizes that Harry is vicious, he has an obligation to protect others from that evil. Knowledge entails responsibility. The opposite of loyalty is not quiet disapproval, which is what Holly means to show toward Harry, but instead condemnation. Explicit judgment is necessary, from Calloway's viewpoint, and Holly is eventually persuaded: he shoots his old friend in the end. Condemnation is not properly private (and loyalty, because its avowal is ready in principle for reiteration, even in public upon request, is not private either).[13] Condemnation is a back-handed form of affirmation of general (publicly held) values on which even personal trust relationships depend. The film explores the unexpected civil consequences of forms of trust that Holly and Anna had reason to think were private. Circumstances

The Third Man (1949)

arose in which they needed to defend their loyalty as civil as well as private, or else defend the privacy of their loyalty in face of the civil damages that Harry had produced. Holly tried but ultimately could not accomplish the former; Anna does manage the latter. The film suggests that Holly's act is right; even Harry nods in mute approval of his own execution. Anna leaves the screen intransigent.

The famous last scene, which Carol Reed invented independent of Graham Greene's script, contrasts the options, condemnation and intransigence. This is the film's thematic schema. After the second and final burial of Harry Lime, Holly misses his plane in order to wait in the road for Anna to come his way. She walks past him as if he were a post. Those two characters instantiate irreconcilable approaches to trust and understanding. She would remain loyal to Harry forever, even after she knew with certainty that he is unworthy of loyalty; she must remain blindly faithful. Holly is the opposite: a friend who trusts, but consistent with what he actually knows; he changes his loyalty to mistrust because of knowledge, irrefutable and consequential information. He does have to see with his own eyes the dying infants in their hospital beds (the slide show was not sufficient). He seems through much of the film merely emotional, quick to lugubrious drinking, and so on; critics treat him roughly. But they shouldn't: he is the one character who grows. He learns that mistrust is a responsibility, once one has appropriate knowledge, and this is a dark, unwelcome lesson. Still more: explicit judgment, even all that condemnation implies, is also a necessary consequence of reasoned mistrust. It is the injury of others that renders condemnation necessary. Holly's stubborn loyalty to Harry facilitates injury to the helpless young. That is, the film suggests that there are conditions—though they are rendered extreme—when unyielding loyalty is unethical and inappropriate to democratic citizenship.

Holly wants Anna for his own—an impossible vision of completeness. Her sense of trust is incompatible with his. For her, loyalty and knowledge are entirely separate, as the private and the public are commonly thought to be. The film critic Dana Polan treats Holly and Anna as realistic characters, potential lovers in a romance plot; on this view Holly is a "loser," as Polan says, who is not respecting his old friend when he tries to charm Anna.[14] But Holly's need for Anna is more abstract. The question for him

The Third Man (1949)

is whether an enlightened approach to trust and knowledge can encompass the intensity of Anna's loyalty. The answer is no. That is what it means for her to walk past him, and that question is behind his entire effort to befriend her. She is proudly intransigent, but also a citizen of no state. There are limits to the enlightened approach to trust, but also to passion, and their failed conjuncture is necessary to show to viewers.

CHAPTER 3

Alone

"Trust thyself," Emerson declares, but his is a figurative sense that too easily makes complacency sound thoughtful. *Reliance* is the better term. Literally, properly, trust characterizes a relationship; it takes two. And yet the great test is the extent to which the trusted, one by one, remain free to pursue their own objectives. Independence plays a large role in noirs. Philosophers speak of it as "autonomy"; I draw on their help in the following analysis. An autonomous individual is left alone to find a way of acting that is deeply his or her own. Such a person may change paths, or err, though whether autonomy is compatible with anything other than rationality is debated by philosophers. The philosophical concept of autonomy depends on rationality above all else—all else. In "Self-Reliance" Emerson wrote, "I shun father and mother and wife and brother, when my genius calls me." "Nothing can bring you peace," he explains at the very end of the essay, "but yourself. Nothing can bring you peace but the triumph of principles."[1] An autonomous life can be a chilly thing.

Change is a genuine problem, because autonomy is characteristic only of those whose choices and actions reflect judgment in accord with coherent principles. Should only rational change count as autonomous action? Philosophers do not claim that autonomous individuals are at liberty to change direction as they wish. To trust a changeable person requires unusual fortitude. Gerald Dworkin asks whether autonomy is "predicated of relatively long stretches of an individual's life or relatively brief ones?" His answer, and Marilyn Friedman's too, is that long stretches *are* envisaged.[2] It should be quite difficult to determine whether an individual's choices and actions over time reflect coherence, because one does many different things. The designation of autonomy is meant to recognize unity of the will.[3] In order to argue that another exhibits that coherence, one must discern some pattern of choice and action. Is such a pattern really strong evidence of independence of judgment and will, if one recognizes its coherence? How does one know that one isn't attributing independence to familiar or conventional behavior?

The problem is yet more difficult because, as Harry G. Frankfurt nicely observes, people "are capable of wanting to be different, in their preferences and purposes, from what they are."[4] To respect autonomy is to recognize not only another's rationality but also the possibility that that person will want to realize an ideal, or otherwise change directions in the future. "The central mark of ethics," according to David A. J. Richards, "is not respect for what people currently are or for particular ends. Rather, respect is expressed for an idealized capacity which, if appropriately treated, people can realize, namely, the capacity to take responsibility as a free and rational agent for one's system of ends."[5] This is to say that autonomous individuals are paradoxically both recognizably rational and significantly unpredictable.

This insight is hard for any truster to accommodate: that a loved one's pursuit of self-realization, or of some new ideal, might jeopardize one's trust. A truster expects a trustee to change only within the truster's expectations. A truster wants a trustee to adjust his or her aspirations to the truster's need for stability. Trusters have their limits. A trustee may deliberately change beyond the range of a truster's expectations. Imagine how a self-realizing individual might be tolerated by those with no avowed interest in trust or mistrust, or how an autonomous person might fare socially. One generally succeeds in relationships when one is of use to others, but an autonomous individual may well reject the constraint of social utility. It makes sense that so many noirs end with a manhunt: a representation of extreme societal unwillingness to leave an individual alone; this is a spectacular alternative to civil trust. The object of a manhunt appears to have gone wild.

A manhunt can obviously be rendered within the conventions of realism, but its significance is allegorical. The concept of hunting a person as one does an animal is objectionable on its face; some abstract framework is needed in order to render this activity decently significant. The most common noir framework is the view that the vulnerable, nasty life of the pursued represents a universal condition; that everyone can expect to come to that. In *Raw Deal* (1948) Joe Sullivan (Dennis O'Keefe) is a prison escapee, holed up in a Sierra inn with no other dwellings nearby. Suddenly the police close in, not because they have spotted Joe but because *another*

Brute Force (1947)

fugitive, a wife-murderer, is crawling toward the door, pleading desperately to enter. Two fugitives, that is, strangers to one another, cross paths in a remote mountain inn: the implication, at the level of realistic interpretation, is that so many fugitives are being hounded everywhere that even in the mountains they run into one another. Or, as Dr. Walters (Art Smith) says directly to the audience in the last words of *Brute Force* (1947), "Nobody ever really escapes."

One is brought to realize that whatever superiority one feels to child-murderers, coarse thugs, and wife-murderers, however remote their actions seem from one's own, they represent not an evil one legitimately observes from an armchair but a familiar condition of ordinary existence. The implication of the hunt is that one's guilt may be exposed, and that, exposed and alone, one will be relentlessly pursued by an organized, self-righteous group, eager for a goat to sacrifice to the continued life of the city. New York needs its Willie Garzah, *The Naked City* (1948) suggests, to fall from a parapet of the Williamsburg bridge; California needs Roy Earle (Humphrey Bogart) in *High Sierra* (1941) to fall from a rock ledge, as Hart Crane's bedlamite dove from the Brooklyn bridge in *The Bridge*

Naked City (1948)

(1930), so that the city's crimes may seem "solved" and the life of the city may continue. The hunt provides a sense of strictly and admittedly temporary closure; but it also represents figuratively the social limits on autonomy, and the fate of the untrusted.

Both evil-doing and predation, that is, are ubiquitous, as is suspicion. In *The Desperate Hours* (1955) Glenn Griffin (Humphrey Bogart) is an especially spiteful murderer being hunted in five states after a prison break. He takes captive the suburban family of Dan Hilliard (Fredric March). Dan tells Griffin that he has in him the same violence that Griffin has in him and will certainly kill Griffin if the Hilliard family is harmed; Griffin realizes that Dan means all that he says. One of Griffin's crew is his younger brother: *two* families are on display. One has been residing in a suburb, the other in prison; it's easy to contrast them. But they are both held together by bonds of tenderness, selflessness, and authority. The important civil action proposed by the film is less the sorting of good and bad guys—that is the work of the optimistic police procedurals—than consideration of the flawed humanity of all evil-doers. A manhunt is a civil nightmare. The protection of individuals at their most vulnerable—even when they

High Sierra (1941)

themselves have forfeited some of their civil rights—is a challenge for a humane polis. That challenge may be met politically by restraining the state's police and yet enabling select noncivil investigations (by Philip Marlowes and Sam Spades) to operate with autonomy. Americans maintain a deep regard for decentralization and the idea that the autonomy of citizens brings practical benefits to the state.

It is a dark art, but how extensive is its gloom? Even shadowy films are products of light. Ambient darkness is their dominant, apparent sense, but beyond that is hope of an exception, which is what I am after: an affirmation of values not plainly evident in urban goings-on. Robert B. Pippin has argued elegantly that noir darkness is indicative of a reduced capacity for agency, for planning and controlling one's acts, realizing one's wishes. One may think that this frustration is caused by a force external to the characters; "fate" is the common expression. According to his analysis, autonomy is irrelevant to many noirs, exactly because adequate conditions for deliberation are lacking. Many noirs give "little evidence" that characters "are much in control of the deliberative criteria at work in their planning."[6] "There is very little opportunity," he explains, "for ex ante deliberation in the scenes we see, and little evidence that responses are the expressions of already deliberated about and resolved general maxims of action. In the simplest sense, events come at characters much too fast and too confusingly to allow such reflection."[7] Noir characters appear to be up against impossible odds, or a system of domination, as Willie Garzah, Joe Sullivan, and Ray "Mad Dog" Earle surely are. One might infer that deliberation is ill-suited to the situations faced by noir characters. However, their difficulty cannot be due to a general deficiency in rational analysis itself, because a number of films make a point of explicitly measuring the analytical powers of one character against those of another: Kathie Moffat is quicker than Jeff Bailey, and Jeff was once quicker than he is during the events on screen in *Out of the Past*; Michael is a "dope," as Pippin says, by comparison to Bannister and his wife in *The Lady from Shanghai*; Sam Spade is highly intelligent and his partner, Miles Archer, in *The Maltese Falcon*, simply dumb; Steve Thompson too is shown to be dumb, in contrast to Anna and Slim Dundee, in *Criss Cross*; and so on. Relative measures of intelligence are explicitly taken because they have consequences. Cleverness, foresight, and consistency count in noir.

Pippin's thesis about defective deliberation meets certain films particularly well: *Out of the Past* is his prime example, but it holds too for some others he does not analyze: *Criss Cross*, *Double Indemnity*, *Notorious*, and *Kiss Me Deadly*. For interpretation of *The Maltese Falcon*, *The Big Sleep*, and *The Third Man*, the claim has less to offer; their inquirers keep pace with the plot. Those plots are puzzles of sequence: characters look for causal explanations, and rational analysis is their only suitable tool. The famous anecdote that Raymond Chandler could not remember who killed Owen Taylor in *The Big Sleep* might be mistaken as evidence that causation is tangential to noirs, that atmosphere alone kills, but the contrary is the case. These films are elaborately plotted exactly because rational analysis is essential to the satisfactions of this art. Joe Brody killed Owen Taylor. That matters, as Chandler knew when he wrote the novel, and Faulkner did too when he worked on the screenplay. The fact that consequences arrive quickly and confusingly, as Pippin observes, raises the stakes on relative measures of intelligence. Even very high intelligence provides no assurance of success. But in the best noirs—the ones that count most—high intelligence does allow some characters, such as Philip Marlowe and Vivian Rutledge, to construct unusual trust, the darkness notwithstanding. Pippin's view is that noir characters are "profoundly opaque to themselves or act without being able to register and respond to what is happening to them."[8] This compelling account has a deep purchase on the thematics of noir. Some characters refuse deliberation—Steve Thompson and Swede Andreson, for instance—but no such refusal dominates *The Maltese Falcon*, *The Big Sleep*, *The Postman Always Rings Twice*, or *The Third Man*. The surprising thing is that nonetheless the opaque characters persist into spy films that succeed noir: think of Jason Bourne. The super-agents a half century after the noirs speak explicitly of their own opacity. Brainwashing, in Bourne's case, and ideology and ambition in other cases, have rendered these characters nondeliberative. But theirs is a condition to be resisted—an illness even— rather than a general property of noir existence.

There are some, as Pippin indicates, who refuse to investigate matters, and others whose equipment does not serve deliberation well, but the great noir inquirers are truly autonomous characters: neither entirely private and self-interested nor salaried state agents. They maneuver for distance from both poles and proceed gradually toward reliable judgment.[9] This process entails incidental trust, phase by phase, as an inquirer determines which bits of evidence to develop and which to set aside, but it often entails as well the testing of a single relationship for a deep trust. Along the way, an inquirer may decide to rely on one bit of testimony or another and have no intention of an enduring relationship with the source of the testimony, who is of merely instrumental value. A relationship of deep trust, however, needs to be preserved over time, and that requires that an inquirer not interfere with the autonomy of a trustee. How does a truster cope, in moments of doubt, with inevitable uncertainty concerning a trustee?

With patience, self-restraint, and humor—this is the substantive answer that *The Big Sleep* offers, and it is the most affirmative account of trust that the noirs present. My argument is not that many noirs despite appearances present a utopian understanding of deep trust. Rather, this one film expresses a vision that is compatible with the conditions of life, the desires, and the frustrations presented in many noirs. One exceptional film sees beyond others, yet its vision expresses something compatible with other films; that too is a form of representativeness. Ernst Bloch's account of the greatness of exceptional art works is relevant: they provide an "anticipatory illumination of something accomplished insofar as the anticipatory illumination could be incorporated into the images and ideas at the zenith of an epoch that was rich in perspective."[10] Marlowe (Humphrey Bogart)

The Big Sleep (1946)

and Bernie Ohls (Regis Toomey), a homicide investigator from the district attorney's office, obligingly share information and discuss most things freely. But Marlowe will not tell all, or not right away. Bernie nonetheless trusts Marlowe and Marlowe, Bernie; Marlowe is nowhere near so open with anyone else. Bernie teases Marlowe about being a suspect in the death of Owen Taylor, a former Sternwood chauffeur, but he does so with a smile. He is all geniality and agrees to wait a day or so for more information from Marlowe.

These details demonstrate the practical possibility of a reciprocal, sustainable private-public collaboration of just the sort that is later lacking in *Kiss Me Deadly* (or, more generally, of two autonomous individuals of different personalities in a trusting relationship). The evidence of Bernie's trust of Marlowe is patience. The cop's humor indicates a manner in which patience can be sustained; one need not take seriously all the merely apparent incriminating evidence against one's trustee that events have to offer, moment by moment. "Do nothing 'til you hear it from me," as Billie Holiday says, "and you never will." Bernie does not demand justifications or explanations. Patience allows one to live through uncertain periods when one's trustee is off on his or her own. This truster is relaxed, cool-headed, and uncomplaining, a model of mature, high-toned trust. One might infer that his trusting manner is necessarily dissociated from sexuality, that the film is skeptical of trust within a sexual bond. But this is not so. The repartee between Vivian (Lauren Bacall) and Marlowe also indicates an aspiration to trust coolly and with more wit than logical conviction; there is no unique strain between that aspiration and their mutual sexual desire.

Some female characters—though certainly not all, nor even most—similarly exercise autonomy. According to Michael Wood, "the activity of women is virtually the only intelligent activity in the movies, because men never have time to think."[11] For women, the path to what philosophers call autonomy is more difficult. They are generally solitary, or friendless; male inquirers have buddies. Vivian Rutledge goes her own way without explanation, as Evelyn Mullwray does too, without the comfort of a confidante or collaborator. Brigid O'Shaughnessy is on her own in *Maltese Falcon*, but less interestingly because she simply wants a payday. However, a desire for money is a conventional way to figure a very basic autonomy: as selfish acquisitiveness—a starting point to be acknowledged without shame. The Sternwood daughters are schematically arrayed contraries concerning autonomy. Carmen (Martha Vickers) is represented as a thumb-sucking adult who flirts like a nubile girl. After first meeting her, Marlowe tells the Sternwood butler that she is old enough to be weaned. She has a drug problem, as we say, and is never capable of exercising sound judgment. When he brings her home from Geiger's cottage, he tells the butler what to tell the police. She is expected to play no role herself in discussion with the police. The grown-ups decide where to put her groggy body. Mere biological existence, even past the age of majority, does not establish autonomy. Not one's being but instead the quality of one's deliberations allows one to negotiate diverse difficulties in an ongoing process of decision-making. The philosopher S. I. Benn argues, as others do too, that "defects of practical rationality" disqualify a person as an independent agent.[12] Carmen, like others suffering comparable defects or compulsions, does not meet the minimum conditions of autonomy. Her importance to the film is her representation of reasonable limits to the distribution of autonomy among adults. One realizes, because of her, that there is no good reason to conceive of autonomy as an inalienable right or entitlement.

Vivian is the one who tests Marlowe's capacity to trust an independent woman; she takes him far into the dark, not by what she says (though she

The Big Sleep (1946)

is quick-tongued), but by what she does. She repeatedly shows up where, as a candidate for his trust, she should not be—at Joe Brody's apartment, then at Eddie Mars's casino. "Shows up" is the pertinent predicate because the film does not amply reveal what she is doing at these sites; muteness is the point. She exercises her mobility, but still more mobility *without explanation*, particularly to Marlowe. Her later presence at Art Huck's produces the darkest of these scenes; there, she is close to Eddie Mars's seamier activities. Marlowe gets there on his own, it must be remembered, not because of Vivian. He imprudently disables his own car, presumes that the villain Canino will not recognize him, and thus leaves himself a fixed target.[13] Then he turns his back on Art Huck. For these errors he can blame only himself. He has exercised his own freedom, and in doing so underestimated his adversaries and put himself in mortal danger, from which Vivian rescues him, but without explaining why she was there. She might have warned him off of these errors, but he discovered his own limited capacity by setting his own trap.

Benn refers to a *"principle of noninterference,* the minimal or formal principle that no one may legitimately frustrate a person's acting without

some reason. In calling it a *formal* principle I mean that it determines neither what a person ought to be free to do, nor what is to count as a reason
for interfering."[14] That good reasons exist to interfere in the activities of
others is certain. However, one must argue for particular reasons when one
wishes to respect the general principle of noninterference but identify an
exception to its applicability. Without explanation and advocacy, there is
no interference. When a character like Marlowe refuses to debate justifications of a trustee's actions, as he does in the car ride from Art Huck's, he is
deferring, in his willed silence, to just this principle of non-interference,
though of course he would not call it that. Earlier Vivian attempts to interfere with Marlowe by telling him that her father wished to terminate his
employment, which is of course untrue. Coercion, deception, and manipulation, Marilyn Friedman notes, are the standard ways in which one's
autonomy is violated.[15] Vivian does effectively terminate Marlowe's relationship with her father, and the good general's role in the film.

An inquirer enters a process guided by certain general, strongly held
views. As a plot progresses, those views are tested and revised. Autonomy
is not properly conceived as mere protection from interference, or sanctu-
ary. As Benn argues, "To be autonomous one must have reasons for acting,
and be capable of second thoughts in the light of new reasons."[16] It is this
process of modification or self-refashioning that makes these films exis-
tentially compelling and difficult. Marlowe is a changed man at the end of
The Big Sleep. Dan Hilliard in *The Desperate Hours* is a revealing character in this regard. His distinctive feature is that he is constantly measuring
risk to his family in terms of a situation that changes unexpectedly
moment by moment. His daughter asks him once whether they are wrong
not to go directly to the police when they have an opportunity to do so. His
reply: "Maybe"—not a word often heard in movies. He cannot be sure of
the wisdom of his policies, but he does not surrender responsibility to
think clearly in every changed situation. He modifies his plans in view of
uncertainty. He is said by his adversary Glenn Griffin (Humphrey Bogart)
to be "a tough old bird," and that is his type. But the point here is that he
does not stay in type. He changes as Odysseus does in order to succeed at
keeping his family safe from the criminals who have invaded the Hilliard
home. Autonomy calls for controlled change or adjustment in response to
engagement with resistance, as Marilyn Friedman observes.[17]

But why do noir inquirers seek knowledge? Is it a mere given that they
want to know who killed whom and why? Are they only doing a job for
which they are paid? The opening sequence of *The Big Sleep* addresses

these questions. As John T. Irwin nicely observes, they are self-employed, and much follows from this fact. They *choose* to solve particular crimes. Yes, they are making a living, but their motivation, evident in their persistence, goes beyond the pursuit of remuneration. Their fees are often said to be the same for one case as for another; money provides a necessary but not a sufficient explanation of their motives. When Marlowe first arrives at the Sternwood residence, he is curious about the lives of the very rich. With Carmen, Vivian, and even Norris the butler, he is playful. Of General Sternwood he is respectful. With the others, his spirit is light, even affectionate. His banter with Vivian concerns exactly the issue of ends sought. She wants to know what he seeks. He won't say, ostensibly because of his agent-client relation to her father. But the film shows in this opening sequence that his motivation in this case is a little mysterious. His playfulness indicates that he is not there only to work, and that the process of interaction with wealthy people is as important to him as the end for which he is to be paid—the foiling of a blackmail effort. Such a person has his own motives for inquiry and action, and he means to enjoy the pleasure of self-direction.

The most influential account of autonomy (as legislating for oneself—and by example for others—that which is generalizable) plays little role in noir. Kant held that "*Autonomy* is . . . the ground of the dignity of human nature and of every rational creature."[18] Detectives generally enjoy negative liberty (relative freedom from state, or other, interference) rather than Kantian autonomy. The idea of living so as to legislate for others is remote from the noirs. One sees in *Casablanca* (1942) what is missing from the noir treatment of trust. Rick Blaine (Humphrey Bogart) tries to live entirely for his own ends, autonomous in the common sense of setting his own direction and caring only for himself. "I stick my neck out for nobody" is his repeated slogan. Even very late in the story, he says to Ilsa (Ingrid Bergman), "I'm the only cause I'm interested in." But he comes to repudiate just that by the great end of the film. What turns him around is her account of her past, because it redeems Rick in his own eyes. He sees that she did in fact love him in Paris, and that she was obliged to leave him abruptly. The important feature of this turning point is that his understanding of her story restores his self-esteem. He does not need Ilsa herself. He needs instead to think well of her and of her attachment to him. With his recovery of that admiration, he is able to renew his idealism.[19] The ideal he embraces is the Kantian one of legislating for others; this distinctive form of autonomy is a sign of his recovery of spiritual health. Ilsa tells him that she does not "know what's right any longer. You have to think for both of us, for all of us." A subtle point lies in that generalizing apposition, the transition from thinking for two to thinking for "all." In a narrow sense, "all" means Laszlo, Ilsa, and Rick, but it also refers more broadly to all those affected by resistance to the Nazis. Rick replies, "Alright, I will." And he does. His concept of the greater good is merely numerical: that which affects the largest number of people. And this shallow concept gives rise to his most didactic and regrettable speech ("Ilsa, I'm no good at being noble . . ."). Kantian autonomy requires some self-sacrifice, which takes a sexual form here. Kant's is not the autonomy of hungry lovers. Rick leaves with Louie (Claude Rains).

Noir types are on their own, but trying nonetheless to form a deep bond with one other person. First they need negative liberty, then someone to trust. The goal of trust among autonomous individuals is fraught with paradoxes. The films do not propose autonomy for everyone, but it is worthy of intelligent friends and lovers. The grandest development of this theme is Marlowe's silence. At the end of *The Maltese Falcon* Sam Spade explains where he thinks the limits of trust lie. But in *The Big Sleep* Marlowe appears to know that to attempt to rationalize his trust of Vivian would be a bad idea; even to speak of her intentions and his expectations would hem her in. Howard Hawks marks Marlowe's development by pairing two scenes, in both of which Marlowe drives and Vivian rides.[20] In the first, he takes her away from Eddie Mars's cowboy gambling salon and asks her without success what Eddie has on her, a question Chandler has him ask her four times ("If you say that again, I'll scream," she finally replies). In the second he is driving to a confrontation with Eddie Mars, he says, to ask *him* to explain. To Vivian, Marlowe says: "I won't ask any more questions. I'm not even going to ask you how you got into this mess."[21] His progress is toward self-restraint: he does not insist that she explain why she has been involved with the perpetrators of evil. He trusts her without any explanation: that is his maturity.

Or, to put it more generally: this is the greatest of noir lessons. To respect her autonomy is to surrender the expectation that one's judgments will be made entirely on the basis of reasons and explanations. The basis of this trust is not adequately encompassed by language. This moment transcends the substance of the film in that the great preponderance of its scenes consist of one character explaining something or other to another; the film is almost all talk. Marlowe means to move, through trust, beyond all that. The philosophers insist that autonomy rests upon rationality, but they do not resolve the contradiction between rational coherence and unpredictable change.[22] Marlowe does not stop for the obstacles in the path of recent philosophy on this topic. He accepts the reach of trust into silence, or he has made his judgment of Vivian's character and trusts that.

However, the film does not end there. The final scene has Marlowe moving around Geiger's cottage, making one decision after another without consulting a silent, witnessing Vivian. He then tells her what must happen: her sister must be institutionalized, and her father must be told that Sean Regan is dead. Vivian observes that he has forgotten to say anything about her. He asks what is wrong with her. Her answer closes the film: "Nothing you can't fix." This is a step backward. The trust he displayed during the ride to Geiger's cottage is a great but in truth a dark thing. He imagines lovers silently trusting partners they do not fully understand; this is not a concept of communitarian dependence or collaboration but of tough individualism. When Vivian pays tribute to Marlowe's enormous competence at the end of the film, she presents herself as a patient, a partner who, like Carmen, needs reparative work. She is surrendering her own autonomy in a scene plump with flattery of Marlowe. The difficulty of this conclusion is not only that a domineering male has resumed control of a capable woman, but further that both characters have lost sight of any sense of equity. Why Vivian, clever, ironic, and rich, surrenders to this arrangement has to do with the extraordinary plot of the film.

Every critic must account for the plot of the film because, without explicable causation behind episodes, the efficacy of rational choice is in question, and with that goes the ground of agency. Howard Hawks, looking back four decades, characterized the plot of *The Big Sleep* as peripheral, improvised during the shooting. It "didn't matter at all," he said. "It was all what made a good scene. I can't follow it."[23] My sense is that the film presents a steady press toward resolution of this story of seven homicides (of Sean Regan, Arthur Geiger, Owen Taylor, Joe Brody, Harry Jones, Canino, and Eddie Mars), though only the first, third, and fifth are controversial, as well as four extortion attempts (Brody and Geiger's separate efforts to blackmail General Sternwood, Mars's blackmail of Vivian, Brody and Agnes's effort to blackmail Vivian).[24]

The film begins with a sequence that establishes indirectly the disappearance of Sean Regan (Vivian's husband in the novel, though not in the film), and directly the merely apparent origin of the plot in Geiger's blackmail of General Sternwood. These are two apparently rival lines of inquiry, but they are soon revealed to be just one. The death of Sean Regan is the true origin of the plot; everything follows from that. The opening sequence introduces Marlowe first to a flirtatious Carmen Sternwood, then to her father who insists on talking more about Regan than about Geiger the extortionist, and finally to Vivian who coyly attempts to learn whether the cover-up of Regan's death, for which she has paid Eddie Mars, is jeopardized by Marlowe's inquiry. Marlowe is indirectly told, as the audience is too in this oblique opening sequence, that the real challenge is to find Regan, and that Carmen's appetite has something to do with Regan's disappearance. The resolution of the plot is tidily foreshadowed by this opening sequence at the Sternwood mansion. General Sternwood is being blackmailed by Geiger, first, for bogus gambling debts allegedly incurred by Carmen Sternwood. In fact Vivian, not Carmen, incurs gambling debts, though these are not her debts either; the confusion about which of the sisters might have incurred such debts establishes ambiguity concerning the distinct agency of these two—might one attempt to answer for the other? Carmen is then used to set up another of Geiger's efforts to blackmail her father: for the return of nude photos of his drugged daughter. (Joe Brody and Agnes try without success to see this effort to completion after Geiger's death.) Carmen's true vulnerability, Eddie Mars tells Vivian, is her culpability in the murder of Sean Regan. Carmen's loyal sister, with Mars's help, conceals what she thinks is Carmen's role in the death of Regan by paying for Mona Mars to live incommunicado in Realito. Marlowe follows the trail of Geiger, and that leads surprisingly to Mars, as well as to Joe Brody. Both Brody and Mars, it turns out, have connections to Vivian. She has a convincing explanation of her relation to Brody: he was trying to blackmail her with the nude photos of Carmen not only drugged but, worse, in proximity to the murder of Geiger. And Vivian has still greater reason to respond to blackmail attempts because of her effort to cover up the murder of Sean Regan.

The film's suspense is generated by the fact that the two lovers have antithetical projects: Vivian to bury and Marlowe to excavate recent events. His annoying question about what Mars has on her resolves most of the film's plot. Only in the final sequence does Marlowe question whether Carmen did in fact kill Regan, and that question sets Carmen and Vivian free. Mars is nonplussed by Marlowe's skepticism and quickly concedes that he himself killed Regan: "What are you going to do about it?" he says. This is the last twist of the plot, and it explains why Canino executed Harry Jones so quickly. Would Canino be ordered to execute Harry

Jones and (presumably) Agnes too only to help protect Carmen from prosecution? He might plausibly take criminal liability for those lives to protect his boss Mars from prosecution, especially if Mars were actually guilty of the deed, for Mars would need all the protection he could get if in jealousy he had murdered Regan. Marlowe's effort all along has been to understand *what* was done in the past. Only very quickly in the final minutes of the film does he engage the question of *who*dunit, and that changes everything. He insulates Vivian and Carmen from prosecution, and Vivian gives him uncharacteristic docility. The various relations among the characters that he uncovers complicate his understanding of the past but not of individual characters. Hawks's characters are made to operate in an elaborate web of connections to one another, but they are not deeply constrained by those connections. Vivian's involvement with shady characters repeatedly surprises Marlowe. But she steps free of those relations at the end of the film. Autonomy is hers to recover, once Marlowe's skeptical, rational inquiry has run its course.

CHAPTER 4

Men You Can Trust

The autonomy of others is an open source of difference and surprise. It is a challenge to one who trusts to hold in constant esteem the autonomy of the trustee. Trust among men, though, is apparently simple because obviously limited, and men trust limits. "If you'll trust me just half an hour, I'll trust you," Steve Christopher (Elliott Reid) says to Detective McDonald (Carl Betz) in *Vicki*. Male codes convert trust into reliance. That simplification is an alternative to the deep trust to be constructed between a man and a woman. What follows here is a mirror image of deep trust, a defining counterterm.

The arrangements movie men make with one another do not challenge what characters wish to know, nor are they designed to enhance life in any deep sense. They are instrumental, strategic. In *Strangers on a Train* (1951), Bruno Anthony (Robert Walker) pitches to Guy Haines (Farley Granger) a limited-liability arrangement, an effort to substitute mutual reliance for trust. When he fails to persuade Guy to sign on to a "criss-cross" murder plot, Bruno pushes ahead on his own and strangles Guy's wife Miriam (Kasey Rogers) in order to obligate Guy to perform a reciprocal murder of Bruno's father. Persuasion and consent, that is, are optional in this regime. Bruno may think that Guy will feel intimidated by such decisiveness and then obligated by the proposed arrangement, even though he did not consent to it. Or Bruno may be willing to rely instead on Guy's fear of the complicity that is his by having even talked about his wife with Bruno. Either way, Bruno feels no need to agonize over his speculative implementation of the arrangement, because he has no regard for Guy's autonomy. A preview version of the film (misleadingly called the British version) renders more explicit than the released one does the homosexual dynamic of the conspiracy Bruno proposes. Bruno's desire goes beyond the practical elimination of his father; he wants an intimate bond with Guy. The mutual murder pact substitutes for a love relationship: not trust but reciprocal reliance, a male version of romance—without need of mutual autonomy. Bruno proceeds on spec, without resort to lengthy persuasion, as if a code concerning reciprocal obligations were in place, and he needed only to conform to that in order to compel Guy to conform. On this view, the behavior of men is relatively predictable; the manipulation of that behavior, a practical matter.

Deep trust can seem impractical, unrealistic, though it is neither. Men quickly come up against the practical limits of trust. The most basic is that in a reproductive economy there is need to protect the identity of family lines; a man must know better than to trust another with his beloved. Men may trust other men with their money or safety, but not with their women. (The plot of *Pulp Fiction* [1994] is built on a counterinstance: Marcellus Wallace [Ving Rhames] does trust Vincent Vega [John Travolta] to entertain his wife, Mia Wallace [Uma Thurman], while Marcellus is out of town. The point, however, is that Marcellus's authority is so great and terrible that he dares to extend this unlikely trust to his subordinates.) Some noir paragons conspicuously resist the charms of a femme fatale in order to honor male-male trust; Ed Beaumont (Alan Ladd) in *The Glass Key* (1942) stoically pushes Janet Henry (Veronica Lake) away, until his infatuated buddy Paul Madvig (Brian Donlevy) gives him the ok. (Ed and Janet then, free from a hardly manageable constraint, run out of the scene.) Johnny Farrell (Glenn Ford) in *Gilda* is a similarly unrealistic buddy. When Ballin Mundson (George Macready) hires Johnny to run his casino, he announces a proviso: "There's one thing that I must be sure of: that there's no woman anywhere." Trust among men has its basis in an act of exclusion intended to ensure stability. In *Brute Force* six men share a cell with a single photo of a woman. She is revered by them all; they share her. They can do so because her image is vague, a nearly abstract face with eyes closed—she is not a single woman. If she were, they would quarrel over her photo on the wall. She can be shared only because she is a face on the calendar after time has stopped, a sign of all women, and none in particular. There is a certain purity about trust among men, but it is simple, fragile, immaterial, and based on an admittedly partial vision of life. This communist idealism seeks to overcome not only pragmatic obstacles to trust, but competition *tout court*. And the overcoming of competition is the overriding objective of male trust.

In what media might straight men construct trust of one another? Men

Brute Force (1947)

and women have sexual intimacy, but what are gentlemen to do? Male trust often entails civic corruption. Men demonstrate trust by compromising professional obligations in favor of their friends; personal interests are allowed to usurp benefits of the public sphere. Ned Racine (William Hurt) in *Body Heat* has two male friends: Pete Lowenstein (Ted Danson), an assistant district attorney, and Oscar Grace (J. A. Preston), a police detective. These characters all mean well toward each other, but only to a point; their trust is measured. Pete and Oscar make a concerted effort, in the privacy of Ned's apartment, to warn him off of Matty Walker (Kathleen Turner), though that unwelcome warning comes much too late. The surprise is that, having once warned him, they feel free to contrive an apparently spontaneous face-to-face encounter with a witness who may be able to establish Ned's motive to murder Matty's husband. Ned must choose, in this test, between a front and back exit from the police station. If he chooses the second door, to avoid the witness in the lobby, his friends will know that he was already Matty's lover two weeks before the murder of her husband, and that he lied to them about the depth as well as the duration of his involvement with her. These two scenes follow one another almost directly—a scene between Ned and Matty intervenes. Their proximity heightens a thematic contrast between public obligations and private interests. Men have public obligations that are expected to restrain private interests; that is the whole point of a public sphere, and men are conventionally charged with its maintenance. Two scenes later Pete tells Ned that Oscar is a principled, relentless investigator who will not look the other way even for his friend. Pete then violates his public responsibility to the state by revealing incriminating evidence against Ned. Ned's two buddies are aligned differently on the axis of male trust, but only a little differently: they collaborate in execution of a test of Ned. Everyone knows that private interests distort the administration of justice and the public sphere generally. The film's surprise is rather the delineation of calibrated but nonetheless severe protocols (warning, trials) constraining the expansion of male trust.

Brittle understanding. What is entailed by trust among men can be unambiguous: loyalty and violence, not more. When a call for loyalty is articulated a trustee is obligated—no matter his own judgment—to stand with the truster. This is why, in *Where the Sidewalk Ends*, Paul must give his partner Mark $300 on a moment's notice, and without discussion. In *Gilda*, Ballin will say almost nothing to Johnny on the eve of Carnival until he tells him that he wants his friend by him at midnight. Johnny has no need to reason why or how with Ballin; his role is just to be there, ready to engage Ballin's adversaries. When they first met, Ballin used his phallic cane-knife to protect Johnny from a robber. This weapon and Johnny too are known as Ballin's friends.

The knife, Ballin says, is a "most faithful and obedient friend: it is silent when I wish it to be silent, and it talks when I wish to talk." "That is your idea of a friend?" Johnny asks. "That is my idea of a friend," Ballin replies. The trust between these men explicitly excludes autonomy. They are obligated to unquestioning loyalty, and Johnny to obedience, because the relationship is hierarchical.

Johnny is fiercely loyal, but Ballin, in contravention of his own proviso, introduces the one element to undermine their collaboration—Gilda herself. Near the beginning of the collaboration, Ballin tells Johnny that women and gambling don't mix. Something profound must be at stake, when so clever a character proposes an obvious falsehood. Real gambles (like acts of trust) entail openness to risk, but Ballin says more than once that he and Johnny instead make their own luck. The gambling they oversee is not a true game of chance—its wheel of fortune is fixed. Women, on

Gilda (1946)

the other hand, truly are a gamble, Ballin means, and his casino is no site of chance. He intends to control access to his wife, but he winds up sharing her with Johnny: one particular woman, two men. To Ballin, she is deferential; to Johnny, alternately ironic and tender. She started at different points in space and time with these two men, and she has rendered them strangers to one another because of their different relations to her. And that arrangement cannot be sustained in the flesh. Yet Ballin, nothing if not deliberate, brought her into his life with Johnny. Ballin *wanted* to construct a triad of the sort his paradox about women and gambling announced.

There are few accidents in this art. The plot is schematic: Gilda's appearance with Ballin is a grandly implausible coincidence. Of all the women in Argentina, he chose Johnny's former lover. Only this particular woman can test the possibility of suppressing the past. Can two men make a wholly new future by sharing a woman? She vigorously undermines the stability of Johnny's relationship to Ballin, and she delights in being a wild card in the deck, avatar of difference in the well-run casino. Ballin proposes a conspicuously false view of their triad: "All three of us with no pasts, all futures." On one level, this may be translated as: "Let's start our lives over

Gilda (1946)

as a social, if not a sexual, threesome." More superficially, one knows, everyone has a past (i.e., a limited future), particularly in the land of Noir. The only question, Ballin learns quickly, is who knows of that past. From the moment he introduces Gilda and Johnny, their deception begins. They lack courage to tell him of their past. That past is still alive, and every day that follows is another act of deception within both the threesome and the twosome of Johnny and Ballin. The indefiniteness and comprehensiveness of the deception is the relevant point. There are no discrete lies in trust relationships.

The film is flawed by Obregon's late revelation that Gilda's promiscuity was phony: she had been in the company of men other than Ballin and Johnny but had taken no lovers. With this information the reestablishment of monogamous heterosexual romance is made easy. The erotic vigor she had displayed in the casino signified no lasting challenge to conventional sexual arrangements. And with the reestablishment of ordinary romance the sexual energy between Ballin and Johnny too is pushed out of view. Not that the film would be better if only it heartily affirmed Johnny's devotion to Ballin or the ostensible promiscuity of Gilda, but it might be richer if it more fully engaged the sexual possibilities raised by this triad of characters. Instead Gilda admires a conclusion in which no one has to apologize: Johnny and Gilda had both been "stinkers," she says. Ballin is the one unrepentant character: he did not renounce his affection for Johnny; nor for the wife who seemed to others promiscuous. He loved them both without regret for the range of his affection. He has to die. The film releases the energy of three relationships—that of Johnny and Ballin, of Ballin and Gilda, and of Johnny and Gilda—but then withdraws all that does not conform to the last of these, as if only that can endure. The film suggests that the end of World War II and its international alliances entails a return to stricter national identities. Only the bond between Johnny and Gilda is suitable to a return to America. Those two are ready to declare their traveling lives erroneous wanderings. The potential partnership of Johnny and Ballin that included a vision of global domination and the willful marriage of Ballin and Gilda are both dismissed as might-have-been after the war; neither arrangement can return the characters to their point of origin. Repentance comes to seem shallow, a convenient adjustment to historical developments. And this element of bad faith renders *Gilda* a noir of the second rank.

Although male trust is comprised of straightforward limits, it is strongly utopian: with women out of the way, men hope for all life to be changed. Easy to think that a society of likeness might be especially peaceful, harmonious, stable, because competition is felt as everything but that. Male trust is always in danger of flipping into a rivalry; that is what Ballin hopes to preclude, first by proscribing women generally and then by sharing a particular one. One comes to understand male trust partly by attending to males' betrayal of one another. That trust is a version of squadron loyalty wholly at odds with any plausible notion of individual autonomy. The great failure of male trust is that it produces only rigid structures for action and judgment. The situation of male prisoners is especially instructive, because prison codes are explicit and definite. One knows just what is expected of one and what consequences follow from untrustworthiness: ostracism and death are always the end.

To every question there is one right answer; in prison, there are no mysteries. But this is obviously a non-elective community, and most of the trust operative there is not freely given. Prison trust is intended not to answer to the emotional needs of trusters or trustees, but to provide practical arrangements for those deprived of autonomy. Nonetheless *Brute Force* gives a strong representation of the efficacies and vulnerabilities of male collaboration. The prisoners live together more or less in harmony with one another, united in contempt of the head guard, Captain Munsey (Hume Cronyn). Men rely on one another with extensive confidence, as they need to do. However, the limits of this reliance are revealed in the course of a prison break. Joe Collins (Burt Lancaster) asks Gallagher (Charles Bickford) to collaborate in an escape plan. Gallagher declines, but says that if he were to collaborate with anyone in such a thing, Joe would be the one. He trusts Joe, but he won't collaborate and he can tell Joe why: Gallagher has been promised parole. That is the one answer to a definite question. When, later, paroles are suspended, Gallagher immediately joins the break without debate, as if all judgment were pragmatic. The break is planned to begin at 12:15 p.m. with an attack on the guard tower by a contingent of prisoners in the yard under Gallagher's leadership. Two minutes later another contingent, led by Joe, is due to attack the tower from the rear. However, Joe is slightly delayed; at 12:22 Gallagher gives up on him and, in desperation, rams a truck at the one gate out of the prison. A couple of minutes later Joe, who does get control of the tower, throws the lever to open the gate, but the crashed truck will not allow the gate to open; it opens inward. Drat! The whole effort fails on this one error of practical judgment. Joe looks down from the tower at the truck with exasperation. For all their practicality, the conspirators failed to allow flexibility in their plans. A seven-minute delay threw everything off. In fact, the conspirators knew nothing of the practical fact that things that can go wrong often do. An unalterable plan, however appealing to these men, does not accommodate the actual lives of others.

The rigid action of *Brute Force* is matched by rigid judgment everywhere evident in films about male trust. Forgiveness or even forbearance is rare among trusting males. They enforce on their trustees instead a code of severe retribution. In *Act of Violence* (1948) former army officer Frank Enley (Van Heflin) betrayed his American soldiers, then prisoners-of-war, by informing a Nazi captor-commandant of a planned escape attempt. In return for that information, Enley was given food. He told himself then that he was motivated by prudent care for his imprisoned soldiers, but he later admits on screen that the food was the real thing. This betrayal cost ten soldiers their lives and made widows of six wives. Joe Parkson (Robert Ryan), one of the would-be escapees, survived with a lame leg, and he hunts down Enley to avenge his comrades. Enley has become a successful small-town California contractor after the war. He tries unsuccessfully to elude Parkson and preserve his new position. He offers Parkson a bribe of $20,000 to go away, as Sam Bowden in *Cape Fear* offers Max Cady a similar bribe; Parkson just laughs that Enley could think that money might test his bond to his comrades. Gregory Peck's Sam Bowden offended Max Cady (Robert Mitchum) by testifying as a witness against him in an assault trial eight years before *Cape Fear* begins. Sam's was the testimony of a private citizen, though as an attorney during the film he is an officer of the court and an exemplar of lawfulness under pressure. Martin Scorsese, in the 1991 remake, draws the point much more boldly: Sam (Nick Nolte) admits to having violated a public trust by suppressing exculpating evidence for Cady (Robert De Niro), his own client whom he once served as public defender. His betrayal was a professional violation, as Sam admits, motivated by zeal to put away a violent criminal. Nothing is open to discussion in these three films. Women discuss everything among themselves; men and women discuss a great deal too. But men among men implement a code: stand by your word. Parkson will have Enley pay with his life. Cady will have Sam pay with his family life.

The coward Enley eventually redeems himself by diving in front of a bullet from an assassin he hired to kill Parkson. Parkson survives and Enley dies heroically, as a Secret Service agent might. This is the only act capable of restoring social and ethical order, i.e. honor, after the war. One

Act of Violence (1948)

might wish it otherwise, but violence is a necessary instrument in the male imagination of restitution after betrayal; it assures genuine sacrifice and incites remorse. Enley is an exemplar of postwar economic expansion, but he cannot go forward because of his past. He failed to honor a public trust, and his victim demands that he pay with his private life. Enley's wife (Janet Leigh) and child will be hurt, but Parkson does not care. Parkson's girlfriend Pat (Mary Astor) tries to persuade him to let this old wartime betrayal rest in the past, but Parkson cannot do it. Negotiations cannot alter the matter; male trust is immutable. Language has no bearing whatsoever on Parkson's mission. He can let vengeance go only once Enley is dead. A righteous man betrayed by another man is a nightmare for everyone, exactly because he has little means to transform betrayal into forgiveness or anything beyond retribution. Pat and Edith Enley are brought together by their understanding that betrayal is not the end of life itself. They want the men to find some transformation that might bring them all into a future. These films about the dead hand of the past all ask what possibilities are open to the future. The men see death as the only end of betrayal. Max Cady in Scorsese's *Cape Fear* has become a fundamentalist Christian minister who dies speaking in tongues. But he knows nothing whatsoever of Christian transformation. He is just another outraged man insisting that the wages of betrayal is death. Noirs depict, without admiration, a grim male vision of trust and betrayal. The avengers make a fool's economy.

Robert Altman's *The Long Goodbye* (1973) pushes for just short of two hours against the constraints of male trust, as if to ask whether greater depth might be manageable. But no, the limits of male sociality are unyielding. The film starts and ends with a single male relationship: two buddies. Marlowe (Elliott Gould) lives across from a half dozen often barebreasted beauties whose calisthenics merely amuse him. These dream neighbors have at their entry an ornamental traffic signal set on green when they first come on screen, but this Marlowe is not especially interested in women. Like Raven in *This Gun for Hire* (1942), he has a cat. The neighbors are a nice invention: they make it obvious that the film's focus is male sociality *not* mediated by women. How far will a trusting male go to protect a buddy's interest? Marlowe suffers abuse at the hands first of the police and then of the hoodlum Marty Augustine (Mark Rydell) to protect Terry Lennox (Jim Bouton). Why Marlowe does this is not obvious. When asked if he knows Terry well, he repeatedly says, quite exactly, that he has known Terry for a long time, too long to say; in their early scene

Cape Fear (1991)

together they play like overgrown adolescents. Marlowe's trust is so great that he drives for three hours with Terry, clawed across his cheek, but declines to inquire after details. No questions asked: a buddy deserves autonomy, which entails silence. The distinctive feature of this relationship is that Marlowe suspends his skepticism: he just *has* faith in his guy. To the police and to Mrs. Wade, he expresses heartfelt conviction that Terry truly loved his wife Sylvia and could not have beaten her to death. For all his brittle wit, Marlowe is a sentimentalist.

Noirs repeatedly expose misleading appearances: the commonplace is that things are rarely what they appear, nor people either. Their faces cannot be trusted. When, in *Charade*, Peter Joshua reveals his true identity to Reggie Lambert in his Paris embassy office, he makes a goofy face and clowns about his deception. Marlowe, in *The Long Goodbye*, also makes faces: for the police, when he is booked and interrogated; for Eileen Wade (Nina Van Pallandt), when she tells him that his face inspired her trust; and then Roger Wade (Sterling Hayden) tells him that he has a good face. This is essential to Elliott Gould's interpretation of the character. Gould (or Altman) sees that Marlowe needs to adjust his appearance to various contexts, moment by moment. Marlowe does this playfully, without anxiety of any kind, as Bogart too does in Geiger's bookstore in *The Big Sleep*. Marlowe has a rubber face, Altman shows—sound equipment for living. Consider the alternative, also conspicuous in the film: three women— Sylvia Lennox, Eileen Wade, and Jo Ann (Jo Ann Brody), Marty Augustine's girl—suffer beatings to the face. Sylvia and Eileen seem to stand up for themselves, but they are beaten anyway; Jo Ann smiles benignly at Marty, and he brutally smashes a Coke bottle in her face. Marlowe is appalled by photos of Sylvia's injuries, mildly concerned about Eileen's, and indifferent to Jo Ann's. No particular pattern. The guard at the entry to Malibu Colony keeps no one out. He good-naturedly greets everyone with an impersonation—Jimmy Stewart, Barbara Stanwyck, Walter Brennan. Marlowe too light-heartedly clowns his way past LA cops and thugs. He just means to get by his adversaries, partly with humor, partly with patience, in order to press his own investigation so quietly that viewers may not notice that his main question throughout the film is, Who killed Sylvia Lennox? That question disrupts the surface plot when Eileen Wade, whom Marlowe has disingenuously drawn into thinking she holds the reins, asks: "Why don't you call me Eileen?" Then he lets her know that his interests are far from romance, that he suspects her of wrongdoing. She is stunned by his questions. Only her husband's suicide gets her off the hook. Walk quietly and wear a rubber face—that is the film's counsel.

Personal judgment seems the basis for Marlowe's lengthy, unpaid investigation of Sylvia's death. However, he does say that he was bound to silence not only by personal loyalty; his business depends on prospective clients having confidence in his discretion. It was good advertisement for him that the press told of his unwillingness to cooperate with the police. Professional interest and male loyalty overlap a little, as they do for Sam Spade in *The Maltese Falcon*. Nonetheless Marlowe is determined still, near the film's end, to defend Terry's honor, if Roger Wade is in fact guilty of Sylvia's murder. Nothing so arouses Marlowe's ire as his friend's damaged honor. When he eventually sees that Eileen Wade has played him, and that Terry, guilty, callously exploited their friendship ("Hell, that's what friends are for"), he goes far from his place of business, and far too out of character (when did Marlowe get—or need—a pistol?) to execute his old friend. Altman puts Marlowe on a tree-lined allée, approaching his confrontation with Terry, to whom Marlowe has been loyal at his own cost. Holly Martins walks down a similar allée at the end of *The Third Man*, after having executed and buried Harry Lime. Both characters come to the end of male trust and accept responsibility for cleaning up the mess made by their misplaced loyalty. Terry, it turns out, was just a shallow guy who considered Marlowe a "born loser." Altman did very little to establish this character; Raymond Chandler's Terry Lennox is a fuller character with a rich and varied personal history. Altman's "Terry Lennox" is little more than an allusion to some distant, unknown past: to the concept of a sentimental bond. This is why Terry can disappear for most of the film: he

doesn't need to *do* anything for Marlowe's trust. Male trust has this inert-
ness about it. A male is trusted by virtue of *being* a buddy. Marlowe stu-
pidly erred in trusting Terry. Men and women haggle, struggle over the
terms of their trust; male trust is a blunter instrument.

The concept of transformation has enormous power; forgiveness is only
one of its forms. Parkson and Marlowe transform betrayal into patriarchal
justice through retribution. One commonly but wrongly thinks of betrayal
as utterly debilitating for the betrayed one. But Marlowe is jolly after he
executes Terry Lennox; he now understands his life more fully than he did.
He has found a limit of which he had been ignorant. Even the pain of sexual betrayal may be turned into a source of unsuspected strength. Noir
buddies often help one hold at bay the consequences of such loss. Tony
(Jean Servais) in *Rififi* (1955), for instance, signs on to do a jewel heist he
had declined earlier in the day as suitable for young men, but he does so
only after he has beaten his former lover Mado (Marie Sabouret) for her
infidelities during his seven years in prison. Tony is rejuvenated by her
betrayal, or by his confrontation of the dark truth of her faithlessness.
There is a sense in which violation may renew moral order, and betrayal
may renew trust. Tony's violent but parental response to Mado's promiscuity gives him strength and recklessness to undertake a risky robbery. A
cold vigor comes of surrendering trust, or of living without illusion of
another's trustworthiness. Mado drives Tony to homosociality, then to a
sense of invulnerability. Finally he demonstrates a steely will to assure the
survival of a heterosexual family, as if mistrust of women might be reconciled with a reproductive domestic order. He does not turn away entirely
from the heterosexual and heterosocial structure, though he resolves to
serve it not as a lover but as a benign father at one remove: trustworthy
Uncle Tony. Betrayal brings him to an abstract, ascetic strength beyond
sexuality. Male trust is often formed in reaction to some betrayal that
collaborating men wish to contain.

Trust and betrayal have an elegant simplicity and economy in this film
about men. First, one witnesses the bright, utopian promise of homosociality.
This is the imagined harmony of collaboration without difference (as in
Ballin's rigged casino without women). Tony's gang members trust one
another easily. Although they have never worked together, they quickly
enjoy each other's company, collaborate uncomplainingly, even silently, and
debate nothing whatsoever. Even when conflict arises, it is easily dispatched.
At their first meeting, Tony and Cesar (Jules Dassin) trade insults, but as a
result of their reciprocated directness they quickly and respectfully shake

Rififi (1955)

hands and become true friends. They demonstrate in words a willingness to conflict with each other openly, when an occasion demands that. They locate each other's limits and then enjoy one another with confidence that, were further problems to arise, they would know of them directly and be able to resolve them without delay. Cesar is an expert safecracker and a cooperative worker whose one vice, libido, leads him to break his gang's trust. He ultimately, though inadvertently, breaks Tony's rule to stay away from the nightclubs immediately after the heist. Once he has betrayed his colleagues, regardless of his innocent motivation, Tony reminds him, the rules dictate that he must die, and Cesar, without protest, takes his bullets like a stoic. That is the male correction of noncompliance.

Cesar's is a simple violation: one rule, broken. A tougher challenge is to extend and deserve trust in a future of unforeseeable circumstances. Compared to Cesar, Jo (Carl Möhner) is an antithetical character, entirely a family man. He is more loyal to Tony than any of the other gang members. But when Jo's son is kidnapped by a rival gang, Jo cannot trust Tony to retrieve the boy. Uncle Tony does in fact recover the boy, but not before Jo crosses him by giving the loot from the heist to the rival gang as ransom

Rififi (1955)

for the boy. Jo suffers a fatal shot in the head by the rival gang leader, who manages to shoot Tony as well before he himself dies. These two betrayals, Cesar's and Jo's, are symmetrical contraries—one a promiscuous, and the other a domestic heterosexual male; together they imply that all hetero-sexual drives are hazardous to male solidarity.

Fraternity works without difficulty through the duration of the job, but these two forces that move Cesar and Jo more generally corrupt male trust: the allure of available women and the protection of male heirs. Both drives overrule manly trust. Jo and Tony die needlessly, only because Jo could not trust Tony sufficiently with the fate of his son. For that matter, Mario and his girlfriend Ida (Claude Sylvain) are dead because of Cesar's foolish pur-suit of the nightclub singer. This is especially ironic because Ida exempli-fies an alternative type of woman who, while joyfully devoted to Mario, casually exposes her breasts before the other gang members, who seem not to notice her allure. However, men are ultimately unable to submit to a discipline of trust and restraint, for reasons derived from an economy of sexual reproduction. Mario and Jo are neither undisciplined nor reckless. Quite the contrary. They thought that their violations were exceptions to rules they meant to honor. Concerning the gang's rules, they express no skepticism. What brought them both down was too strong and too sexual a sense of individual agency.

The objective of male trust is to overcome individual agency, to render autonomy irrelevant. Cesar and Jo hit their limits in this regard and must be executed. The failure of male trust to generate flexibility and forgiveness is especially meaningful. Forgiveness is a crucial test of any concept or practice of trust. Without it, trust is indeed impractical, because of course people fail to uphold their trusters' expectations, and their own. What is to happen then? Is trust itself simply doomed to failure? Male trust of males has seemed, in the stories I have told, to be blocked at just this point: when a male trustee fails a male truster, the trustee must be killed, as Enley, Lennox, Jo, and Cesar all are. When they are eliminated male trust is reduced to a mere code, not a real practice for people who inevitably fail some of the time. Because everyone fails eventually, the enforcers of the male code would have to eliminate all males; that would be the generalization of the male trust code. However, one neo-noir does conspicuously establish a connection between male trust and forgiveness, and its success is instructive.

The mystery plot of *L.A. Confidential* (1997) is rapidly explained by Ed Exley (Guy Pearce) and Bud White (Russell Crowe) who, after both (separately) making love to Lynn Bracken (Kim Basinger), have an athletic fight that reconciles them. This violence not only establishes the sort of restitution discussed in connection with *Act of Violence*, it loosens their lips so that they can narrate for viewers and for one another the resolution of the mystery. Then they team up to bring the film expeditiously to its conclusion. Their entrance into Pierce Patchett's (David Strathairn) home is

L.A. Confidential (1997)

choreographed like no other scene in the film. These cops suddenly seem made to be dance partners; their collaboration, a long series of coordinated right moves. Until Exley had sex with Lynn, he and Bud had been completely antagonistic. But sharing a woman has a transformative effect, more or less opposite to that of Johnny and Ballin, who did not knowingly and sexually share Gilda. Knowing is everything. Ballin was deceived and tried to kill her when he learned of her intimacy with Johnny. But Bud's situation was different: he was deceived, though only briefly; Lynn was a prostitute, so long as Pierce Patchett lived, not Bud's wife. She managed, that is, the equivalence of lovers; her acknowledged profession keeps the concept of substitution in constant view for Bud and Exley, and for viewers of the film. Exley was told explicitly by Lynn that fucking her was, for him, an indirect effort to fuck Bud. Exley accepted that insight and moved ahead. She could see all along that Bud and Exley were the film's real lovers, though they could not talk about it. Bud's jaw is wired shut at the end: obligatory taciturnity! The film lets Lynn end her career as a prostitute, but not as a mimic. All Hollywood rests on substitution, and so does male-male trust. In the final sequence she is no longer a Veronica Lake type. She wears shorter hair and Ray-Bans, as Marilyn famously did. Bud has certainly forgiven Exley and Lynn for their intimacy, and all three lives have moved ahead, with evident trust in one another—a transformation achieved by sharing a woman. The film closes with a tender, juvenile farewell between the two men.

The objective of male trust? An end to rivalry. Men trust one another in order to relieve themselves of the burden of competition. It is a remedy to a problem, not a good in itself. What if one sought trust as a resource rather than a remedy? Bud cannot say a word about the life he expects in

L.A. Confidential (1997)

L.A. Confidential (1997)

L.A. Confidential (1997)

Bisbee; that is unknown territory to him. The noirs expose various hazards to trust between men and women, but that is the site of noir hope. The trust of men in one another focuses more narrowly on reducing the costs of rivalry.

CHAPTER 5

Women You Can't

In the last quarter century the noirs have been sharply reinterpreted by feminist critics. This has been the dominant direction of noir criticism: the films as psycho-political allegories. Elizabeth Cowie recapitulates the now-established notion that film noir presents a "masculine scenario" of a man "who suffers alienation and despair, and is lured by fatal and deceptive women."[1] This account is widely shared, and with reason. It has a purchase on many relevant films, but, as Cowie observes, "the duplicitous woman is essential neither to the group of films designated *noirs*, nor to the thirties crime fiction from which many were derived." She argues further that the sense of noirs as committed to a masculine fantasy "obscures the extent to which these films afforded women roles which are active, adventurous and driven by sexual desire."[2] Even scholars who are critical of the masculine scenario appreciate the strength of characterization in noirs. Janey Place, for instance, observes that film noir "does not present us with role models who defy their fate and triumph over it. But it does give us one of the few periods of film in which women are active, not static symbols, are intelligent and powerful, if destructively so, and derive power, not weakness, from their sexuality."[3] There is much to like in these films without denigrating women—including particularly memorable characters like Kathie Moffett, Vivian Rutledge, Brigid O'Shaughnessy, and Gilda. My difficulty with the now-conventional view is that it focuses on the psychological needs of a single person and does not adequately deal with the significance of relations among characters in the films. As the title *The Big Sleep* comes up, Bogart and Bacall are shown in silhouette. He lights her cigarette and his own. Two cigarettes, side by side in an ashtray, are on screen at the end. This stylish little frame stresses that Vivian and Marlowe have found terms for meeting each other's needs, chiefly for autonomy. My interest is less in male fantasies than in the construction of hope by means of trust established between two characters at a time.

In love one trusts, as if it wielded power beyond that of any one or two lovers. Insofar as lovers are *made to* trust one another, one questions the reaches of a lover's will, and at its farther reaches one encounters cruelty and betrayal. *The Postman Always Rings Twice* depicts the cruelty to which ordinary people may resort just to have their way in more or less ordinary matters. What makes the subject engaging is not cruelty itself but the ways that people can *share* responsibility for cruelty. The story of a single evil-doer is one thing, but when two collaborate their rationalizations, on the one hand, and their shamelessness, on the other, enrich the story immensely. The sharing of shame—as Frank and Cora, Walter and Phyllis, and Martha and Walter all do—requires that these partners trust one another to keep each other's shame secret. Still more, lovers who collaborate in an evil act—murder obviously, but the same is true of adultery—trust their collaborators to dissociate the deed from their character. That is, lovers who come together in wrong-doing usually need their partners to have faith in them *despite* shared knowledge of the misdeed. And this happens every time that adulterers marry after betraying former partners. Willfulness must be renamed as something else. One marries a beloved who has been adulterous on the premise that untrustworthiness derives from a moral lapse, or from local circumstances, but not from character. Trust and betrayal, not cruelty, make a story. The difficulty of the film is whether a corrupt will can be sufficiently rehabilitated to support mutual trust.

Frank Chambers (John Garfield), Cora Smith (Lana Turner), and Nick Smith (Cecil Kellaway) are presented as reasonably careful and self-aware. Nick is a largely jolly fellow—anything but villainous or loathsome. He is inattentive, parsimonious, and drinks excessively, but he is generous with his young and implausibly beautiful wife. The two of them married with a frank understanding that their relationship might develop into love but was to begin as a mutually cooperative arrangement. (James M. Cain, in the novel, was less thoroughly committed than the screenwriters later were to the topic of willfulness; he provides no such information about Nick and Cora's arrangement.) Frank is a cocksure drifter who likes to get his way with others on the sly, but he admits all this to Cora. She is a cool, vain young woman who claims not to like her own looks; there is that minor duplicity about her. She is sufficiently romantic or sincere, however, to leave her marriage to wander with Frank, though they get only a few miles away before she admits that she needs the financial security of

her arrangement with Nick. One noteworthy feature of the characterization of the film's evil-doers is that neither is particularly intelligent. Cora
refers to Frank as smart, but he shows little sign of that to the audience.
They are ordinary people who want things that are unavailable to them
without an act of murder: so murder it is, then. They suffer from no complications of desire, and their past is unremarkable. They just are not intelligent enough to escape punishment. The lawyers are the only smart ones.
Working people are simple and shallow in the film. Because working people can be frank about their desires and pragmatic in their deliberations,
they should be controlled by clever guardians of the law. I say *should*
because the film represents the power of the state in lean fashion (none of
the homicide detectives and squad cars of other noirs). Such a low-budget
state needs all the intelligence it can muster.

Lana Turner's performance effectively conveys a little bad faith now and
then: in particular, when she proposes killing Nick, she coyly guards her
glance and reveals her intention hesitantly but nonetheless deliberately in
order to manage Frank. Jessica Lange in 1981 presented an especially lusty
Cora (close in that sense to Cain's original character), whereas Lana Turner
found some innocence there. On their first night-swim, Cora horses around

The Postman Always Rings Twice (1946)

with Frank in the surf, as a teenager might. She shows no extraordinary sexual appetite, and she wants only to own her own labor-intensive business. She means to work hard for modest financial security, but she does want it. She has to manage Nick and Frank in order to get her way. She is willful, even driven, but those are altogether common characteristics. Cora does actually love Frank, and she wants a family with him. To realize her goals, she is willing to collude in the murder of a man who clothed her well and trusted her far more than he should have. Her essential vice is not appetite of any sort, not even cruelty, but rather a willingness to use all others as instruments in her own self-realization. Hers is a sin of management, banal and recognizable, but an utter faith-breaker, as Martha's Walter comes to understand.

This film's power derives in large part from the representation of social class. Cora is waitress and cook in her husband's diner. The diner is on a side road off the coast near Los Angeles. Frank is a drifter who owns but one suitcase. These characters have no reason to think that their financial or social prospects are bright. But in the comprehensive California sunlight that seems not to matter greatly. Remember that the opening dialogue is about aspiration. Frank is chipper about his future, unworried about his prospects. And Lana Turner is robed in clean white for most of the film. She too has a sense that her future should be unobstructed—and easily could be. She wants to make something of herself, she says. The plot is a working-class variant of a court intrigue. The characters want *more*: Frank wants the girl, and she wants the diner; neither fame nor power but just the things that ordinary working people want. Frank and Cora are conspicuously secular people without religious conscience; the commandment not to kill warrants no mention in their deliberations before they actually kill Nick (even though Frank is telling his story to a priest). They fear only the state. James M. Cain's novel was preemptively censored by the Production Code Administration as early as 1934. Sheri Chinen Biesen tells the story of an ultimately defeated ban that lasted over a decade.[4] The production of the film was a milestone in the reduction of industry censorship. Biesen attributes the ban mostly to the book's sexuality, but what makes the film genuinely subversive is that it frankly presents the instability of working-class ethics. That aristocrats and very rich people connive without compunction to seduce and kill one another is not news, but that ordinary people do so as well for a blonde or a diner is more immediately troubling.

The meaning of individual noirs usually derives from plot, character, and dialogue, but the great ones make their meaning felt nondiscursively

The Postman Always Rings Twice (1946)

as well. *The Postman Always Rings Twice*, for instance, has a distinctive rhythm: Cora and Frank oscillate between passionate hope to be free (but financially secure) and hateful mistrust of one another, back and forth without progress. Frank is repeatedly faithless and shallow; and Cora, rancorous and proud. Their relationship began in betrayal and deception; from that core, they can develop nothing truly positive. They repeatedly betray one another and call the score even, as if that might be a basis of a fresh start. Little good comes of wrong-doing. The film's rhythm seems about to change, though, when Cora returns from her mother's funeral in Iowa and announces a change of heart toward Frank. At first one thinks that a new awareness of mortality may have made a difference to her—a deepening touch of death. Later one learns that the cause is inadvertent pregnancy. She imagines that raising a child might serve as restitution for the murder of her former husband. Frank and Cora both turn to a commercial model of Christianity and imagine a comforting God who balances deaths and births arithmetically. However banal, this theology frames their misplaced trust of one another and of their own powers.

Despite her venality, Cora has greater strength of character than either

Frank or Nick. A sense of closure and change allows her to take her life into her own hands. She is unambiguously courageous in her willingness to accept public responsibility for her misdeeds, as she does when she reopens the café after her conviction for manslaughter and faces down her infamy. "Would you kindly give me your autograph?" a gloved lady asks this proprietress-waitress. Cora accepts responsibility again, in a different manner, when she requires of Frank a new ground for their relationship. She deliberately leads him on a long ocean swim, recollecting the night-swim that occasioned her first consent to their love affair. She tests his devotion by telling him, out in the ocean, that she is too tired to swim back on her own, that he might easily leave her out there to drown if he wished to do so. She actually asks him to do just that if he does not trust her: "Frank, what I wanted to be sure of was whether you trust me, whether you believe that I can never turn on you again." When they get back in the car to drive home, after he has towed her to shore, he asks her: "Are you sure now?" "I'm sure," she says. He does trust her, and she him; they have both risked loss to continue together. Moreover they have renewed their faith in the notion that a single deliberate decision can turn life on a dime.

They are poised for a new beginning, when a car accident reestablishes the film's rhythm. What this catastrophe suggests, in the eyes of their god, is that trust alone is no adequate justification of life. Frank and Cora (and their fetus) die, on this view, because all they have is mutual trust—a great but not a sufficient good. The lives of these ordinary predators serve no worthy end. Their trust, their wills are extinguished by a road hazard, a just god, or just a larger view. The surprising feature of Frank's narrative is its innocence. Walter Neff and Jeff Bailey narrate their past with some realization of their own errors. Not Frank; his story is crisp, buoyant, unre-flective. He is executed because instead of breaking past the cycle of betrayal and reconstituted hope that has plagued his relationship with Cora, he runs the car into a concrete wall. His last hope is that he will be with her in a Christian afterlife. "If you've got this far," the closing sentence reads, "send up one for me and Cora, and make it that we're together, wherever it is."[5] It takes religion to break out of their cycle; trust cannot do that, for these two. They need more metaphysics.

Conventional representations of men and women in film start with eros, but that is not where trust begins. And trust pushes back against familiar categories of interpretation. Eros certainly draws one to intimacy, but between eros and trust is a basic enmity. Everyone wonders—over and over—how to harness the force of eros with bonds of trust. Is eros the true

The Postman Always Rings Twice (1946)

basis of the collaboration between Phyllis and Walter in *Double Indemnity*? She first appears wrapped only in a towel; once she is dressed, the camera and then Walter focus on her legs and an anklet. She and he understand each other well enough to act decisively in concert. Their repartee shows their ironic imaginations moving at the same tempo and in the same direction— though for a moment Phyllis surprises him. In words they do very well with one another. She seduces him by letting him think of himself as not only a rake but also a wit. After his second visit to the Dietrichson home, he is at his apartment, thinking that she will approach him again about a plot to murder her husband, and then she is at the door, as if on a stage cue. He says in the voice-over that he already knew she would be there. "Suddenly the doorbell rings and the whole setup is right there in the room with you. . . . That was it, Keyes. The machinery had started to move and nothing could stop it." It seems to him utterly "natural" that she should be at his door. Does he feel destined by a force of nature to commit this crime? By his own nature? Or is it rather a particular femme fatale?

Cora enters her first scene even more dramatically than Phyllis does hers in *Double Indemnity*. But Lana Turner's Cora is an earnest and ordinary miscreant. She wields no mysterious allure. Very good looking, yes, and that is all. She is self-disciplined, hard-working, and ambitious in modest terms. The concept of a femme fatale refers to a particular woman having unusual power to arouse in men unusual desire and compliance. This figure has erotic charisma. But some of the greatest noirs reveal the thinness of that appeal; they invoke a more matter-of-fact account of motivation.

One infers wrongly that the basis of Walter and Phyllis's mutual attunement is erotic; in fact it is intellectual and shallow at the same time. Eros is only a point of origin for Walter's involvement with Phyllis, and even for him that dissolves almost immediately. She arrives at his apartment at 8:00 p.m., he says, and she must be home by 9:30 to meet her husband, she says. The implication is that in about an hour they have made love for the first time, and he has been persuaded to murder Dietrichson, which is quick work on both fronts. Surprisingly, the film represents no great transformation of the characters during this time. Their lovemaking appears not to have been sufficiently extraordinary to require any distinct comment from either of them.[6] She asks only if he will call her, and he fails to hear her because his mind is elsewhere. He is scheming the murder of her husband and the deception of his employer, Pacific All Risk Insurance Co. But in reverse order, because his long-standing fantasy has been crooking the house—not bedding a blonde. Faulkner thought of Cain as a smutty writer, but the story makes no mention of sexual intimacy between Walter and Phyllis (Phyllis and Nino, yes). In an abstract sense the film is close to Cain's story in this regard.

Walter and Phyllis are both clever, it's clear. He is on the make, and she means to be desired. Their sexual frankness might lead one to think that they would be imaginative lovers. But they are evidently only ordinary, conventional lovers with one another. When they express devotion their language is dull. "I'm crazy about you, baby," Walter reports to her on their first embrace. Later he tells her: "I'm thinking of you all the time, baby." She assures him, "I love you, Walter." And he replies, "I love you, baby." Barton Keyes (Edward G. Robinson) is utterly free of such banality. His language conveys genuine wit and distinctive judgment. "You're not smarter, Walter," he says famously, "you're just a little taller." This is funny, quite true, and therefore altogether memorable.[7] His language presents a standard of intellectual honesty by which others are to be judged. Walter and Phyllis say nothing particularly funny, true, or memorable about their affection for one another. Their intimate expression is thoroughly conventional.

Double Indemnity (1944)

There is a larger-order conventionality too about Phyllis's analysis of her marital situation. The main characters have substance, yet they are dissolving too in some broth of habit and aspiration. Phyllis, for instance, reports to Walter at his apartment that her husband is "so mean to me," that "he's always been mean to me," that he begrudges her every shopping trip, and so on. When Mr. Dietrichson (Tom Powers) comes on screen, he is in fact a mean guy, or at least one who has settled with satisfaction into an ordinary grouchy husband and father. He barks resistance at his wife and daughter and seems thereby to make himself feel important in the household. Phyllis is simply correct about him, even though her analysis sounds self-serving and juvenile (unless one credits her with an allusion to Billie Holiday: "Why must you be mean to me?"). Phyllis and Lola Dietrichson (Jean Heather) oddly cannot do without that grouchiness. When Walter drives Lola to meet Nino Zachette (Byron Barr) at Franklin and Vermont, one learns that the forbidden suitor Nino is much like the forbidding Mr. Dietrichson: he puts his head in the window of Walter's coupe and barks resistance at Lola, much as her father had just done at the family home. The daughter needs a complaining, domineering male. The

Double Indemnity (1944)

big surprise is that Phyllis too needs her mini-Dietrichson. Walter is
amazed to learn that Nino pays late-night visits to her after the murder of
Dietrichson. The characters and their ideas are not particularly distinctive; the film makes a point of the recirculation of language and experience. Phyllis was the murderous nurse of the first Mrs. Dietrichson; then
she becomes a murderous second Mrs. Dietrichson. Walter first uses the
expression *straight down the line* to indicate assiduous compliance with
his supposedly masterful plan for the murder. Phyllis repeats the phrase
several times to indicate her deference to his plan. Keyes independently
invokes the idea of a "trolley line" to the cemetery. This is the dominant
figure for the plot, as one learns in the opening shot of Walter's car speed-
ing down streetcar tracks as if he were aiming at construction workers for
the Los Angeles Railway Company. Those deterministic expressions bleed
into one another toward the end of the film; the impulses of these characters are so ordinary that even the figurative idioms of one will serve for
another. Instead of extraordinary lovers or villains, the film presents
phrases and types in circulation.

And yet Phyllis and Walter collaborate in murder and grand larceny.
They rely on one another practically in order to execute their plot. Their

reliance is without any deep or exceptional basis, however extraordinary the plot. This is mutual reliance masquerading as trust. The film suggests that much of what is commonly called trust between men and women is largely a procedural arrangement having to do with timed meetings, and that eroticism is too trivial to warrant more than perfunctory representation.[8] Even collaboration in the commission of extraordinarily consequential acts does not require deep trust; the most decisive agents are egotists, however they patter of love. What Walter comes back to is not passion, not a woman but a man. He devotes his last free moments, as he bleeds into incapacity from a bullet wound, to a proud explanation of his actions to his friend and colleague, Barton Keyes. Walter is a lover only in a shallow sense; he is an insurance worker who effectively chooses to die at the office rather than live free in Mexico. And this industry of massive record-keeping is riddled, like other industries, with the ordinary corruptions of ordinary people.

Walter tells Keyes that he murdered for money and a woman, and that he got neither. But he has a third motive, stronger than the others: Walter is competitive. He is the top salesman at his firm, and a proud, cocky fellow. Keyes thinks at least for a while that Walter is smarter than the others

Double Indemnity (1944)

in the office. Walter acknowledges to Keyes that he fantasized about deceiving the firm, and that he imagines that Keyes has done the same: "One night you get to thinking how you could crook the house yourself, and do it smart." When he returns to the firm after having been shot, he is responding to the greatest pressure he knows. He is not very lustful, and he shows little sign of material greed. But he is intent to tell the one to whom he is closest that he has tricked the firm and bested Keyes's "little man" of suspicion. Walter has several engravings of pugilists hanging on the walls of his apartment. Two amateur sports trophies serve as bookends there as well: one for basketball, one for boxing. Walter is an athlete. He wants to win. His real passion is for the game he plays with Keyes and Pacific All Risk Insurance. After Phyllis shot him, he was three hours from freedom and medical attention in Mexico. He spent that precious time not at the wheel but at the office, boasting to Keyes of his cunning. Sparring with his employer and his best friend: that is his supreme delight. His objective, like that of a pugilist, is victory over men he has faced.[9]

Romance, intimacy—much of this is really social and common, not distinctively personal. Greed is a social vice, and that is what Phyllis feels most deeply. The most painful consequences of misplaced trust are met by those who know each other intimately and are yet surprised by what they fail to anticipate. Their lovers become strange to them, when their bonds stand revealed as more truly social than intimate. There are, however, many occasions when one trusts strangers or acquaintances in social settings, as Walter and Phyllis sense (while the housekeeper looks on!) that they might possibly trust one another largely because they relish clever innuendo. How does one determine when to extend good faith as a beginning, or withhold it as a prophylactic doubt? Prognostication is inevitably inexact. Is a hunch, therefore, as firm a basis as a rational inference for a leap of faith—or perhaps for a small one? What kind of information might count for one betting on rational inferences? An inference depends upon a capacity for recognition: some particularity seems evidence of a general phenomenon. How fully, then, do socially identifiable types govern perception and inference, even concerning romantic experience? And what potency does the concept of a femme fatale have when even she is an ordinary self-seeking person among other similar characters?

Something surprising happens to the two lead characters near the end of the film: each experiences a moment of release from self-interest. Two consistently egotistical characters abandon caution and endanger their survival. The first incident comes when Phyllis refuses to fire a second shot to stop Walter's advance on her. She knows that he means to kill her; that her life is at risk, but she lets him come all the way to her and take her gun. "Why didn't you shoot, baby?" he asks. "Don't tell me it's because you've been in love with me all this time." "No," she answers, "I never loved you, Walter. Not you, or anybody else. I'm rotten to the heart. I used you, just as you said. That's all you ever meant to me—until a minute ago. I didn't think anything like that could ever happen to me."

This is just what it seems, a frank moment of truth—and her first. Armed with his customary cynicism, Walter misses this single recognition of his autonomy: "I'm sorry, baby. I'm not buying." To which she is indifferent: "I'm not asking you to buy. Just hold me close." He embraces and kills her. She is surprised by the shot, as audiences should be too, because this moment of self-recognition runs counter to all that has preceded it, and it is without consequence. Minutes before she methodically prepared to shoot Walter in her living room. For no apparent reason, she abandons that plan halfway through, and with nothing to gain from the reversal. The very next scene shows Walter confronting Nino Zachette, whom he planned to frame for Phyllis's murder. Instead he reveals himself at the site of the murder and gives Nino a nickel to call Lola. Like Phyllis, Walter has nothing to gain and much to lose from this moment of selflessness. Audiences have little reason to expect selflessness from Walter; he is as out of character here as Phyllis was a moment earlier. Raymond Chandler and Billy Wilder invented this set of reversals for the screenplay. Wilder years later explained it a little (characteristically, without mention of his writing-partner): "I just wanted the audience to go with Walter, to make him a murderer all right, but with redeeming features. The Keyes relationship and ultimately the gesture of letting the innocent man off the hook. If he confesses, then it has to be motivated by him, by his sense of justice. Perhaps he'd done it, but within that murderous act there is still an element of compassion and decency." [10]

Nor has he a word for Phyllis's reversal. Whether Walter or Phyllis seems to audiences more sympathetic for these reversals, the film is certainly enhanced by them. What they contribute is an unavoidable recognition that the categories of judgment one derives from stories, those that artists construct for audiences, however coherent and responsive to social behavior they seem, leave behind some remainder of human complication, even of warmth and, as Wilder says, decency. At the end, the plot turns against itself, and what one reasonably thought one knew is mightily qualified.

Categories of all sorts, even stereotypes, facilitate thinking about

Narrow Margin (1952)

romance, yes, but about matters of life and death too, as Keyes's actuarial tables indicate. Or do they *govern* thought? His point is that social planning goes far beyond what is commonly acknowledged.[11] Decisions one considers personal and private are predictable. *The Narrow Margin* is lean and firmly pointed toward one particular site of this issue: how one spots the right woman within the grid of social types. The strength of the film derives from this very tight thematic focus. The confinement of a moving train is a perfect setting for an analysis of settled judgments. One feels the presence of strangers there and cannot easily step aside to avoid encounters. Who are they who sit and stand so close? An inevitable question there.

At the outset two Los Angeles police detectives, Walter Brown (Charles McGraw) and Gus Forbes (Don Beddoe), travel to Chicago to pick up a witness, Mrs. Frankie Neall (Marie Windsor), the widow of a crook; she is to give testimony to a California grand jury. The gravel-voiced Detective Brown anticipates that she is a cheap moll and bets his partner five dollars that he has her pegged properly without even seeing her. He trusts social categories: crooks and molls are only that, crooks and molls. (The point is not only about physical appearance.) His partner thinks, on the contrary, that various kinds of women might fall for a crook. As soon as Marie Windsor is presented as the widow of the crook, Brown is sure that he has won his bet. "Was I right?" Brown asks. "Don't rub it in," Forbes replies. The surprise comes much later in the film: this supposed moll is a decoy, an undercover Chicago Internal Affairs officer, not a femme fatale. The real Mrs. Frankie Neall (Jacqueline White) is a straight-looking, principled, and intelligent mother of a small boy, and Brown suddenly falls for her during the train ride across the plains. Aside from Marie Windsor's character and Jacqueline White's, the bad guys stay bad and the good guys, good; everyone, that is, looks the part. Only the two women are misleading, which is Johnny Farrell's complaint about women in general.

Why does the film not represent male characters as comparably misleading? This has to do with the enforcement of the occupational structure. Men are detectives, crooks, or trainmen: character is fitted exactly to occupational function, that is, to the judgments that determine the payment of working people. The corpulent special agent for the railroad (Paul Maxey) is anatomically equipped to control the movement of passengers through a train's narrow passages. If the cast were all men, the world of the film would represent only work, as if only that were worthy of preservation.

Narrow Margin (1952)

Narrow Margin (1952)

Noir women, though, preserve a dimension of character that is less determined by occupational categories and social types. They value the possibility of a freely elected ethical character that is not on display—a kind of perfume of privacy and particularity. Phyllis's dalliance with Nino is surprising in just this way. Men shallowly prefer to embody and display their occupational functions. They enjoy hegemony over the labor sector of social life, and that is where they foolishly invest themselves most fully. They avow consistency. Walter Neff needlessly sinks into captivity in an insurance office after hours; he might have been closer to Mexico when he lost his legs. The hardened Detective Brown is no smarter than Walter (and he's not even so tall). The point is not about gender alone: rather, the film represents a rivalry concerning the value of a distinctive element of intelligence not governed by the division of labor.

Like the much greater *Maltese Falcon*, *The Narrow Margin* is organized to examine critically the ground of mistrust: Is hard-boiled skepticism as reliable as it is purported to be? Can a skeptical inquirer learn to trust a woman, and how might that trust be grounded? The film has only this one problem to study. Detective Brown shows consistent contempt for Marie Windsor; he learned nothing from his interaction with her, which does not speak well for him. However imaginatively the Chicago Police Department plotted, its deception was brutally inefficient. The decoy stratagem cost two detectives their lives, and a crook was killed too: three corpses for a ruse. At the end, Jacqueline White refuses to be escorted by the police to the courtroom. She prefers to walk with Detective Brown in the open—no tricks. I said that Detective Brown falls for Jacqueline White's character during the train ride, but the development of his feeling for her is not represented. He has a sudden moment of recognition during a quick train stop, after which he is ready for marriage. "When [the train] is moving," she tells Brown, "everything's a blur." The film is not concerned to track his attraction to straight-seeming women—or to any women; the point is rather that social categories lead his judgment astray when it comes to Marie Windsor's character. The romance with Jacqueline White is rather stipulated than represented by the film; it is not—unfortunately—a real interest for the film. This is one of those films that suggests that not everyone is corrupt, that a straight life is accessible and valuable, that the public sphere is still a place of security.

For all its dark cinematography, its violence and cramped scenes, the film opens out at the end to civic hope. The police turn out to have been working more earnestly, if not skillfully, than even the detectives knew to preserve the legitimacy of judicial procedures. Marie Windsor died (unnecessarily) for this end. And in their walk to the courthouse Detective Brown and the real widow of Neall demonstrate sufficient civil courage to ground hope in a future in the city. That hope arises in the nonprofessional character of the one surviving female character. She is direct in her self-presentation and, however respectful, skeptical of the capacity of the state. Nonetheless she is about to fulfill her civic obligation at considerable risk to herself and her child. How she came to marry a crook remains thoroughly mysterious. Hers is the intelligence that survives the test of the train, and it is at once apparently conventional and anomalous too. She displays no eroticism, but she has had a surprising private life as the intimate of a major criminal. She and Phyllis are not what they appear to be. Social categories have been thoroughly confusing, misleading. There seems, at the end, no such thing as *social* knowledge, though men continue to believe in nothing else.

A femme fatale enters a scene memorably, as if she were the only woman: Brigid O'Shaughnessy in *The Maltese Falcon*, Phyllis Dietrichson in *Double Indemnity*, Cora in *The Postman Always Rings Twice*, Rita Hayworth in *Gilda*, and Kathy Moffett in *Out of the Past* all have a craft.

Narrow Margin (1952)

Brigid labors to draw Sam Spade into trusting her (so that she may elude the police), but he resists, discounting her account of adversity with explicit irony and amusement: "Oh, you're good," he says, apparently well-armed against her wiles. He tells her too that he and his former business partner Miles never believed her story about her sister: "We believed your $200." It is obvious that her interest in Sam is instrumental: he may even help her recover the bird. She means to make an impression: she halts momentarily, as if stunned by his appearance, as she first enters his office. His true interest in her is ambiguous. Like Miles, he is erotically drawn to her—though how strongly, or more important how blindly, is unclear throughout the film. Dashiell Hammett found ten ways to say that it was impossible to read Sam's face or voice.[12] Sam is charmed by her bizarre inconsistencies, and at the same time exasperated by her inability to tell a plausibly coherent story. The strength of his characterization is that one cannot know with certainty what he intends for Brigid and him. He is an enigmatic character who labors to apprehend the murderer of his partner and yet admits to being relieved by Miles's absence.[13] The opening scene closes firmly with Sam's utterly false words about Miles: "You've got brains, yes you have."[14]

The Maltese Falcon (1941)

Brigid learns that she is making headway with Sam when he tells the police at his apartment that she is an operative in his employ. She has reason to smile at that particular prevarication, because it seriously compromises his own defense against the charge that he murdered Miles or Thursby. He could not, after misrepresenting Brigid as his employee, claim that he was investigating Thursby on her behalf. The true origin of the plot is cut off by that lie. He's lost sight of his self-interest. That she herself lies frequently enhances her allure. "You *are* a liar," he remarks in astonishment. Her disarming reply: "I am. I've always been a liar." Then he asks, "Is there any truth at all in that yarn?" "Some," she answers. "Not very much."[15] Nearly all the characters lie to one another frequently—except Wilmer (Elisha Cook, Jr.), who rarely speaks at all. And yet the realistic representation of urban life—the activities of criminals, the police, and the court—and what John T. Irwin rightly speaks of as the film's conspicuous theatricality are actually at some variance. Lying and role-playing obstruct the explanatory mission of realistic narrative. When Brigid first comes to Sam's apartment there is a blank space on the wall where some sort of picture had presumably been (though no such blank, and no picture, is on the wall when the police first visit Sam). Huston thought to register

The Maltese Falcon (1941)

visually the fact that Sam gives neither Brigid nor anyone else the full picture. He conceals his designs from other characters, and from the audience too.

Prevarication is the medium of social exchange. Misrepresentation dominates the film; nearly every scene displays some duplicity. Lying and city life seem just to go together, though this is not a cause for regret. The spectacle of enterprising liars contriving intermittent collaboration with one another is a continuous delight; without that, no film. Why Brigid's particular misrepresentations charm Sam is revealing. They share a knack for dissembling, as others might for juggling. Neither is shamed or inhibited by being caught in a lie. For both, speech is less expressive than instrumental, a means of pushing ahead. They presume a world of amnesiac others who forget the latest lie and just start over with them, as if everyone expected everyone to lie constantly. They take pleasure in prevarication: it is delightful that one may get ahead in this manner. In Brigid he has met a woman who requires of others as much tolerance as he himself does. She briefly seems his near peer, and that charms him. In truth she is no match for this athletic improviser.

Lies present a very particular obstacle to trust. Not suspicion but "deception is the real enemy of trust," according to Onora O'Neill.[16] And for good reason, because it prevents one from securing the ground on which one stands when extending trust to another. The most crafted sequence in the film is when the cast is gathered in Sam's apartment to transact the sale of the falcon. (Is there elsewhere a comparably engaging scene of extended exposition?) No one is permitted to leave there before the deal is done. Brigid exits the room to make coffee and Gutman (Sidney Greenstreet) palms a thousand-dollar bill to cast suspicion on her. All transactions among known liars must be constrained within primitive boundaries. Those deserving of mistrust are wisely kept before one's eyes. Wilmer's eyes are closed, and he awakens to find that he—the one who does not lie—is to be the goat. This marvelous assemblage of rogues reveals dramatically that each individual is alone and vulnerable in a trustless world. Sam is not committed to protecting his "precious" love Brigid, nor will Gutman stand by his "son" Wilmer. They are a herd of cats, and the falcon is a fake. There is great theater in this sequence, but miserable human relations. At its end, the action of the film evaporates. Three corpses, and just for lies.

Trust is most meaningful when one takes responsibility for it, through avowal, not when circumstances oblige one to rely on another. From Holly's experience one sees how important true knowledge is to trust. One wants ideally to establish with confidence all that one knows about a trustee and then, with faith, leap further into an unknown future. As Onora O'Neill observes, "Deception . . . undermines and damages others'

Chinatown (1974)

capacities to judge and communicate, to act and to place trust with good judgment."[17] The surprising point in *The Third Man* is that Harry's deception of strangers undermines his friend's trust of him. Holly might think, as Anna apparently does, that Harry's deception of others need not count against Holly's own trust of Harry. Holly learns that injurious deception of others does properly count against his particular trust of Harry. Lies, as I indicated earlier, are not entirely discrete; their consequences spread. Lying is the true theme of *Chinatown*, not political corruption. Until near the end, Evelyn Mullwray is lying to Jake, and Jake to Lou Escobar. From Curly's promiscuous wife to Noah Cross introducing himself to Catherine as her grandfather, lies and betrayals enshroud the film (just as they did Huston's *Maltese Falcon*). Duplicity in families (incest and infidelities) and in business (valley land and water deals) runs across class and gender boundaries. "Chinatown" is nearly a common noun for inscrutability—unavoidable, because duplicity is ubiquitous. Life comes round to China-town, even though Jake had tried to stay away. There is no one original or determining lie, but rather so many lies that one cannot know much with certainty. A single misstatement and one sinks into a ready morass of misrepresentation from which there can be no leaps. Calloway is quite definite about what is false and what is true; he fixes responsibility accordingly. But Noah Cross, in another world, tells Jake: "You may think you know what's going on, but you don't." Even Hollis Mullwray, rich, powerful, expert, does not know where the water is going. He seeks enlightenment (as in a parable) from a small boy on an old horse. Ignorance is a condition of existence—for everyone. The story of the water is about LA politics, but more important it renders the film's enigmas universal, comprehensive. The limits of knowledge are there in the elements of the locale: land and water, both visible, both mysteries. Without a prospect of sorting lies from truth, there is no hope for a future, nothing really to be done. Jake's trustee is dead.

Sam gradually sorts truth from lies and in the meantime is rightly amused by Brigid's zany admissions, as he is too by Joel Cairo's (Peter Lorre) buoyant audacity. Brigid, Cairo, Gutman, and Wilmer are a theatrical troupe passing through a merely realistic fiction.[18] They caper around the edges of realism, each one bidding for the notice due to an eccentric. Dramatically they are irresistible. No one else in the film can bear comparison to Brigid, Cairo, and Gutman. Brigid and Gutman flatter Sam with the assertion that he is a wild one: "You're absolutely the wildest, most unpredictable person I've ever known," Brigid tells him, though he is

The Maltese Falcon (1941)

altogether tame by comparison to them. His attraction to her is partly a response to the exotic troupe from Istanbul and Hong Kong. Does he trust them? He says that he is trying to find reasons to trust Brigid, but that is talk. He certainly mistrusts the others, and he makes sure that they mistrust one another. His motivation for befriending her—that she is constantly worthy of his attention—is no reason to *trust* her; it is rather reason to keep her around, along with her three partners. As the troupe leaves the screen, the film must quickly end, and the ordinary characters clean up after the circus. His own task is to determine how far he will go for an exceptional woman.

Trust is more prudent than eros, but then anything is more prudent than eros. Sam wants to maintain intimacy with Brigid, but he knows that he cannot trust an admitted liar. His powers of detection would be useless: he would daily stumble over her contradictions. He explains, in the end, that their bond is unsustainable because of the absence of solid ground for trust. "I've no earthly reason to think that I can trust you," he says. "And if I do this [viz., help her to evade conviction for the murder of Miles], and let you get away with this, you'll have something on me that you can use

The Maltese Falcon (1941)

whenever you want to. Since I've got something on you, I couldn't be sure that you wouldn't put a hole in me someday." This is the skeptical rational analysis he employs in dueling with Gutman; they both presume self-interest as an enduring and overriding motivation. He looks for general reasons to guide his decision, and he recognizes that they all militate against trusting her. He also has a professional obligation to see Miles's murderer prosecuted, and he takes that seriously, though viewers may not realize that he does so until the end of the film. He says, "When a man's partner is killed, he's supposed to do something about it. It doesn't make any difference what you thought of him. He was your partner and you're supposed to do something about it. And it happens we're in the detective business. Well, when one of your organization gets killed, it's—it's bad for business to let the killer get away with it, bad all around, bad for every detective everywhere."[19]

Against such general considerations is the fact that he loves Brigid in particular, loves exactly her odd particularity, which renders the calculation difficult. If the quandary stopped there—with a conflict between general and particular value—he would be paralyzed. But it doesn't. What resolves the issue is his Kantian sense that Brigid has used him. She has not respected his autonomy: "I won't [let you go] because all of me wants to, regardless of consequences, and because you've counted on that with me the same as you counted on that with all the others." She may in fact love him, but he knows that he has been her instrument, and that all by itself is sufficient to quell his impulse to trust her with his own well-being. "Someday," he says: that, the indefinite future, is the crux of romantic trust. What a lover wants from a trusted beloved is some limitation of future uncertainty. Passion surely cools in time, and the heart changes too. One cannot trust a lover always to love, certainly not passionately, but one may expect a lover to be restrained always from regarding the beloved as an instrument for some purpose or other. This is to say that romantic trust may have as its ultimate objective the stability of a lasting ethical pact. This is Sam's final point: Brigid used him. She surely will succumb to temptation and do so again *someday*. As the past was, so shall the future be.

John T. Irwin's claim that noirs focus on making a living, or self-reliance, has everything to do with privacy. Private detectives "need to conceal their motives or identities from others in order to do their job."[20] Sam's role-playing follows from this obligation to conceal his activities. Until his final speech, one cannot know his intent with certainty, or his feeling for Brigid. She naïvely trusts in her own seductive power to render him manageable, predictable. Irwin writes eloquently about the literary value of Hammett's *The Maltese Falcon*: "It's a work so intelligent, with dialogue so witty and a view of life so worldly-wise, presented with such formal economy and flawless pacing and yet such fun to read, that it continually renews my belief in the principle that art and brains can transform just about anything, no matter how lowly or unpromising that thing might seem, into something intelligent, moving, and worthy."[21] Something similar can be said on behalf of Huston's version, which is faithful to the novel. Then one wants to question the admirable artistic intelligence behind the work because it closely resembles the protagonist's cunning and underhanded procedures. Hammett spins a yarn out of a hoax statuette, as Sam (while being paid by three of his four suspects) spins out an elaborate trap to apprehend his partner's murderer. Intelligence does not require much to begin with, as Irwin observes. The intelligence that one admires here is insistently practical, apparently too practical for the project of trust. The cunning femme fatale gives first her money and then a gun to the one who betrays her. The resolution of Sam's affection for Brigid is costly. He is shaken by conflicting impulses. What strikes me is that he has not actually transformed his erotic desire to hold on to Brigid. Instead he represses that and constrains her. Off she goes to Tehachapi. The astonishing thing thematically is that in the first noir, professionalism, of all things, keeps him from getting the girl. A private life is out of reach.

The stories I have told about trust between men and women explain failure. In what sense is that failure instructive, general? Failed trust follows largely from misrepresentation, deception, false labeling. Is candor, then, an effective antidote? One might be easily convinced that men and women need to identify their interests more directly, openly, that a Confucian correction of the relations of names to things might enhance the orders of trust. But the opposite may be more true: that the less said, the better. One remembers the Kid at the end of *Out of the Past*. Male taciturnity may be a great resource in the struggle for trust between men and women, if the resistance to self-expression can be transformed into a reluctance to press inquiry on a trusted other. There is an ethics of courtship, easy to overlook and painful to practice. Near the end of *Daisy Kenyon* (1947) Peter Lapham (Henry Fonda) says that, concerning "modern warfare," Daisy (Joan Crawford) and Dan O'Mara (Dana Andrews) are babies. Theirs was a triangular love war. Peter seemed not to be putting up a fight to keep his wife, Daisy, from O'Mara, but he actually fought quite effectively. He pressed not directly against his rival, but instead against his own instinct to overwhelm her autonomy. O'Mara, on the contrary, took the liberty of drawing up a divorce settlement on Daisy's behalf, though she had not asked him to do anything of the sort. That was his manly approach to rivalry. Peter knew that marriage—or trust that lasts—depends on respect for the autonomy of one's spouse. He restrained not his rival but himself, and he trusted Daisy's perspicacity to assess properly the difference between her suitors. His is an ethical effort, and he gets the gal.

To reckon with the autonomy of another, especially a lover, is a challenge. It is hard to begin from the premise that a beloved is entirely justified in pursuing his or her own ends. The corollary is that the beloved owes to the lover no explanation of these ends. Not to be told the intentions of one's beloved is very hard, especially when one is committed on principle to accepting those intentions wherever they lead. Holly Martins's trust ended when his trustee's intentions endangered the well-being of innocent children who obviously need protection. One may draw a line at the point at which the beloved's intentions endanger others, but otherwise hold tight to the autonomy of the beloved. Another way of putting this point is to note that the romance of taciturnity goes very far toward a principle in this matter: one may trust the trustee so extensively that one refuses to ask where the trustee is headed. That may be a principled refusal to demand self-justification from the one whose existence, just as he or she is, requires of the truster no justification at all. This is the point at which Marlowe arrives in his relationship with Vivian Rutledge in *The Big Sleep*, and it is the high-water mark of noir trust.

CHAPTER 6

Quick Change

One wants to admire art that refines or at least expresses humane understanding. The truth is that film noir is severe; humane is not a term that properly comes to mind. The end of *The Postman Always Rings Twice*, for instance, suggests that Frank and Cora are too venal to live. The inhumaneness of noir is generally evident in the many representations of cruelty, extreme adversity, and especially of modest problems that become catastrophes. The proportions of recognizable experience are often lost to noir's exaggerations. One variety, for example, is a cautionary tale about male faithlessness. Such films register the costs of maintaining trustworthiness, but also reveal the small, routine, imaginative betrayals so easy to justify, or at least rationalize. *The Big Clock* (1948) is the grandest of these, but *D.O.A.* (1950), *Black Widow* (1954), *Woman in the Window* (1944), and *Scarlet Street* (1945) are thematically comparable; all of them examine libidinous curiosity, as though testing what a guy might expect to get away with. Edward G. Robinson appeared in both of the last two films, directed by Fritz Lang. In *Woman in the Window*, as Professor Richard Wanley, he is punished harshly for a moment of quite limited faithlessness: he agrees to a single drink with a woman met on the street. In *Scarlet Street*, he commits the same sort of infraction. His punishment for these betrayals mushrooms far beyond his initial intentions. The films suggest that the first little betrayal is the one that counts most, exactly because events have a life of their own, and because adverse consequences are compounded by the intentions of faithless others too. The male leads are punished for self-serving mindlessness: men fail to acknowledge, even to themselves, all that they imagine with these women from the street, and they fail to reckon too the cost to their marriages of their corrupt imaginings. They are punished for sinning in spirit beyond what they do in fact.

The Woman in the Window (1944)

Beneath this severe ethics runs the determinism that Robert B. Pippin analyzes. "How did I get into this rat race anyway?" George Stroud (Ray Milland) asks in the opening monologue of *The Big Clock*. "I'm no criminal. What happened? When did it all start?" The answer, never uttered to the male leads in this subgenre: you were not thinking honestly about the implications of your casual infidelities. Faith is broken first at the edges, in little pieces. In *Angel Face* (1952), Frank Jessup's (Robert Mitchum) difficulties begin with a callous, ordinary lie to his girlfriend. She missed a call from him while she was in the shower, and that becomes sufficient justification for him to cancel a date and go out instead with the murderous Diane Tremayne (Jean Simmons). Even *Out of the Past* is set in motion by Jeff Bailey's initial faithlessness not to a wife or girlfriend but to his client, Whit Sterling. Jeff fails to notify Whit that he has located the femme fatale in Mexico: the Western Union office was closed for siesta. That slight contingency leads eventually to Jeff's death. One likes to think that one has many opportunities to stop short before decisively violating a trust. Betrayers imagine that they preside over an ethical terrain of evenly distributed sites for rational decisions. But no one truly presides over his or her own ethical tests. T. S. Eliot speaks of "The awful daring of a moment's surrender / Which an age of prudence can never retract."[1] A single impulse takes one a long way because events themselves are causally connected.

These men endure stunning punishment without much opportunity to correct their decisions, even after they recognize their errors.[2] Jessup is made to acknowledge his faithlessness in front of his rival for his beloved's affection; he casts his eyes down at his lap while he is scolded—and to no avail. Noir punishes faithless perpetrators mercilessly: Jessup dies for his error. These films are melodramatic, harsh—without charity or compassion. Otto Preminger kept the camera on the car crash that kills Frank and Diane in *Angel Face*, as if that horrible death were what audiences wanted most to see. Men and women repeatedly come to a very bad end from their efforts to trust each other. Noir expresses not sanity but ravenous hunger for moral judgment.

What might count, in the land of Noir, as sound moral judgment? Strauss and Wanley make errors; their minds are fogged. Wanley has a few drinks and a meal and slips into an erotic fantasy. Stroud has more than a few and then forgets his wife and family. Alcohol gives eros an edge over good sense—conventional wisdom. Sound judgment requires clarity of

Angel Face (1952)

Where Danger Lives (1950)

mind, but even more than that. The plot of the rarely discussed *Where Danger Lives* subjects Jeff Cameron (Robert Mitchum, then Hollywood's most conspicuously self-sufficient male lead) to a physical beating that reduces his fortitude and impairs his power of concentration. The point is that, however snappy his judgment, the real work of mind requires ongoing labor. An ordinary brain concussion disables his powers of deliberation. He struggles heroically, though intermittently, to resist Margo Lannington's (Faith Domergue) machinations. The *execution* of judgment is shown to be a Herculean task. This demure but erotic woman is more than the large, powerful, and only apparently devious Jeff had imagined. He has to fall and roll down a long flight of stairs, because he cannot walk, then stumble from one post to the next in order to confront her at the border to Mexico. There she shoots him, but he persists in limping toward her.

The theme of trust is directly named early in *Where Danger Lives*, but first a counterweight is set in place. Jeff is introduced as all professional mastery: a cool, competent hospital physician who charms a little girl in an iron lung and a boy without arms—and does so without sentimentality. The girl nods off, and he tells a nurse to complete the story later . . . in the usual way. He is not particularly moved by the children, not really

Where Danger Lives (1950)

charismatic. His skills are managerial; his actions, directed at specific ends—until the femme fatale appears. She is wheeled into an examining room, after a suicide attempt, and this doctor quickly believes his medicine has saved her life. A few days later she tells him her real name (after lying about exactly this to the hospital staff), and he asks, "Isn't that putting an awful amount of trust in a stranger?" She replies that she doesn't think of him as a stranger—music to his eager ears.

One expects trust to flower slowly, after good faith has been demonstrated. The truth is that eros effectively promotes sudden trust not just in the absence of evidence to corroborate trust, but in the presence of incriminating evidence of faithlessness. Jeff trusts Margo—before his concussion—only because he wants her. The camera presents her face in a velvety focus as she lies on a gurney, and he is a goner. Why trust one who misrepresents her own identity? Well, she is that gorgeous, and he, unaware that eros is hell on managers, trusts his eyes. Moreover lovers extend trust suddenly to express consent to intimacy—or is it the other way around? Signs of trust are exchanged in courtship to display, of all things, autonomy. Jeff cancels a date with his fiancée Julie (Maureen O'Sullivan) in front of his new flame. He misleads Julie into thinking that he is treating an emergency patient at the hospital. Why *exhibit* such faithlessness (as Mitchum did again in *Angel Face* in 1952)? He means to display control of his own life, even of his love, as if eros were not his master. He steps in with both feet: a red rose every time he sees Margo, apparently to suggest some romantic sophistication. At deception, noir men consider themselves masters, though they are novices. Margo, on the contrary, is openly apprehensive, not smug. She remains constantly alert that no information concerning her mental incapacity is conveyed to Jeff's ears. Just when men think that mastery is established, they expose their vulnerability. Not Margo but Jeff trusts the wrong stranger.

He does, to his credit, confront the fact of her untrustworthiness, when he learns that the man she called her father (Claude Rains) is in truth her husband, and her husband warns him that "scandal can be quite damaging to a career." The script holds a constant focus on professional ambitions—as if they were the solid ground of male rationality. His "life and heart," she says, are in his work. Suddenly Jeff has sufficient prudence and character to drop her. The male fear of degradation can be essentially professional: joblessness. Nothing from her can renew his trust. "You lied to me," he says, and without ambivalence puts her behind him. He errs characteristically, though, in overestimating his own competence. Margo screams, and he runs back into the house, as if he might save her from calamity.

The calamity is all his. After an altercation with her husband, Jeff is dazed by a blow from an iron poker, and Frederick Lannington lies on the floor, unconscious, soon to die (smothered by Margo). Before his head injury, like Ajax, Jeff towered over both Lanningtons. Afterward he is crippled, physically and intellectually. He realizes that he has no reason to love or trust Margo, but he repeatedly rubs his head, befuddled, and goes along with her every dumb proposal. He diagnoses himself as suffering from a concussion: "I may talk rationally but my decisions may not make any sense." It takes a blow to the head to get these words out of Mitchum (they might serve as just commentary on his character in *Out of the Past* three years earlier). Thereafter Jeff moves through the plot as her patient, though he has the strength not to trust her again. "You lied to me once. Maybe you've lied a hundred times," he says in their bridal chamber in Arizona.

When he is almost completely incapacitated, from the floor he expresses dismay at Margo's character: "You're horrible, you're sick"—in a tone uncharacteristic of Mitchum. His judgment of her is firm and sharp. The erotic basis of trust is deep and confusing. A male inclination to go along with eros, to call it trust, is powerfully resistant to skepticism. The film takes him to a point where he thoroughly renounces his erotic imaginings.

Where Danger Lives (1950)

But to get there he has to be beaten and abused, made to imagine himself the object of a police hunt. Margo can manage this—even though he was a socially secure physician just days earlier—because now he is a large wounded animal.

Pursuit, the enforcement of social judgment, is a prominent feature of noir. From *M* (1931) to *Night and the City* (1950), small, weak, guilty characters are hounded by groups. These goats are stigmatized, and their hunt and flight scenes are base, painful to watch. However guilty the prey, one takes no pleasure or satisfaction in the urban hunt. They are so alone as they scramble for shelter, and their predators lack all nobility. These victims are debased, but from what better situation are they pulled down? This is an awkward formulation, but it exposes the meaning of these scenes. The hunts represent an abstract alternative to trust relationships. The hunted are undeserving of anyone's trust. That is their isolation. Those beyond anyone's faith may dart right or left, but their end is assured. They are small prey for wolves. It's trust or death, these films suggest: and the death of the untrusted is ugly and demeaning. One of the best of these films, *The Killers*, gets the hunt out of the way in the first thirteen minutes, when Swede Andresen (Burt Lancaster) famously acquiesces to his own execution. "I did

The Killers (1946)

something wrong once," he says as an indication of the cause of his execution. He failed to secure trustworthiness from Kitty Collins (Ava Gardner), failed to be trustworthy too, and was willing to accept the alternative, when his professional predators arrived.

Noir holds out a grim view of existence: greed, graft, and cruelty are extensive. Not just the bullets, the fists, and the chokings, but Mike La Figlia at the produce market in *Thieves' Highway*, the imbibing beat cop at Wanda's speakeasy in *Call Northside 777* (1948)—they are figures of familiar, acknowledged fakery, like the costumed hawkers of Hollywood Boulevard, or the sighted "blind" beggar in *M*. Still worse than empty pretense, shame hangs over many of these films, a modernist embarrassment in the face of precedent. The Strangler who murders Harry Fabian (Richard Widmark) in *Night and the City* understands the nature of honor, recognizes the nobility of the wrestler Gregorius, and fears infamy. He does not want to be known as the man who killed Gregorius, because he knows the value of the Greco-Roman traditions that Gregorius reveres. Gregorius is necessarily an *old* man; viewers must see up close his aged, sinking face and wrinkled flesh. "Honor," as Emerson says, "is venerable to us because it is no ephemera. It is always ancient virtue. We worship it today because

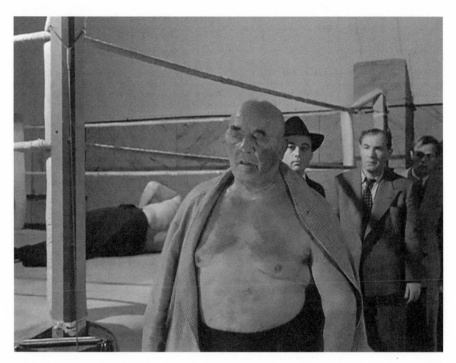

Night and the City (1950)

it is not of today."[3] Gregorius's thematic function is to *exit* the contemporary scene. The corruption of *Night and the City* is modernity itself.

There is a pressure on narrative and drama to represent some change at the end. A story needs to declare a direction, not just track a process. Harry first appears in flight from a collector. Then he is caught trying to steal money from his lover Mary (Gene Tierney), and he feebly lies his way out of this betrayal. She, secure in her dignity, recognizes his meanness without condemnation. In the course of the film he exploits others, even the noble Gregorius, who dies as a consequence of the contest that Harry has mismanaged. Unchanged, as base as ever, Harry repeats, near the end, even more boldly this time, his shameful effort to steal from his beloved. But he gets one last "bright idea": that Mary might benefit from the bounty on his head, if his pursuer Kristo were made to acknowledge that Mary exposed Harry to assassination. This is Harry's effort to achieve a little nobility, once he realizes that he must die. He does not understand love or honor, however, and that limits his effort at redemption. This is all the self-transcendence that this character can manage, but it is something. He knows that he has dwelt in shame all his life and would like to go out with something different. The darkness of noir, like fakery and self-loathing,

The Third Man (1949)

clears very little room for the generation of hope. A number of characters come to see that an honorable life is out of reach; they settle for death with honor.

In making *The Third Man*, Carol Reed hosed down the streets before shooting. He wanted them to glisten—just a touch of brightness. Must these films promise so little? Is the measured correction of error not to be considered? One basis of hope and exhilaration that these films occasionally produce is a sense that however structured, or set, social life appears, the lives of individuals may change very quickly, up or down. "Thirty-six hours ago I was a decent, respectable, law-abiding citizen with a wife and a kid and a big job," George Stroud (Ray Milland) says in *The Big Clock*. But now he is a skulking fugitive in his own workplace. Large raises, high salaries—these are sources of apparent quick change for executives. With new money one can decide suddenly to buy what was unaffordable, only imaginable, yesterday. That's a conventional basis of hope: sudden change, no delay. A new life. For crooks, the equivalent is a valise full of cash, or plastic surgery. These are metaphors of transformation without work or persistence. Marlowe's $25 a day plus expenses,

Jeff Bailey's filling station—they are just the opposite: structures for ripening character. Sudden change is the state religion in the land of Noir. Some films keep an eye on the dissenters, though; most of the faithful are fools.

So many noirs reveal why trust falters, but what then? What hope is plausible after disappointment or betrayal? Rififi beats Mado and feels young again. Bud White hits Lynn Bracken and Ed Exley and then seeks domestication in Bisbee, Arizona. The truth is that those whose trust has been betrayed ask not only why trust failed, but also whether it might be recovered, and if so, how. Even after betrayal, bruised, in pain, one wants a way to trust. Violence may be the first thing that comes to mind, but not the second or third. William Carlos Williams puts the matter well in a late poem:

What power has love but forgiveness?
In other words
by its intervention
what has been done
can be undone
What good is it otherwise?[4]

"Love" is an indefinite signifier, like "it," open always to resignification—hence its utility to those constrained by failure. The underappreciated *Criss Cross* is unusual among noirs in focusing, at the very start, on the practical project of reconstituting trust after obvious betrayal. Can failure to sustain a trust relationship be corrected? One wants to think of betrayal as a lapse that occurs, like other events, in time, something that at another moment might turn out differently, even though one knows that *trustworthy* is a term that is poorly modified by *mostly*. Or perhaps if one understood the immediate cause of a lapse, one might correct something to ensure trustworthy behavior in the future. A project of reconstitution rests on the presumption that faithlessness derives from nothing so settled and enduring as character, but instead from a situation. Situations can be altered. That, at least for a while, is a hope felt after betrayal.

This film begins with a shot from a plane apparently descending into a filled parking lot in Los Angeles. Among the bulging fenders of 1940s sedans is a couple in embrace; then come alternating close-ups of Steve (Burt Lancaster) and Anna (Yvonne De Carlo). She is assuring him of their bright future. And this is exactly what he wants to hear because he has been painfully unable to forget his past with her. This is their hope scene. The rest of the film consists of Steve's recollection of the weeks that led up to her promise, then of the heist, and finally its aftermath. The screenplay is taken from a pulp novel by Don Tracy; the film is vastly superior exactly because it complicates the characters of Steve and Anna. They become studies in ambivalence.

Steve Thompson returns to Los Angeles from a working-class *Wanderjahr* following a divorce from Anna. When he arrives at his family home, no one is there; like Odysseus, he checks that the dog still recognizes him. He visits the local hangout, nearly empty in the afternoon, and is received suspiciously, as an utter stranger. The film captures a sense of blankness surrounding his desire to recover a marriage: he has no reason to expect a different outcome from reconciliation. His vague, ungrounded expectation embarrasses him, and he tries to cover up his own intentions. He cannot admit to friends and family the irrationality of what he wants. He conceals even the simple wish to phone Anna. When he does see her, he is thoroughly conflicted and unclear about his intentions, though she is expressly eager to renew their relationship. The indeterminateness of his love, after a divorce, has rendered him strange even to himself. A desire to forgive and reconcile, against his better judgment, makes him a spook. Because he has not thought things through, or has not reconciled his feelings and his plans, he is repeatedly surprised by events, caught off guard by one encounter after another.

Anna's betrayal of Steve, within the action of *Criss Cross*, is that, while dating him after their divorce, she suddenly runs off without notice to marry the villainous Slim Dundee (Dan Duryea) in Yuma. "She really did go to Yuma, Mr. Thompson," Frank, the great bartender (Percy Helton), tells him. "You see . . . well, she got married." Just two scenes back, Steve and Anna made a date to swim at Zuma beach. Zuma to Yuma in four minutes. Steve is first shocked, then bitter, but four months later they reconstitute their intimacy yet again. And then they are caught in a compromising situation by Slim. Steve concocts on the spot a plan for a heist, as a distraction from his feeble lies about the immediate situation; one lie, that is, leads to another, the second worse than the first. Slim, greedy and crooked, however jealous he is about Anna, is effectively deflected by the ambitiousness of the heist. Then the real plot is underway. The heist is more deeply necessary, Steve knows, because Anna is a material girl; he needs money in order to have a life with her. He has come to understand *why* their marriage failed and means to do something different this time.

Criss Cross (1949)

In the opening scene, in a stolen moment together the night before the heist, she pledges faithfulness to him: "Steve, all those things that happened to us, everything that went before, we'll forget it. You'll see. I'll make you forget it. After it's done, after it's all over and we're safe, it'll be just you and me. You and me, the way it should have been all along from the start." They pin their hopes on a plan to leave the past quickly behind them. Steve proposed this heist without forethought. His plan has no connection to the life he lives: he has never had criminal connections and is incompetent at criminal strategy. He tries to go out of character in hope of changing his life suddenly and completely.

For all her assurances to Steve, Anna has a faint sense of her own agency. Her marriage to Slim is a thing that happened to Steve and her, rather than her own deliberate act. And her imagination of a renewed relationship with Steve rests on her ability to induce amnesia in him, not to change herself. Although she is sincere, loves Steve, and truly wants to make another go of it, her character is too weak to take responsibility for her actions. Steve's character is stronger (he has courage that she lacks), but his intelligence is weaker than hers, and Slim is much smarter than both of

Criss Cross (1949)

them. The film repeatedly denigrates Steve's intelligence, and Anna's too. For characters of limited intelligence, there is no way to reconstruct trust. They come up against exactly the same difficulty each time they try. Anna is selfish and materialistic. That is what makes her run off with Slim to Yuma and try to run off alone at the end. Steve is selfless in his love of her, and stupid in his plan to overcome his adversary and live with Anna. Whether more intelligent characters might find ways to reconstitute trust is a question not met by the film. Steve asks her why she married Slim. She tells him that she wanted gaudy wealth, that Steve's respectable family and friends tried to run her out of town, and that her spirit was tired of coping with Steve's anger. Besides all that, Slim wooed her with material goods when Steve was away. After she gets all these "causes" out, she breaks down in tears and asks herself how she got so mixed up: "How did it happen?"

Anna truly worries about Steve's well-being, but her love is faint too. Her trust of him conforms to what Russell Hardin describes as an "encapsulated interest" model.[5] She trusts him insofar as she has encapsulated his interest in her own. She does intend to wait for him to recover from his

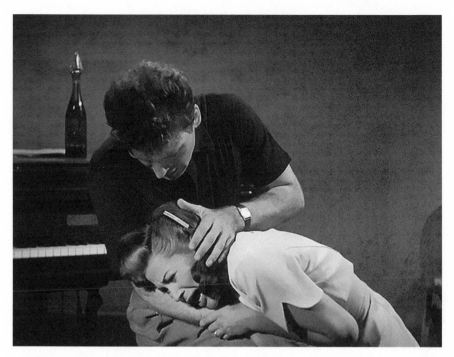

Criss Cross (1949)

gunshot wounds and to flee with him and the loot from the heist; she does not plan to return to Slim. She obviously prefers him to Slim. However, when Steve shows up unexpectedly in a way that will lead Slim to her, she knows that she must dissociate his interest from her own, because he cannot travel as easily as she (he needs medical attention). Practical considerations require that she make her own way to freedom from Slim. She tries to take the loot and leave Steve to face Slim alone. The world runs on self-interest, she explains to Steve; he has never understood this basic point. She apologizes that she is just not a selfless person. Steve is, with regard to her. He never cared about the money from the heist; his only objective was to satisfy her appetite for wealth. He has subordinated his interest to hers, and done so irreversibly. He dies with composure holding her. He makes no effort to dissociate himself from her as he faces execution by Slim. The film exposes the encapsulation model as a temporary arrangement driven by self-interest. When this model of trust inconveniences her, Anna removes the capsule and reverts to naked self-interest. Steve's trust went much further. He was not limited by consistency between her interest and his own. When their interests did not match up, he held by her interest at his own cost. He makes this commitment to her not as part of any scheme; he is a poor planner, driven by heart alone. Without intelligence, his trust leads only to self-sacrifice. *Criss Cross* is unusual in that it focuses sharply less on ethical problems than on failures of mind. The characters are insufficiently thoughtful to produce their own happiness. Making trust work for two people requires not just heart but intellect too.

The film makes the point not that Steve and Anna have no reasons for their acts, but rather that they have various motives and no sound way to distinguish reliable from unreliable motives. The moment when Steve proposes the heist to Slim is unique to the film; in the novel the heist is entirely Slim's idea. Steve has two motives that I have mentioned (to distract Slim from Anna's infidelity and to secure cash to satisfy Anna) and one that is revealed in the scene at the armored car depot when he talks about methods of protecting against robbery. Like Walter Neff, he has imagined larcenously how to rob his employer. Given the particular circumstances, he goes ahead with something that had in some sense crossed his mind earlier, though he never planned the crime in detail, as Walter did. Steve made a sudden decision against his own lawful nature to proceed with something ill-considered. Anna's decision to marry Slim was also rash. This is the way ordinary people navigate their lives, according to the film. And that is frighteningly plausible.

Most noir characters, like Steve, Anna, and Harry Fabian, are looking for a quick change; even very different characters seem to think that something big is just around the corner. Their sense of impending possibility seems to counterbalance the determinism that is a more widely recognized feature of noir. For instance, Dixon Steele (Humphrey Bogart), of *In a Lonely Place*, is highly intelligent, quite different from Steve, but also an angry, violent man, fearful of rejection. And he too, like Steve, Anna, and so many others, is banking on a sudden turnaround. As soon as Laurel Gray (Gloria Grahame) acknowledges an interest in him, he pursues her frankly and forcefully; before that acknowledgment, he hadn't noticed his beautiful neighbor. He is moved by evidence of the possibility of changing his life (i.e. by will) not by a free desire. The film, like Dorothy B. Hughes's novel on which it is loosely based, concerns an ill-tempered man, but it is more revealing concerning the limits of willfulness.[6] A modest act of trust makes Dix and Laurel both think that they can remake their lives entirely. She tells him that she won't be rushed, but they both rush into intimacy. Marriage is his means of reversal because, without patience or peace in

In a Lonely Place (1950)

himself, his hell is solitude. When he is waiting for a response to his proposal from his beloved, he is demonstrably ill at ease, wringing and clutch-
ing his hands. Fear of rejection, of betrayal, and recent combat experience
drive him quickly to violence and repeated suspicion.

Dix manages to destroy the trust that his beloved originally shows him.
There is ambiguity about how much trust she extended to him originally.
She testifies on his behalf when she barely knows him, but does not tell
police detectives, for instance, that she heard Mildred Atkinson (Martha
Stewart) call for help while Mildred was at Dixon's apartment (Mildred
was quoting a novel, but Laurel would not have known that). Nor is it
entirely clear that she did in fact see Mildred leave Dixon's apartment, as
she told the police. Detective Lochner (Carl Benton Reid) does not believe
her. As Laurel gets to know Dixon, at a breakneck pace, and witnesses his
many rages, she begins reasonably to fear him. She is so frightened that she
lies to him when he proposes marriage to her; she accepts his proposal
without intending to marry him. She learns that his obsession with
betrayal is wholly unmanageable, and then she does betray him by arrang-
ing to leave him just before their elopement. "I don't trust him," she says.

In a Lonely Place (1950)

"I'm not even sure he didn't kill Mildred Atkinson." The terrible thing to watch here is not only the unnecessary destruction of intimacy and love, but finally Dixon's dejection. He knows that he has failed to make anything good of the trust he was given, and he is not angry, just sad and ashamed, as he returns to the solitary life he had hoped to put behind him. He had intended something altogether different, but at the end of the film he must live alone, in hopeless regret, with the consequences of his compulsions.

Quick changes rarely produce happiness, and that qualifies what one can say for the hope that the noirs support. But these films nonetheless engage deeply with a need to hope for a better life. Many noirs try to see the city from the perspective of the working- and underclass; set mainly at night, after the legitimate economy has largely shut down, their focus is on the lives of those who are poorly protected by social institutions. The noirs look into the dark. As Wallace Stevens puts it:

Weaker and weaker, the sunlight falls
In the afternoon. The proud and the strong
Have departed.

Those that are left are the unaccomplished,
The finally human,
Natives of a dwindled sphere.[7]

The wish to push past the darkness to something different—that is where one finds a recognizable spirit in noir. "Nothing is more human," in Ernst Bloch's words, "than venturing beyond what is."[8] I find two orders of utopian imagination in the noirs. The first is a complex concept of trust between lovers. The second proposes quick changes in the immediate future. The first constitutes an aesthetic discovery, and the second is familiar, even banal. The first is presented in a single great film, *The Big Sleep*, and the second in many. Noirs draw on the elements of melodrama, polarized forces, but they rise to serious art by resisting familiar configurations. Many characters believe that their hopes may be immediately realized. Quick change is candy for the imagination.

The somber truth is that stability and happiness are long-term labors; that quick changes are destabilizing, destructive. To live in trust of another person, even of only one, is a state of glowing exceptionality. Some of the lead noir characters want that life instead of the lives represented as fact by these largely realistic films. The films reveal the dark world as it is, but they tend toward an alternative of mutual trust that begins with two people. The hasty, hungry imaginations of noir characters are chastened by these plots that end in execution, beatings, homelessness. In 1800 Wordsworth complained of the corrupting influence of urban congestion and gothic fiction. He would have understood that the artistic objective of noir is the correction of imagination. And so should we. The wonder is that complex trust may arise, with effort, while one is on the job. Even dubious snooping in the pay of wealthy, interested parties may lead one to a partner in trust. On what ground, then, would one ever turn down a job? Even the shadiest corners of the working world respond to the needs of the spirit. The noir environment seems deterministic, yet the camera is held to regions of experience that are accessible even to those of little or no means. The changes imagined by this art are set there in the dwindled sphere.

PART II

Spies

CHAPTER 7

State Service

C ritics agree that classic film noir ended with *Kiss Me Deadly* in 1955. When Mike Hammer surrenders to the police a key to a locker with nuclear fuel, noir is over as a credible imaginative form, as Robert B. Pippin puts it. The noirs are realistic films, but they are more deeply credible as proposals about how life may be constructed. However dark, they express hope by figuring ways that two unusual people may trust one another. Mike realizes that his autonomy is less than he had imagined, that the state's authority requires greater deference than he had formerly given. He can no longer, in John T. Irwin's terms, work for himself alone.[1] He curbs his independence in order not to interfere with the state in a world threatened by nuclear war. He does not pledge allegiance to the state, but he surrenders some autonomy. In December 1971 Richard Helms, then director of the CIA, told the National Press Club: "You've just got to trust us. We are honorable men."[2] Helms says not only that the press should trust the CIA, but that necessity requires submission. A noir inquirer may try, after the war, to trust the state, as Regina Lampert (Audrey Hepburn) comes to trust Peter Joshua (Cary Grant). *Charade* eases the difficulties of submission by positing a handsome and witty representative of a benign state. Two decades later the notion of a benign state was not credible. A number of still more recent films have undertaken analysis of the difficulties that arise when enterprising inquirers—characters who decades ago would have appeared in noirs—give to the state, rather than to their lovers or buddies, a very great trust. Mike Hammer's descendants go to work not for themselves but for the CIA.

Myself, I suffer from an allergy to authority. One whiff, and my eyes water. Even in ordinary academic meetings I grow bleary. A colleague speaks of one of us as "a leader in the department," and I sense a fleecing.

The students I teach wish to become leaders in finance, or enterprise, the law, public administration, or the military. The college brings in speakers every month to keep notions of leadership in constant view. The college ROTC van has on its side: "Developing America's Leaders in the Inland Empire." Ominous phrasing for a local obsession, but in truth all colleges prepare students to serve as leaders of some sort. Mine is only more explicit about this project. The revealing term may well be *service* rather than *leadership*. One hears often about an ideal of public service. Former CIA agent Robert Baer reflects, "We were all adventurers . . . but a public service ethos burned in us too."[3] Those who serve seem to subordinate their own wills to those of others. Such apparent humility effectively permits a leader to decline requests for justification: I do not make policy; I merely serve another. Those who lead government agencies speak of themselves as public servants—often in just these terms.

For over a decade, mainstream films have cast a cold eye on state service; honorable leadership has come to seem implausible. What alternative to leadership is imaginable for young people? Sheepishness is not alluring. Maybe the implicit alternative is that of a comrade, a willing member of a greater collective. Even those who mean to become leaders may imagine themselves as team leaders. The ambition to lead gains respectability in proximity to a concept of service: one serves some larger objective or collective "in a leadership capacity," as we say. Those entering the military plan to serve the nation as officers. This is the strong version of leadership and service—the motto on the van. No other sector of society is so explicit and definite about concepts of leadership and service. That makes sense, because armies actually move and require leaders and justification for their movement, especially if they go far. The films I discuss in this chapter focus on service to a democratic, secular republic in all but one instance. The significance of extreme service is the topic under scrutiny. But it should be understood too that since *Missing* (1982) the boundary between private enterprise and state authority has been represented as porous. According to Hollywood films, those who run law firms or direct corporations find themselves up against contradictions familiar to CIA agents.

Given that students intend to become civil leaders, what should they know, especially the ones who mean to go far? This question about imperial citizenship is examined in the Bourne trilogy, *Syriana* (2005), *Munich* (2005), *The Good Shepherd* (2006), *Traitor*, and *Body of Lies* (both 2008). Thucydides explains that Athens became an empire by specializing in shipbuilding and navigation. Athenians collected tribute from other cities to support the navy during the war against the Persians. The elements, or trees and the sea, made Athens an empire. Pericles states that regardless of how Athens came to be an empire, it must continue to expand in order to survive. The territories it fails to dominate will be dominated by its adversaries, and ultimately Athens will have to fight those adversaries, strengthened as they will be by their subject cities. This was the argument that made Thucydides a prominent Cold War theorist, and he has not yet left Washington. In 2009 I asked a freshman humanities class whether they considered themselves citizens of an empire. I had hoped to establish the political and historical relevance of Thucydides's *History*. Only two of about twenty so considered themselves. I did not ask this question in order to provoke any self-loathing—far from it. One can certainly debate the sense of the term *imperialism*, but the fact that the great majority of these well-educated young voters felt certain that the term does not apply to their nation surprised me. The United States has not created a colonial administration, it's true, but it has instead an agency, however ineffective, that seeks to determine the outcome of coups and elections in distant nations.

US expansion accelerated quickly after World War II when, among capitalist nations, only the United States was sufficiently strong to reconstruct markets and governments. The United States did not enter the war in order to acquire an empire, but after 1945 it felt economic and political pressure to ensure room for its continued economic expansion. Most American citizens recognize that prosperity depends upon access to foreign markets and resources, even though they do not consider the nation imperial on the British or even the Roman model. The argument is often made that clandestine connivance and force are necessary to secure access to material resources, markets, and labor pools for US entrepreneurs, and that this is the most efficient way to improve the standard of living for the largest population. Before one goes very far in condemning US expansion, a literary critic has to acknowledge that the history of Western literature is unimaginable without imperial themes and the institutions of cosmopolitan cultures. T. S. Eliot said that he was all for empires, apparently for literary reasons.[4] US expansion has provided subject matter and a nervous, self-questioning perspective to postwar literature and film for which one may be grateful.

One presumes that American audiences consider the consequences of expansion after viewing these mainstream films. Particularly in the last decade, but earlier too, filmmakers have asked: For what must we answer?

The films I have in mind are justly interpreted as fables about political responsibility. This analysis goes back to Sydney Pollack's *Three Days of the Condor* and to Costa Gavras's *Missing*, but it is more acute in the recent films I mentioned. In *Traitor*, Nathir, leader of a terrorist group, says that "the Americans love to brag about how their government represents the people. So we should accept that every American shares equal responsibility for their government's crimes. Nobody is innocent." That strenuous proposal has acquired wide currency, and filmmakers recognize that it is terrifying to US citizens. Ed Hoffman (Russell Crowe), a CIA case officer at Langley in *Body of Lies*, repeatedly tells his field agent, "Ferris, nobody's innocent in this shit." It's clear that much damage is done in the name of US citizens. These films have helped to shape discussion of complicity for citizens about a decade older than my freshmen. It's not clear, however, that the films have affected the generation that now puts boots on the ground. One may reasonably object that my freshmen had it right, that the term *imperialism* does not suit US foreign policy, but then one is at a loss for a substitute. What might better characterize the far-reaching economic and military activities of the United States since 1945? The traditional term has the advantage of frankly acknowledging not only US appetites, but also its responsibilities—and ultimate vulnerability.

Students signing up for ROTC reasonably expect to be protected against illegal commands. There are understood limits to service proper to a state. The military hierarchy of command systematically subordinates individual judgment to the objectives of the state, but civilian oversight ultimately checks that authority. Students who respond to CIA recruitment efforts, however, proceed without that protection. They realize that they may be asked to provide service beyond the law. The CIA may refuse responsibility for the commands that have passed through its chain of command; agents themselves may be entirely disavowed by the agency they serve. The CIA expects a grand order of service, to which one must add that such service is secret. A recruit's will to serve should be so strong that he or she can bear being known not as one who served with honor, but instead as one who did not serve at all. The agency's avowed values are, "We put Nation first, Agency before unit, and mission before self."[5] Service with *acknowledged* honor—that of police, firefighters, soldiers, and others—is a less compelling subject for writers; the sacrifices such workers undertake are compensated in an immaterial but more or less durable and traditional manner.

Recruitment to the CIA is a special subject, but not because this agency is unlike all others. The issue is rather that the agency requires ultra loyalty without worldly recognition. The motivation for this service must come from within. A naïve account of service is expressed in *The Recruit* (2003), by Walter Burke (Al Pacino), who presumes that young agents seek above all self-approval. He offers them engagement in a broadly conceived moral battle. This is his orientation address to a class of recruits: "So, why are you here? . . . It ain't the money. . . . It ain't sex. . . . What about fame? Our failures are known; our successes are not. That's the company motto. . . . So . . . what is it? I say we are all here . . . because we believe. We believe in good and evil, and we choose good. We believe in right and wrong, and we choose right. Our cause is just. Our enemies [are] everywhere. They're all around us. Some scary stuff out there. Which brings us here." The film undermines these bromides by exposing his hypocrisy, but beyond that his account fails to explain why agents commit acts they understand to be immoral and illegal—and this does need to be well explained. He provides no account of what distinguishes the forces of light from those of darkness, nor of how to recognize one or the other party when labels are unreliable. About political objectives, he is again silent. Former CIA assassin Mitch Leary (John Malkovich), in *In the Line of Fire* (1993), tells Frank Horrigan (Clint Eastwood) that he "used to think that this country was a very special place. . . . Do you have any idea what I have done for God and country? Some pretty fucking horrible things. I don't even remember who I was before they [the CIA] sunk their claws into me." He recalls only that he once was a patriot.

The power of ideas to motivate extraordinary agents has always been controversial. Traditional representations of exemplary valor do not support a model of rational agency. Achilles is no patriot; the concept of Greek solidarity does not move him. He has to suffer intimate personal losses and be promised enduring honor before he willingly sacrifices his well-being. Countless detective stories, films, and television serials use personal motivation to explain the assiduousness of investigators, as if the notion that a service ideal alone might drive one to extraordinary lengths were inherently implausible. This is why the CIA as subject matter is especially important: this agency proposes an impersonal commitment that brings no reasonable gain to those who serve it. Achilles had a recognizable appetite for glory, and that helped move him to fight the Trojans, though that alone was insufficient. Jake Gittes, remember, had a practical sense of the value of reputation. But CIA field agents remain anonymous. They must serve for the experience itself, or for a concept of the state. Achilles refuses without a second thought the sort of service that the CIA proposes. Directors understand well the constraints of service. Several films have undertaken to test the role of ideas as motives by representing agents who stumble into service. In *Three Days of the Condor*, Joseph Turner (Robert Redford) inadvertently becomes an agent by going out for sandwiches; he returns to a decimated workplace, and the plot begins. Why are his friends dead? In *The Amateur* (1981), Charles Heller (John Savage) too is a desk analyst at the CIA, a cipher specialist who wishes to become a field agent in order to avenge the death of his sweetheart. She was executed by terrorists, and he means to punish them, though he has no relevant skills. He must trick the CIA into training him and then assisting him in his project. Neither Turner nor Heller expresses commitment to the state or the agency. Their motivation remains entirely personal. They do not fit the agency, exactly because they have little regard for impersonal values. They are figures from other narratives dropped into a CIA story in order to demonstrate just what is extraneous to service. Their motivation is situational, and their autonomy, unsustainable. They depart at the end for another life. Like Achilles, they refuse abstract values and thereby modernity itself.

The familiar claim of several films is not that the state's agents are fanatics, nor that they are driven by mistaken beliefs, but that on the contrary they are without convictions. Commitment to a secular state seems tantamount to having no convictions. Mussawi (Mark Strong), just before torturing CIA agent Bob Barnes (George Clooney) in *Syriana*, asks, "What if I had to get you to recant, Bob? That would be pretty difficult, because . . . if you had no beliefs to recant, then what?" Jason Bourne is a zombie who cannot recall how he got where he is. The US state is extended far beyond the conscious will of its agents. This fog around motivation extends even to infantry soldiers. In *The Hurt Locker* (2008), Sergeant Sanborn (Anthony Mackie) asks Sergeant James (Jeremy Renner), "How do you do it, Will?" James replies, "I don't know. I guess I don't think about it. . . . I don't know. Do you know why?" And Sanborn: "No, I don't." The film makes a fierce and contested claim: that soldiers (James is an army ranger) are unable to say why they risk their lives, why the interests of the United States deserve vigorous defense elsewhere in the world. In *Syriana*, Dean Whiting (Christopher Plummer) says that Barnes has been used by the CIA throughout his career without knowing why. The CIA, in need of a scapegoat, has turned on Barnes. He replies: "I didn't used to need to know." His aspiration to loyalty alone was adequate for many years of hazardous service—until the agency betrayed him. The films suggest not that there are no good reasons for extreme service, nor that Bourne and these others are insufficiently thoughtful individuals, but rather that loyalty is no substitute for conviction. The postwar liberal vision of a state free of ideological zeal, sixty years later, has gone too far. Ideas matter on the ground. This critique of liberalism was expressed long ago by the poet and New Deal–liberal Charles Olson, when he visited the incarcerated fascist Ezra Pound. Olson felt at a loss to assess Pound's crime: "[Fascists] know what they fight against. We do not yet know what we fight for."[6] The real issue in these diverse contexts where motivation seems in doubt is the liberal notion that political convictions are best held with moderation—that politics is not a just center of civic life.

A mundane, familiar sense of service within realistic limits (what ROTC students expect) is explicitly rejected by these films as insufficient. In *Green Zone* (2010), Miller's (Matt Damon) pragmatic subordinate advises against engaging a sniper. "We're here to do a job and get home safe," he says. "The reasons don't matter." This is the voice of an ordinary soldier—not of a true leader. Miller wants to do more. "They"—the reasons—"matter to me." He pushes beyond his immediate orders, and that attracts the attention of a CIA agent, Martin Brown (Brendan Gleeson), who enlists him in the intelligence work that drives the narrative. The difference between performing one's narrowly defined duty and seeking a general policy or truth behind one's orders is exactly what takes Miller from the army to the CIA. The agency is for inquirers, even intellectuals, not administrators. In *Green Zone*, as in *The Good Shepherd*, Damon is unwilling just to serve; he is eager to do so effectively. His reasons? "I came here to find weapons [of mass destruction] and save lives." In a different film, as a different character, he is reported to have said much the same thing: "You said you'd do anything to save American lives, Jason." Inquirers learn that extreme actions performed by ultraloyal, compliant agents are necessary to alter the course of events. One comes around to a familiar pragmatism that can justify all deeds. But one gets there by seeking general accounts of motives and objectives.

The issue arises with the thought that CIA agents, and Marlowe too, work alone; they are not team players. They are all exceptionality. Their autonomy is exactly what action films represent best.[7] This is why off-the-books agents are the focus of such films as *Munich*, *Traitor*, and *Body of Lies*. Agents undertake risk ostensibly for an idea about the state and its needs. William Sullivan (Robert De Niro), a character modeled on William J.

Donovan in *The Good Shepherd*, says, in good faith, that a conception of the nation motivates him: "this is for America." Edward assures him that the next generation loves the country too: "We all do, sir. We all do." This nation rests upon Enlightenment ideas, not blood, not earth. Traditional societies have a different coherence and stability; the United States repeatedly renews itself with immigration and social legislation. Sullivan has faith in the Constitution's checks and balances. He advocates a check on the growing power of the agency, what promises otherwise to be a hazard to the republic. The crucial element of this scene is the assertion of collective identity. Edward's hollow words propose what needs to be believed: that the nation is held together, from one generation to the next, by consensus concerning state power. But Sullivan is a dying father, rapidly losing his footing in this political allegory. The director (also De Niro) includes this dialogue between Sullivan and Edward in order to establish a philosophical decline from the CIA founders to the very next generation that administers it after 1949.

The film suggests that an idea of the nation ensures endurance, survival. Edward means to mollify Sullivan by speaking patriotically as a representative of a younger generation, but De Niro the director reveals how patronizingly Edward manipulates Sullivan. Fifteen years later, in a rare moment of pique, Edward expresses the mistaken belief that only the white nation will survive. The director presents a scene with an Italian-American Mafioso, Joseph Palmi (Joe Pesci): it is utterly irrelevant to the plot, but thematically crucial because it exposes Edward's corrupt concept of the state.

> Palmi: Let me ask you something. . . . We Italians, we got our families, and we got the church; the Irish, they have the homeland. Jews, their tradition; even the niggers, they got their music. What about you people, Mr. Wilson, what do you have?
> Wilson: The United States of America. The rest of you are just visiting.

The CIA is represented as an elite New England preserve—with all the racism and class privilege once associated with that milieu. Edward loses a chess-like struggle with the KGB exactly because his racist version of the nation has not survived even in his own family. Not that each generation starts from scratch; De Niro's point is subtler. The convictions of one generation are mere proposals to the next.

This film begins with a single question, never explicitly posed, but

The Good Shepherd (2006)

governing its structure all the same. Imagine Edward, examining his past, asking, *Where did I go wrong?* The first sequence is a grainy black-and-white surveillance film of a young man and woman making love; then a color close-up of Edward's enlarged eyeball looking through a magnifying glass. These juxtaposed shots are about scrutinizing private lives, his exact line of work, though his own private life does not do well under such scrutiny; this is what destroys his sense of honor. The deeper theme of these opening shots is male lineage. (Mothers are more or less dispensable to spy films—though the KGB peculiarly refers to Edward as "Mother." These films focus on the continuity of male reproduction. What is a man to do?) This is a way, however presumptively sexist, of focusing films on the long-term viability of service to the state. Are conditions in place to assure the needed service to the state we know? Certainly not, is the damning political judgment spoken by recent films. The young man in the surveillance film is Edward's son, though the father cannot recognize the son without technical enhancement of the film. Junior, in bed, is passing information to a dark-skinned KGB agent—a life that Edward barely dares to imagine. From his father the son wants recognition, and he means to get that by trading in his father's currency. In the film's second sequence Edward is examining a tiny clipper ship he has built and is inserting in a bottle. The clipper is a figure for his own father's failure, and for his son's betrayal of Edward's trust.[8] Edward's father's betrayal of public trust is visited upon his son and then his grandson. The male line is cursed, and the family can reproduce, at best, only the wounded: Junior's intended is pregnant when she is pushed out of an airplane. The film presents a Greek sense of the incompatibility of family and state honor. There is no viable private sphere

The Good Shepherd (2006)

for those who serve as Edward does. Two lovers in the Congo cause the failure of the Bay of Pigs invasion of Cuba. Sullivan is quite wrong: the CIA offers no place to raise a family.

Edward rises to power at the CIA through a social network he entered at Yale; those born to that milieu condescend to him. His particular strengths are drive, self-control, and retentiveness. This is why he catches his poetry professor's plagiarism and recognizes the KGB presence in Guatemala. He is more grind than strategist. He marries Clover (Angelina Jolie) as a consequence of having accepted her sexual advances at a social event; he accepted induction into Skull and Bones (the Yale senior secret society) at an earlier social event. Neither of these crucial changes in his life did he initiate. The leadership cadre he joins expects an ambitious outsider to deliver whatever is asked of him, and he does. He ships out of his marriage, without consultation, a week after the wedding. He represses his loves, his spirit, almost completely. He becomes cipher-like, even before joining the CIA, so incommunicative that his son's fiancée is assassinated because Edward would not utter one word, nor even nod his head, to prevent her death. His KGB opposite presents him with a choice between nation and family. Edward refuses to respond, and that costs his son's intended bride her life—and blocks the next generation of his family. A single word might encumber his power at the CIA.

"I am the good shepherd," Christ says, "and know my sheep, and am known of mine" (John 10:14). Edward means to be a good shepherd, but he neither knows his family nor is known by them. His mode of survival is silence, even when spoken to; a stern prudence is his only guide.[9] He trusts neither himself nor others. Were he to speak, he knows, he might lie, and his father's last words warned him against that. He is at ease only with women who cannot hear well, cannot easily hold him to his words. Just before his father shoots himself, he counsels young Edward. "He asked me if I knew what trust was," Edward later reports. "And I said, 'trust is when you feel safe with someone.' . . . And then he said: 'Don't ever lie. If you lie to your friends, they won't trust you. And you will have nothing. And you'll never be safe.'" The first words of the film are those of Edward's son's KGB lover: "You are safe here with me." Junior asked Edward in 1946 whether Edward had killed anyone while he was at war. Edward lied by saying no. This lie was among his first words to his son. In truth he killed the one woman he had slept with during the preceding six years. (He discovered that her hearing in fact was not impaired, that she recorded his words for the KGB.) Neither father nor son felt safe. Edward made mistrust the basis of his professional life, as CIA agents routinely do. (The actual James Jesus Angleton—the model for Edward—so mistrusted even the staff at CIA that the Soviet division of the agency was frozen for a decade [1964–1975], while he searched for a mole.) Exactly because Edward had so little experience in trusting others, when he did convey his trust, he did so poorly. (Kaspar Gutman [Sidney Greenstreet] observes exactly this about speech itself in *The Maltese Falcon*.) *The Good Shepherd* suggests that trusting is an art that requires practice; but the cost of withholding it is high. The one Russian whom Edward trusts, Valentin Mironov (John Sessions), turns out to be a mole. (The model for Mironov was Anatoliy Golitsyn, who was not a mole, but Angleton nonetheless grossly overestimated his significance. Shortly before his retirement Angleton himself was suspected of being the mole he could never identify.)[10] Edward takes to heart the advice that Sullivan gives him: "No matter what anyone tells you, there'll be nobody you can really trust. I'm afraid that when all is said and done we're all just crooks." He had heard something similar from his college professor: "I hope you're lucky enough to find someone you trust. I regret to say, I haven't." Mistrust stunts life itself, and Angleton's career demonstrates that it ultimately disables even the intelligence services.

One often hears doubt turned against the very project of truth-telling: And what *is* truth? Bernard Williams asks how far are "the narratives that support our understandings of ourselves and of each other, and of the societies in which we live, capable of truth?"[11] Skepticism, he observes, too easily grows boundless. But spy films—and noirs too—are conservative in examining the damage done by definite lies. Edward Junior *did* hear his father's conversation with Philip Allen about the site of the coup planned against Fidel, though Junior denied that he did. And Junior conveyed that bit of information to his KGB lover. As a consequence of one particular lie, the Bay of Pigs coup was a fiasco—in the film, that is. Many causes contributed to the actual failure of the coup, but the film is a handsomely shaped work of art focused on this one fictive "fact." Junior lies, despite his father's admonition to maintain confidence concerning that particular overheard conversation, as Edward lies, despite his father's final admonition not to do so, lest others mistrust and dislike Edward. Male lineage turns round the same issues, generation after generation; the shapeliness of the film suggests that such betrayal is inevitable, part of one's growing up. Men lie in order to distinguish themselves from their fathers, but they resemble their fathers by virtue of their lies. No one lives up to the model set by the father of the nation. Cherry tree? Not me. They are ordinary men, or all just crooked.

The decline of the CIA, or more generally the failure of mind to serve the state effectively, is the subject of *The Good Shepherd*. Intellectuals in state service have produced an institution sick at its core. Edward came to the OSS and then the CIA from the study of poetry at Yale. The most canonical modern poem is relevant. Eliot's *The Waste Land* represents the most general consequences of impotence. The sign of this particular pathology is a failure to establish continuity from one generation to the next. Much is made of the clannishness of the CIA, and one might think that any variety of solidarity might help to hold the agency together over time. But just this is the film's critique of the US intelligence service: its pathology prevents a sustainable idealism. Only doubt persists. The eastern seaboard effort to recruit the brightest of young scholars to the nation's intelligence service comes apart within the duration of a single career. The sons (daughters are altogether neglected) cannot continue the work of the fathers.

The Good Shepherd is organized in a literary manner, almost like a poem. The narrative does not reconstruct Angleton's life in a literal sense; nor does it represent many of the significant events in the history of the CIA between 1949 and 1961, though this is the dual subject matter of the film. The determining historical events, radically condensed, are present in the film, though some are mere references.[12] In a verse couplet the second rhymed word reveals the structure of an expression. That such order obtains at the level of sense—that a rhyme is meaningful—may be a revelation. A couplet reminds one that words have consequences; beginnings, ends. Nothing memorable stands alone. A string of couplets persuades one that, as Whitman said, "It avails not, time nor place—distance avails not." The film's structure, despite many shifts of time and place, is intricate in this way. It is marked by narrative and character rhymes (Edward's two apparently hearing-impaired lovers, for instance), but also by verbal echoes (the rhymes on "protect" and "safe"). The subtlest echo is on the term "cardinal." Early in the film, on a bus to his office, Edward receives a dollar bill from a little boy who seems to want change. Edward provides coins, then gets off the bus. At the office his assistant, Ray Brocco (John Turturro), matches the serial number of the bill to a table of code messages. "Cardinal is interested," he reports. Who is the asset named Cardinal? That question, one word, hangs in the air until late in the film. When Edward meets with Ulysses (Oleg Shtefanko), his KGB counterpart, to refuse to collaborate to protect his son from exposure, the KGB bodyguard for Ulysses asks for a dollar to buy a gift for his daughter. Edward provides a dollar bill and says, "It's a cardinal rule to be generous in a democracy." Ulysses registers the remark, but so does his bodyguard. One of them has received a message that confirms collaboration. This matters, because Edward has just acknowledged defeat in the matter of Cuba—the one political adventure represented on screen. Junior's betrayal of his father cost the United States a victory at the Bay of Pigs that had otherwise seemed, to Edward, "fairly certain." The passing of this message indicates that Edward is in fact running either Ulysses or more likely his bodyguard as a double agent, a rhyme across the two intelligence systems. The beauty of Edward's line is that even if Ulysses is ignorant of the code sense of the word *cardinal*, he has warrant to think that Edward means to indicate that, when Ulysses has a modest need for collaboration, his capitalist counterpart will be generous. The message itself is ambiguous. Who will work for whom in the future? A fog rolls in at the end.

Hollywood has given audiences ideological artifacts like *The Good Shepherd*, and they apparently want more of the same, which is a wonder. The films exploit obviously political subject matter timed to the fears of the last decade. Very few of them propose unfamiliar causes and consequences of events recognized as constitutive of the nation's recent past (as *The Good Shepherd* does, concerning the Bay of Pigs fiasco); most instead give memorable form to the unresolved contradictions of a democratic and expansionist republic.[13] They construe the affective dimension of public events by providing a narrative shape not only to fears but to reformist hopes as well—in particular, for an effective and honorable intelligence service. The challenge facing directors like De Niro is to render radiant the inert matter of political controversy. The Bourne films are weighted down by bent and crushed automobiles. However, the obvious alternative to trivial thrills—namely, analysis of politics and economics—is so abundant in print that film audiences reasonably resist explicit analysis. Directors seek a meaning in public events that film illuminates more effectively than political commentary can. These films vie directly with discursive prose, as one often sees in the opening sequences, when directors most want to establish the general significance of the scenes on screen. *Body of Lies*, for instance, opens with a neat discursive frame. First, a video of Al-Saleem (Alon Aboutboul), a jihadist pledging death and destruction in Europe; second, a failed police effort to prevent a bombing in Manchester, England. The logic of the juxtaposition is simple cause and effect. Al-Saleem is at the controls. The titles then appear on screen followed by a now conventional zoom shot from a satellite and a label "Samarra, Iraq"; and finally the prone body of CIA field agent Roger Ferris (Leonardo DiCaprio) and a voice-over by his case-officer at Langley, Ed Hoffman (Russell Crowe). Hoffman is using voice-recognition software to dictate a policy memo displayed as a digital text on a computer screen: a screen within a screen; an essay on both screens. He acknowledges that the Iraq War began with obscure and mistaken objectives, but states that it will continue nonetheless "because we are there." It doesn't matter how we got there—pragmatics, not principles. Everyone has heard or read that over and over. (Clark Poundstone [Greg Kinnear] repeats this in *Green Zone*.) This is the ideological frame for what follows, and it derives largely from the archive of print journalism. The job of the film is to rise well above such familiar discourse. That, it certainly manages. This opening makes the further point that the CIA spins out its theories with little input from civilian sources. Ed Hoffman has an audience of two who listen, skeptically, it appears, but silently, as he leans toward them and speaks conspiratorially about the jihadist challenge to western civilization. Those auditors may well be Congressional representatives, but there is no opening for them to speak back to the CIA. Intelligence agencies control their overseers in the War on Terror.

A modern state takes an abstract view of human activity, according to James C. Scott.[14] It looks down, as from a satellite, on those circumstances that can be altered. Individuals have curiosity; they assume responsibility, make commitments, feel sympathy. One might think that a state perspective, because abstract, would be oriented on principles or stable values, but the contrary is the case. Principles are irrelevant; all is open to practical

Body of Lies (2008)

calculation. Hoffman explains that the interests of the CIA are global, not local, not personal. Despite the apparent particularity of his expression (a southern drawl and a singularly coarse imagination), he is a spokesman of an imperial state. The sequence of shots on screen in the first five minutes establishes a logic of juxtapositions: CIA headquarters is to agents like Roger Ferris as Al-Saleem is to his foot soldiers. The information technologies of West and East, state and sect, differ, but they control all the same, with the consequence that those on the ground are expendable; their particularity, illusory. His analysis is not subtle, only bold. He callously dismisses concern for the locals who facilitate his agents' work. Ferris is once offered collaboration with Hani (Mark Strong), head of Jordanian intelligence, based on a single principle: no lying. But Ferris's case officer forbids compliance. A modern state masters contingent events, scenario by scenario. The term *foreign policy* is a misnomer: US policies abroad are plural, mutable, and insubordinate in regard to any principle. This is difficult for citizens of a nation of Enlightenment ideals to understand. The objective abroad of a modern state is *not* to bring social and economic structures there into conformity with an imperial order. The CIA expresses no faith that democratic reforms or free-market economics will bring progress abroad. Instead it seeks diverse and local outcomes. "Global," in Hoffman's usage, is a geographical term that means extensive, not universal.

The film's title holds an abstract focus on mendacity—beyond all the bloody action. One expects a democratic republic to aspire to transparent procedures, but very recent events have reminded us that representatives of the executive branch systematically misrepresent the actions of the state in public testimony to the legislative branch; the government lies to itself about its activities. "Home to old lies and new infamy," Ezra Pound wrote in 1920. One generation after another pulls up short in the face of state mendacity. After the Gulf of Tonkin resolution in 1964, and a half century after Pound's complaint, Robert Bly wrote that "These lies mean that the country wants to die."[15] Mendacity damages the heart of the nation, because meaningful democratic citizenship requires reliable information. A decade later Jürgen Habermas argued that the democratic public sphere depends upon confidence that language adequately communicates truth. The truth is, though, that lying in political contexts is widely expected. John Mearshimer observes that lying is "accepted practice": statesmen lie either to other states or their own people for "compelling strategic reasons."[16] Martin Jay has argued further that, "To the extent that democracy is always a condition to come rather than a state of being already realized, we cannot avoid a certain duplicity—and perhaps a necessary and even healthy one—in our claim that we live in one in the present."[17]

Jay admires the "aesthetic play" in political discourse that renders truth-telling "marginal, if not irrelevant."[18] From this point of view, Lyndon Johnson's machinations leading to the Gulf of Tonkin resolution and Bush's invasion of Iraq on behalf of weapons of mass destruction can be criticized as bad art but not as assaults on democratic process. The film reveals the effect of such mendacity on voluntary state service. Hoffman's lies to Ferris are factual, not profound, though they make Ferris's job more difficult than it needs to be. Hoffman's duplicity ultimately erodes Ferris's commitment to serve the state. And that is the consequence of routine mendacity: that only those comfortable with shifting explanations and objectives will serve voluntarily a state that lies to them without compunction.[19] The state advances toward greater cynicism; as ultra-agents withdraw from service so too presumably will ordinary citizens in less demanding roles. *Body of Lies*, *Traitor*, and *Munich* all propose that mendacity is unsustainable. These films insist that the greater challenge to the intelligence services is not outwitting the nation's enemy but retaining the faith of the state's servants—and ultimately of its citizens. *Body of Lies* suggests that Hoffman could, at little cost, be franker, that his mendacity is unnecessary. In this sense the film concentrates on remediable, not systemic, problems with US intelligence procedures.

Body of Lies articulates a practical, straightforward critique of US counterterrorism. Two principal characters pursue alternative methods of espionage; a third, the protagonist, must choose one as a model. Hoffman operates by remote control from suburban Virginia—but to merely modest effect. He relies not on charisma, as Hani does, but on the blunt authority of the state to persuade his allies and subordinates to comply with his wishes—and this fails him. He treats his agent as a subordinate who does not need to know all that is known. The liability of his manipulation is that it is not only "results-oriented," as he puts it; it is oriented on *immediate* results. Unlike the Bourne films, *Body of Lies* displays no war room of analysts screening data banks. He and Garland both reach out from their homes, not from headquarters. The camera shows no interest in institutions. Intelligence gathering is more personal art than institutional procedure. Hani is an antithetical character who identifies his values as "Middle Eastern." The film presents his approach as essentially wise, humane, and effective. He punishes severely those who cross him, but he does not seek information through torture. Instead he respectfully and cleverly exploits local cultures. He recruits a young jihadist by making gifts to an aged mother in her son's name. This imitation of filial piety is offered to the jihadist as incentive to spy on Al-Saleem. Hani recognizes the young man's ideals and challenges him to live up to his own best self. "Go and be a good Muslim," he says. Whereas Hoffman precipitously exploits others, Hani knows to wait for his schemes to mature.

In the Middle East, Hani tells Ferris, friendship can save one's life—as it does save Ferris's. Hani's one rule for collaboration is extremely tough on spies, because they try to trust no one. As an agent of the US government, Ferris is not free to confide in the head of the Jordanian service, even though Jordan and the United States are close allies in intelligence gathering; the US Congress annually appropriates funds to support the Jordanian service.[20] Bernie Ohls works for the Los Angeles district attorney in *The Big Sleep*. He can confide freely in Marlowe, because they are friends. Bernie is not severely constrained as an agent of the state. A decade later, in *Kiss Me Deadly*, Los Angeles police detective Pat Murphy cannot confide in his friend Mike Hammer, because the federal government forbids public-private collaboration. Nuclear weaponry is the warrant for the nation-state's new authority. All individual relationships, professional as well as personal, are rendered subordinate to state control of the means of mass destruction. Weber says that the state is "the sole source of the 'right' to use violence."[21] As the force at the state's disposal increases in magnitude, the autonomy of individuals (even of state agents) is sharply reduced. Ferris can construct trust relationships only after leaving the agency.

Body of Lies seems a dark film in political terms because, despite US

technological superiority, US relations with foreigners are entirely instrumental, ignoble, predatory. However, the film expresses significant optimism too about the quality of life accessible even to US agents. Two
considerations reveal this. First, Ferris is capable and committed to his
work, curious and hardworking, anything but cynical. His is the good faith
of a recent generation from the universities. He has learned some Arabic
and is admirably respectful of local cultures. Second, although he has to
leave the agency, he is able to do so and seems to move toward a full and
healthful life—with a woman who likes children. His last appearance on
camera shows him shopping for food. That is life outside the agency. His
case officer tells him that there is nothing to like about the Middle East.
Ferris replies that that notion may be a problem in itself. Failures of attention and curiosity may lie at the root of US foreign policy. Ferris, though,
enjoys life there—pastries, customs, language, women, children. And he
values highly his opportunities to found trusting relationships with others
there. Aisha tells him that he is not the CIA, and he tells Hoffman that the
CIA is not America. Ferris's faith is in a cultural nation independent of
state institutions. That is a basis for much optimism.

Other agents who leave the agency—Samir, Bourne, Mitch Leary—carry
a burden of responsibility, remorse, which does not encumber Ferris. In
2001 President Bush famously declared the United States at war with an
indefinite enemy. When Ferris feels guilty after executing a collaborator in
order to preserve his own cover, Hoffman reminds him that "we are at
war." The point is to win: it is not hard to justify dubious means in order
to achieve victory in war. Nearly all's fair there, we say. One takes for
granted that innocents will suffer. Most war casualties are noncombatants.
As the poet Robert Hass observes, "In the first twenty years of the
twentieth century 90 percent of war deaths were the deaths of combatants.
In the last twenty years of the twentieth century 90 percent of war deaths
were deaths of civilians."[22] Who is to answer for the—no longer incidental—civilian victims of war? Three decades ago, in *Missing*, an American
ambassador to Chile addresses the complicity of ordinary citizens: the US
Embassy protects the interests of over three thousand US firms doing business there—"in other words, your interests," he tells New York business-
man Ed Horman (Jack Lemmon). "I'm concerned with the preservation of
a way of life," he adds. This is another kind of support for Nathir's notion
that "every American shares equal responsibility for their government's
crimes." So long as the benefits of economic expansion—foreign markets
or oil, cheap labor—are distributed to a desiring population, civilians are

engaged in a struggle for economic hegemony. Hollywood filmmakers for at least three decades have used their art to inform US audiences of the adverse consequences of economic expansion; a concept of collective responsibility is by now entirely familiar. Ignorance is not the issue. Even US consumers make meaningful choices; a global economy is not being thrust upon an unwilling populace. What then remains of the concept of innocence?

In 1981 President Reagan issued Executive Order 12333, which forbade CIA agents from committing assassination. Gerald Ford had earlier issued an order forbidding political assassinations. Reagan removed the word *political* and extended the order to cover not only staff agents but all CIA employees, including contract employees. There is reason to think that CIA operatives took this order seriously before 2004.[23] Robert Baer says that he never violated it, though in the opening sequence of *Syriana* the character Bob Barnes (based on Baer) assassinates with equanimity some purchasers of missiles. Nearly all CIA films represent agents as ready assassins, and yet the government tried to curb assassinations. Audiences have shown no skepticism about state assassinations in these realistic films, despite the laws of the nation. They seem to *want* to regard assassination as a state resource. At the end of *Three Days of the Condor*, Higgins (Cliff Robertson) says that when oil or food becomes scarce the American people will not want to discuss the propriety of an invasion of the Middle East; they will instead expect the state to secure the future by invading nations that can supply desired resources. The nation now expects the state to commit assassinations in order to fulfill its security mission. It is only a short step to the same arsenal, as Higgins said, to secure access to resources. That is the grim prediction behind filmic representations of CIA assassinations.

Assassination is a set topic in US film. Before 2001 it was illegitimate for US agents. The representation of it as common practice has an important indirect consequence. The worst that can be alleged of a democratic republic is not that its agents are assassins, but rather that its accounts of its activities are generally unreliable. The representation of assassination promotes general cynicism concerning government testimony; that is the main meaning of this topos. The Bourne films, for instance, persuade audiences that the imagined state is not only extremely powerful and remorseless, but that it has every reason to obscure its functions. If the state were responsible for assassinations, before 2001, its agents and officers would diligently avoid publicity concerning the one crime that is systematically prosecuted in the civil justice system. Where their efforts to conceal misdeeds might end would be hard to determine. My understanding is that the assassination topos is ultimately allegorical, that it concerns the status of language in a democracy. Robert Bly in 1970 wrote wittily about state mendacity as a contagion: "Now the Chief Executive enters; the press conference begins: First the President lies about the date the Appalachian Mountains rose. Then he lies about the population of Chicago, then he lies about the weight of the adult eagle."[24] The poet's familiar point is that, as one lie leads to another, mendacity spreads through political discourse until policy debate is moot.

The corresponding topos is that of a free press. Narratives about civil misdeeds can be resolved easily by resort to a critical press. This is the notion that journalists stand ever ready to effect changes in state policy by exposing misdeeds and failed policies. Instead of public debate about competing policies, the press intervenes to embarrass the state concerning some program or event. Citizens may not need to assess the relative merits of competing policies; they need only read the paper concerning a fiasco. This is critique by exposure rather than debate—the B-version of democratic transparency. It rests on the premise that there is at least one thing that a state cannot admit: assassination had that significance, until 2001. In the second season of the Canadian television series about surveillance, *Intelligence* (2006–2007), the US Drug Enforcement Agency plans a sting arrest in Seattle of Canadian drug lord Jimmy Reardon (Ian Tracey). In fact execution, not arrest, is the intent behind the sting. When Mary Spalding (Klea Scott), the director of the Canadian Organized Crime Unit, threatens to take to the press evidence of a US mole in the Canadian secret police, she invokes the second of these corresponding topoi. The press does in fact follow the DEA effort to arrest Reardon, and eventually the lead-agent commits suicide rather than face exposure of his attempt to execute Reardon. The US agency is represented as ready to execute rather than prosecute; this is the first topos—apparently more plausible after 2001. And public exposure is the ultimate weapon of public servants who mean to hold the state to avowed procedures; this is a slightly more venerable topos. They work together. The implicit claim is that only the power of the press can stop a democratic state that has corrupted its own policies; debate cannot do this work. And the local point is that various US state agencies, not only the CIA, are lately more cynical than agencies of other democratic states.

Spy films confront a small set of familiar quandaries. I say *confront* because, film after film, their problems neither change much nor go away. At the heart of espionage is one intractable ethical contradiction: agents regularly use others in order to secure restricted information. The idioms of espionage are frank about this: a case officer "develops" an "asset." Moreover, agents make pacts to forego apprehension of a malefactor, likely to do more harm in the future, in order to secure useful information in that future. In some instances, they knowingly sacrifice the lives of those they are charged to protect in order to render protection to a greater number at a later date. This is known as the Coventry calculus. Because British intelligence had cracked a Nazi code, Churchill might have protected the citizens of Coventry from a planned aerial attack, though to do so would have indicated to the Nazi command that its code had been compromised. This is a particularly painful and hazardous calculation: a greater good is merely a hope or expectation concerning an indefinite future, whereas the necessary sacrifice is a present certainty. What is remarkable is that spy films rarely discover surprising features of these ethical dilemmas. The same contradictions between service to the state and Kantian ethics are repeatedly identified, but without analytical development. Spy films constitute a kind of serial: Heartaches of the Guardians. Plato is a constant presence, but so too is Kant. And that makes for problems. This is only to say again that the films are ideological artifacts. Their work is to render clear just what the political activities of the modern state displace.

State servants regularly surrender Kant and avow Bentham, the greatest good for the greatest number. Once a state admits the felicity calculus as a legitimating criterion, nearly anything can be justified. Hoffman excuses the execution of an informant who "was always going to get killed. Besides you had milked him and he was dry." But because espionage is conducted in time, and the future is uncertain, the outcome of the calculus is inevitably doubtful in any particular circumstances. The exploitation of one and all for political purposes is axiomatic to Hoffman. The state must survive in its current form in order to deliver prosperity to an increasing number of its citizens. This poses no quandary for Hoffman, though it does for Ferris and virtually all field agents in CIA films. The film has Hoffman meet with Ferris and Hani in Jordan to make the point that Hoffman's sangfroid derives from considered views. The miles between Langley and Amman matter not at all; Hoffman will cashier anyone to achieve the objectives of the agency. The drama derives from the fact that Ferris deals with others face to face, and that is the life he wants. He is discontent with a state policy that has him lying to those willing to trust him; nor does he regard that policy as an efficient way to pursue US security interests in Jordan. He is personally and professionally ashamed to discard those who help him. In order to secure the help of others he must build limited trust with them. Hani is there to remind Ferris of that fragile, daily process. The Jordanian approach to counterterrorism entails individual responsibility. A Middle Easterner, Hani tells Ferris, must stand by his word. Hoffman recognizes the practical obstacles to candor and prefers to speak less of truths and more of immediate effects. When Bassam (Oscar Isaac), Ferris's collaborator, is blown up, shards of his bones are embedded in Ferris's own body. Ferris reproaches Hoffman and the agency with the charge that they should do more for Bassam's family. Hoffman poses the relevant question: What are *you* doing for the family? Responsibility belongs to single persons. Hoffman understands this, and Ferris is learning the lesson from others. No comfort is to be had from investment in institutions. Even Hoffman works from a cell phone.

Body of Lies is an especially didactic spy film. It goes beyond analysis of the failures of the CIA to propose alternatives to US covert procedures. Hani is a major character because he explicitly articulates an approach to espionage that the CIA neglects.[25] He understands the private lives of his people, and that allows him to maneuver for leverage without shooting anyone. He knows that Mustafa Karami (Kais Nashif) would feel better about himself if he enjoyed the admiration of his own family. Hani arranges for Karami's mother's approval of her son, and Karami will do anything for Hani. Hani distinguishes his policies from Hoffman's in terms of a longer view, or patience. Or one might say that Hani more fully understands the motives of his assets. Hoffman himself says he wants a quick payoff for his investments; he thinks that he needs only shallow acquaintance with his assets. The narrative is structured to show not that Hani's methods are more honorable, only that they work where Hoffman's do not. American audiences appreciate the value of success.

CHAPTER 8

Privacy

John Wayne learned to fight from an Indian—in life, I mean. A pioneer stuntman taught him to make it look real. "I spent weeks studying the way Yakima Canutt walked and talked. He was a real cowhand."[1] Bogart took a lesson from boxers. In *The Big Sleep* he stops one of Eddie Mars's thugs from robbing Vivian by throwing one little punch. With his right hand he fiddles a lapel, then lets it go directly to the chin. Boxers know that vulnerable spot: take one there and your legs buckle. The thug is down and out. Marlowe recovers Vivian's purse without missing a breath. The objective of fisticuffs in Westerns and noirs is to validate the manly efficacy of the protagonists. Jason Bourne takes fighting to a level never imagined in those films; his matches are fantasies of a tech era. In a hallway at the Waterloo train station he has no difficulty dispatching three armed CIA agents. They lie on the floor like swatted flies. His fight with Desh in *The Bourne Ultimatum* (2007) is still more revealing. Desh is a formidable adversary exactly because he and Bourne have received the same training. Their match is long and close. The blows between them come rapidly, and both agents are masterful at blocking, slipping, and countering; they make Floyd Mayweather Jr. look slow. Exactly because these adversaries are well-matched, the fight ends in a brutal, artless way, when Bourne slowly strangles his opponent. All these fights are unrealistic, but Bourne's is more so than those of his noir and Western predecessors. Who taught this guy to fight? The state provided training that took these athletic but otherwise ordinary men to a level well above rivalry from even armed professional thugs. This matters greatly because the efficacy of the modern state is exactly the subject under scrutiny in spy films as in noirs.

Hollywood filmmakers are certainly critical of state power, yet they solicit admiration for it too. Bourne's proficiency is a pornography of

The Bourne Ultimatum (2007)

The Bourne Ultimatum (2007)

willfulness. Under every scene of his exploits is a whisper: the state can make you great. That the state archives knowledge of effective combat techniques is plausible. Comprehensive mastery of information is the mission of the CIA. Bourne's martial skills demonstrate CIA competence at the level of individual agency. His fights do not illustrate *character* (he has little of that). They authenticate state power. The spectacle of the CIA war room of projected screens and ready analysts is meant to represent instantaneous access to massive data banks. Insofar as information counts as knowledge, the state appears omniscient—a consequential lesson, and obviously false. The agency's record reveals that ordinary ignorance has repeatedly hobbled US diplomatic and military efforts. A decade was required to locate its most notorious enemy. The CIA was originally mandated to acquire and analyze information about the world. This work is performed largely by analysts at their Langley desks. Grafted onto this charge is the objective, not written into its charter, of conducting covert actions abroad. For nearly its first two decades, the agency gave much more to the latter than to the former.[2] Covert action—not data analysis—makes plots. Analysts appear in films like *Three Days of the Condor* only when they stray into cloak-and-dagger activities. When action films represent the acquisition of intelligence as comprehensive, and its analysis as rapid (if not acute), they serve audiences just what citizens of a republic understandably wish to believe about national defense. Those who follow the history of the CIA, however, realize that generic conventions are misleading audiences into a patriotic illusion of security.[3]

The competence of the CIA (and, by implication, the efficacy of the US state) is undercut, however, by another thematic convention: a sharp line between case officers and field agents. Daring individuals make their own power through technique; the agency is nothing without cowboys—a point made in any number of films. The Bourne films show a single agent repeatedly outwitting wicked but gullible guys at headquarters. Bourne is able to empty the safe in Noah Vosen's (David Strathairn) office; he observes CIA offices from an adjacent building when executives inside are unsure even what country he is in. The headquarters officers cannot secure their building—let alone protect the nation—despite their costly apparatus. *Spy Game* (2001) is exceptional in its representation of the capacities of an old-school case officer. Nathan Muir (Robert Redford) is a weathered agent turned Langley case officer. He initiates a naval operation to rescue from a brutal prison in China a young agent Nathan originally recruited. The measure of Nathan's proficiency is that he manages his task by connivance against the directorate of the agency—and does so on his last workday before retirement. The executives mean to sacrifice the young agent in the interest of upcoming trade talks with the Chinese. Nathan's motive is loyalty to his agent, whom he once warned not to expect personal loyalty. This is a central soft spot. Bob Baer refers to the agency's former commitment to its own agents. That policy drives Nathan, though the agency itself no longer adheres to it.[4] The lesson of the fable is not that the CIA is incompetent, nor that its resources are inadequate, but that the agency is now guided by inhumane, timidly conceived policies. Mere economic considerations—local ones, not political ideals—determine agency priorities, as formerly they did not. Nathan gives an impressive demonstration of what the spy game can accomplish: he is an audacious Odysseus, and he is devoted to an ideal of freedom—not so different from Sam Spade in *The Maltese Falcon*.

I referred to a misconception of CIA *proficiency*. This apt term keeps in focus a modest, definite objective; it describes an ability to get something made or done, but also a sense of advancement. *Efficiency* focuses still more on the production of effects, but it lacks a sense of progress. To be proficient is a utilitarian way of engaging what was traditionally spoken of as excellence: those who excel outdo the competition. This sense is close to that of proficient, but the latter term, focused more steadily on effects, offers a pragmatic version of excellence. Moreover a proficient person does not excel generally; he or she does one thing quite well. Jason Bourne was told by Dr. Albert Hirsch (Albert Finney), "Your acts will save American lives." His proficiency is aimed at that particular effect; an inventory might measure his proficiency, numerically. However, in order to achieve proficiency as an agent, he must relinquish his former identity as David Webb and become a different person. His new identity is focused entirely on his function as a servant of the state; it has no other dimensions. All else in his life is erased. He excels at work, but as a semi-person: mateless, no past, all present and immediate future.

Exactly this specialized excellence is promised to those who serve the state absolutely. Edward Wilson, in *The Good Shepherd*, also sacrificed parts of himself in order to serve the CIA. The full person was a comic performer, a cross-dresser even! In the black hole of his household safe is a program from his college performance of Gilbert and Sullivan's *H.M.S. Pinafore*. That is the lost Edward's marker, comparable to David Webb's dog tags. The appeal of spy films is partly a thrill of living dangerously, but still more a dream of towering over others in one's knowledge. "I'd joined the CIA hoping to get at a slice of truth not available to everyone," Robert Baer admitted.[5] Spies are supposed to have the real dope. But espionage agents on film are repeatedly in the dark. Most noir inquirers, like Sam Spade and Philip Marlowe, are quick-witted. Jeff Bailey in *Out of the Past* is exceptional exactly because he is slow to get it; he's been living in the mountains too long. CIA agents are *kept* ignorant; their case officers often know more than they do. Remember Hoffman and Ferris. Bob Barnes is made to stumble around even more than Jeff Bailey. The CIA seems not to insist that agents stay sharp.

Steven Spielberg's *Munich* concerns the hunt for the Palestinian terrorists responsible for planning the kidnapping and murder of eleven Israeli athletes at the Munich Olympics in 1972: it breaks pointedly with the fantasy of state proficiency. Spielberg's agents are off the books of Mossad, as ultra-agents usually are in recent spy films. The difference is that these characters lack special training and experience. Avner (Eric Bana) is a low-level agent with what he calls "the most boring job in the world." His father was a national hero, but he is a state-salaried bodyguard. The bomb expert of his squad of assassins knows little of bomb-making. In the Israeli army he dismantled bombs, but he never made them. The film's claim is that this team is comprised of former citizen-soldiers, amateurs whose actions are to be understood in relation to ordinary civilian life. This particular point about amateurism is unique to the film. George Jonas's *Vengeance* (1984), Spielberg's source, makes clear that all five members of this team were in fact fully trained Mossad agents. Many recent films ask whether the state's special training incapacitates its servants for civilian life. Can the agents of counterterrorism be expected to return to civilian life? Are their violations of civil order so grave as to damage them permanently? Or more abstractly: Is the rift between the avowed norms of civil society and the techniques of counterterrorism so deep as to undermine the constitutionality of a democratic republic?

Munich engages these questions in terms of a contradiction between state service and family life. The families of doctors, lawyers, coaches, musicians—of all those who give themselves over to their work—come under pressure, but state servants face a sharper contradiction, as Plato understood. Women and children of the guardians were to be shared in the republic. Seventeen minutes into the film is a close-up of Avner's wife Daphna (Ayelet Zurer), cheeks flushed, arms held down by her husband as he makes love to her. Their most private acts are exposed to public view. She is seven months pregnant, and their love life is central to the film: a handsome couple enjoying one another erotically and reproducing. Into that situation comes the head of Mossad, General Zamir (Ami Weinberg), who brings Avner to a meeting with Prime Minister Golda Meir (Lynn Cohen), and still other generals. Zamir then addresses Avner: "We want to ask you, Will you undertake

Munich (2005)

a mission? An important mission. You'll have to leave the country and your family. Maybe for years. You can't talk about it with anyone, even your wife." Avner says conspicuously little. "So this isn't about guarding tourists on El Al jets?" he cracks, amusing only himself. "Now you should say something," he is told. "Do you have any questions?" Golda Meir reminds him that his wife is approaching full term. "Family matters," she remarks. But Avner accepts his mission, without questions. "It's a good sign," his control later tells him, "that you didn't ask questions."

The contrary must be the case. He undertakes service uncritically, ignorantly. *The Bourne Ultimatum* develops this theme further. Dr. Hirsch tells Jason: "We didn't pick you. You picked us. You volunteered. . . . Even after you were warned . . . you didn't even blink. . . . You said you wanted to serve." But then David Webb repeatedly resisted the CIA's effort to train him into his new identity as assassin Jason Bourne. "Will you commit to this program?" he is asked by his trainer. Several times he replies "I can't" before he executes a hooded stranger to indicate his commitment to following even a lethal order contrary to the laws of his nation. Why does he commit? Why, for that matter, does he resist? The film leaves a near blank concerning Webb's motivation. Avner is at a point in life where he has good reason to refuse ultra-service. His family obligation is maximal just when he leaves his wife to assassinate terrorists. The prestige of the state is so great that the individual volition of these needy men, in their minds, is as nothing. Both films—*Munich* and *The Bourne Ultimatum*—indicate that those who undertake ultra-service to the state rarely deliberate the consequences of their commitment. They are driven by their particular needs, not by a principle. About Webb's life, nothing is known. But *Munich* makes clear that Avner lives without his father. He was orphaned, in a sense, because his mother had him raised in a kibbutz while his hero-father was in prison. He often refers to his father, but he does not see him. His wife, he says, is the only home he has known, whereas his mother speaks formulaically of Israel as a home for all Jews. He develops to a point where he needs neither parent nor parental state. This Sabra agent becomes a cosmopolite and raises his family in Brooklyn.

Early in *Munich*, before her meeting with Avner, Golda Meir reacts to the Black September attack in an odd manner. "We have laws," she tells a table full of generals or state ministers. "We represent civilization." (The film, however, shows Avner's targets to be particularly courteous, cultivated individuals—civilized, in the ordinary sense.) Of her adversaries, she says, "I don't know who these maniacs are and where they come from.

Palestinians—they're not recognizable." All parties to her discourse know well where Palestinian terrorism came from. This implausible speech raises a question about exceptionality. Must a constitutional republic consistently enforce its own laws, or do extreme events warrant deliberate departures from legality? The film gives no suggestion that the existence of the republic is in jeopardy. The issue is not to be resolved on pragmatic grounds: the point is made repeatedly that the assassination of nine Palestinian terrorists costs Israel many more lives in retaliatory attacks. The objective of Avner's mission is abstract, idealistic in a sense. "Forget peace for now," Golda Meir says. "We have to show them we're strong." The citizen-assassins are an extralegal squad whose goal is to demonstrate Israel's fierce resolve. Avner's political function is to communicate only that the state of Israel will violate its own laws and use its citizens—regardless of pragmatic calculations—to punish Palestinian attacks. (Keyser Söze.) Civil order has limits. Beneath the laws of a republic, a state is an instrument of force. Golda Meir communicates to her adversaries that this fact is an idea, one unaffected by practical considerations, but Spielberg communicates to audiences doubt about the long-term compatibility of state force and a civic life worthy of affirmation.

Mainstream filmmakers suggest that the practice of democratic citizenship has gone wrong. The problem is less that modern states overpower individual citizens than that citizens do not adequately reflect on their own responsibilities. Dr. Hirsch tells Jason near the end of the trilogy, "You knew exactly what it meant for you if you chose to stay [in the ultra-agents program]. . . . You cannot run from what you did, Jason. You made yourself into what you are. [In a flashback:] "You said you'd do anything it takes to save American lives." Jason was a citizen-soldier with dog tags. He gave up this status voluntarily when he decided to serve under any terms whatsoever. This is what the film criticizes. Jason and Avner could have done otherwise, had they duly considered the political consequences of ultra-service. The optimism of these apparently dark films lies in a belief that rational understanding is a solid ground for reform. They instruct citizens to be wary of ostensibly temporary suspension of a nation's laws.

Edward Wilson, in *The Good Shepherd*, is extremely compliant: in silence he does what is expected of him. His understanding of service obscures all else in his life, though he vigilantly guards his personal privacy. It is locked in a household safe. Like other ambitious people, he sets boundaries around what he considers his private life. The same actor, Matt

Damon, in *Syriana* plays the part of a financial analyst whose professional ambition overruns his family life. He loses one son and nearly his remaining family before he gets the message and returns home. In *In the Line of Fire*, Frank Horrigan (Clint Eastwood), as a young Secret Service agent, once hesitated to sacrifice his life for that of the president. At some level he refused ultra-service, if only for a moment. In the thematic system of the film, he is educable; he realizes that he must resign in order to maintain an intimate relationship with another agent. Two servants of the state cannot manage such a relationship; at least one must serve a partner more than a state. Spy films often make the point that the private sphere is more capacious and demanding than ambitious professionals care to acknowledge. Sullivan wants civilian oversight to check the agency, but what is to check the consuming ambition of ultra-servants? Only one element of the concept of the nation limits the efforts of those who serve and lead: legality. And the intelligence services constantly compromise the nation's laws in the name of security. The guardians of the republic are understood to constitute a class of exceptional citizens.

A distinction between public and private spheres is ancient, but confidence in a wall between them may be modern. Ezra Pound looked to ancient China to resolve tension between the two. In Canto 13, Confucius is asked the question Edward asks of himself: What should one sacrifice to protect one's family?

> If a man commit murder
> Should his father protect him, and hide him?
> And Kung said:
> He should hide him.

A subtle, indefinite distinction is offered between protecting and hiding. A father rightly goes some distance in contravention of civil authority, but not all the way. Pound admired the coherence of Confucian thought. Private and public spheres overlap directly. Obligations to state and family are inseparable.

> If a man have not order within him
> He cannot spread order about him;
> And if a man have not order within him
> His family will not act with due order;
> And if the prince have not order within him
> He cannot put order in his dominions.[6]

The film represents the family life of Edward, Clover, and their son as miserable because of claustral repression and denial. Edward's silences wall him off from his family. The son betrays the confidence of his father, of the household, and of the state in a fantasy of collaboration in Edward's work. He wants entry into his father's life. When a man's family is in disorder, his public life is over.

Near the outset of *The Bourne Ultimatum*, Noah passes through eight doors on his way to work; the shot is comical—one door leading only to another. This is the house that Edward built: a series of blinds. Noah and Edward are bureaucrats removed from public scrutiny, just what William Sullivan feared in *The Good Shepherd*; he wanted civilian oversight of the CIA, which sounded impractical to Edward. Edward and Noah naïvely trust in walls, safes, but "there are no secrets," as Racine observed, "that time does not reveal."[7] When government institutions move beyond the law, a free press can check the state by provoking embarrassment. Responsibility for correcting the state lands heavily on individuals, because intragovernmental mendacity has so weakened the process of Congressional oversight. The penultimate scene of *The Bourne Identity* (2002) shows Ward Abbott (Brian Cox) prevaricating in a perfunctory fashion at a Senate briefing about the political assassination program that trained Bourne. He dismisses it as a training game that did not yield results, and the committee moves on. Audiences are to infer that Congress is wickedly deceived by the CIA. Yet the senator being briefed facilitates the deception by prodding Abbott forward: "What's next?" he asks. The scene indicates that Congress lacks the requisite patience for close scrutiny of the intelligence services. When Senator Ron Wyden, in March 2013, asked James R. Clapper, the director of national intelligence, whether the NSA collects "any type of data at all on millions or hundreds of millions of Americans," Wyden already knew that the government was in fact doing just that, because he had been briefed in closed session of the Senate Intelligence Committee of NSA practices. Clapper knew what Wyden knew, but nonetheless answered, "No, sir," then added, "not wittingly." In June, when Edward Snowden's leaks exposed Clapper's lie to the public, Clapper notoriously commented, "I responded in what I thought was the most truthful or least untruthful manner, by saying no." Clapper, Wyden, and the other participants in the March meeting all knew that oversight entails neither regulation nor public candor. Wyden's provocative question lessened his responsibility for concealment of the surveillance and put that more squarely on Clapper's desk, but Wyden did nothing further to restrain the NSA. Senator Wyden and the rest of the Intelligence Committee did not dispute Clapper's lie. Oversight itself is corrupted by performative mendacity. Clapper continues to serve—without charge of perjury or even a reprimand—and will no doubt continue to testify to the Senate. Ward Abbott's perjury in *The Bourne Ultimatum* is not a satiric moment; it is just realistic representation. The mendacity of the intelligence services is proverbial.

By faxing documents to the press in *The Bourne Ultimatum*, Pam Landy (Joan Allen) does what is not done in the CIA. Her objective is not to overturn the state but to compel it toward self-correction. She advises Noah, "You better get yourself a good lawyer." The courts check the executive branch, for a while at least, when the press presents viable evidence to that effect in the public sphere. The same sort of scene, decades earlier, resolves *Three Days of the Condor*: only there Higgins (Cliff Robertson) suggests how fragile is the protection provided by the press. What if the editors of the *New York Times* were not to print a story given them by a whistle-blower? They will, Turner (Robert Redford) asserts. But the closing shot freezes this still-open question about the integrity and security of a free press alongside the supplication of the Salvation Army for the voluntary magnanimity of passersby. The film, based on a 1974 novel, was released in 1975. This concluding scene, outside the offices of the *Times*, is original to the film. It had been only four years since the *Times* had published the Pentagon papers, and only three since Woodward and Bernstein's articles on Watergate began to appear in the *Washington Post*. Pam assures the survival of a republic of laws in the way best known to her generation—that of a whistle-blower. Dr. Hirsch had said to Jason during his indoctrination, "The republic lives on a knife's edge." The figure holds.[8]

Syriana's art is more synthetic than analytical; its success is in its scope. It engages political issues by weaving together distinct narrative strands. The grandest narrative concerns collaboration between an energy conglomerate and Washington lawyers in and out of government. The second strand reveals the role of the CIA in facilitating the exploitation of Persian Gulf oil and natural gas resources in Kazakhstan. The third—surprisingly poignant—follows the exploitation of displaced Pakistani laborers in the Gulf, first by the energy company, then by jihadists. One experiences the film as a montage of artful cuts from one narrative to the other. All three are kept in play as the film builds slowly to two junctures where the separate strands cross one another. The first of these comes when Bob Barnes (George Clooney) asks who is responsible for his estrangement from the CIA. Stan (William Hurt) whispers in Bob's ear the

Three Days of the Condor (1975)

name of Dean Whiting (Christopher Plummer). One might expect an oil magnate to prevail upon the CIA to make Barnes a scapegoat. The more interesting notion is that the legal intermediaries of foreign trade are the most nefarious agents in the industry. The CIA is effectively controlled, according to this analysis, not by civilian oversight (as Sullivan had wanted) but by a law firm.[9] The confrontation of Whiting and Barnes across a diner table joins the first and second narrative strands. This conjunction closes with a fatal missile attack on Prince Nasir. The second juncture brings together the CIA and the jihadist narratives. As soon as Langley's missile lands on the prince and his family, the Pakistani teenagers use Barnes's missing missile against an oil freighter, as if the CIA by the implicit logic of montage *caused* the attack on the freighter. No question that audiences have difficulty weaving these strands into a clear argument. Make the connections, the film urges, and it meets audiences where they feel strongly, in families. All three strands bring home to fathers and sons the unintended costs of a global economy.

That a corrupt energy industry is a national hazard: not surprising. *Three Days of the Condor* and *The Kingdom* (2007) make this point too, but their formulaic plots draw attention away from economics. The screenwriter (Lorenzo Semple Jr.) and the director (Sydney Pollack) of *Three Days* injected the subject of oil into James Grady's plot. In the novel, CIA agents turn against the agency because of personal, ordinary greed; they wish not to be caught using agency resources to transport opium for profit. The film concocts instead an artful scheme for managing oil resources by sending coded messages in literary translations. Twelve minutes short of the end, Turner recognizes the cause of the plot: "Oil fields. Oil. That's it, isn't it?

This whole damned thing was about oil. Wasn't it? Wasn't it?" At just this point of enlightenment, master-assassin Joubert (Max von Sydow) enters and shuts down the explanation. Similarly, the early scenes of *The Kingdom* establish the US need for oil as a motive for ignoring Saudi jihadists. The film develops away from analysis of the economic pressure on counterterrorist investigations to focus instead on growing respect between a Saudi officer, Ferris, and the lead FBI field agent, Floury (Jamie Foxx). It elaborates a buddy-plot in which US and Saudi citizens learn in short order to respect one another while trying to manage losses due to an inexorable conflict between the oil-rich Saudi nation and its Islamic traditions. The underlying issue of the oil economy is unaffected by the sentimental outcome of the film. Citizens must simply bear losses due to a conflict of cultures. The one consolation on offer is that fair-minded individuals on both sides, in modest leadership positions, learn to respect one another.

At the end of *Three Days*, Higgins tells Turner, "It's simple economics. Today it's oil, right? In ten or fifteen years, it's food." Oil or food: systematic management of scarcity is the constant (opium smugglers are irrelevant). *Syriana* is a greater film than the other two because, unconstrained by an action plot, it presents a richer analysis. According to simple economics, the most potent agents are those who command capital. That is exactly *not* the case here. One of a half dozen CIA officials at Langley pushes a button and in the desert minutes later an extremely rich, clever, and American-educated Gulf prince explodes with his wife and children. The officials then stand around and calmly chat, as after a committee meeting. This is their work, and its effects overcome the reach of capital. The yet more potent agent is not an emir, an oilman, nor a government bureaucrat, but a lawyer—Dean Whiting, or Lucifer himself. *Syriana* indicts not the capitalist but the administrative tier of US society. The crisis generated by the plot is resolved by means that are made to seem ordinary. The effects of economic and political organization are predictable. When Bob's plot to assassinate Nasir is exposed to the press by Mussawi, the CIA faces a crisis, or "embarrassment." The solution formulated is boilerplate: Bob as a rogue agent overcome by 9/11 resentment—a politically plausible lie. The film analyzes the capacity of the federal legal system (and those administrators in the agency who help it to work) to regulate corporate mergers and offshore transactions. Nothing is conceded to quietism (of the Money-Rules variety). Citizens of a democratic republic can alter administrative structures. This much can be done.

Critics refer to *Syriana* as epic because of its scope. But epic characters are grand. Georg Lukács observed that the historical novel—think of Walter Scott and Stendhal—developed "middling" characters.[10] Exceptional ones are not prominent in this film. The protagonist is certainly not a prime mover of the plot. Within the first five minutes, he manages to lose a missile. The role of this central figure is only to orient the diverse events of the action. He *causes* almost nothing; he is more an object of the actions of others. The most distressing scene of the film is his torture by Mussawi. Neither Bond nor Bourne, Bob is certainly no rogue; even his son wants what is "normal." This pudgy character is without extraordinary abilities or even appetites. The same is true of the Woodman family: husband, wife, and children are thoroughly familiar to US audiences. Their ordinariness (a burden on dramatic art) is necessary to director Stephen Gaghan's analysis of economic overreaching. The film presents only one rogue: Dean Whiting, an exceptional character in that he is uninhibited, contemptuous, and mean-spirited. This is a soft spot: he is the one character able to bring legal and corporate organizations into collaboration. Behind the misdeeds of the CIA and the energy industry is an untypical miscreant. One cannot properly infer, therefore, that the legal system itself is corrupt. An honorable person at the head of a powerful law firm might make all the difference. Leadership may be the answer.

And yet *Syriana* is a dark film; the first cause of its plot is corruption. Bennett Holliday (Jeffrey Wright), a young investigative attorney at Whiting's firm, tells Jimmy Pope (Chris Cooper), "We are looking for the illusion of due diligence." The Justice Department, he assures Pope, will gladly settle for that illusion. It is also true, however, that the film presents a war of ideas formulated by idealists. One wants to understand the role of ideas in politics and economic transactions, if only in this film. Bryan Woodman (Matt Damon) speaks for a secular, capitalist future. Prince Nasir asks what his rival brother and the American lawyers are thinking about.

What are they thinking? They're thinking that it's running out. It's running out. And 90 percent of what's left is in the Middle East. Look at the progression: Versailles, Suez, 1973, Gulf War I, Gulf War II. This is a fight to the death. So what are they thinking? Great. They're thinking, keep playing. Keep buying yourself new toys. keep spending $50,000 a night on your hotel room. But don't invest in your infrastructure. Don't build a real economy. So that when you finally wake up, they will have sucked you dry. And you will have squandered the greatest natural resource in history.

Bryan's sarcasm veils a deep and immature sincerity. He is about a decade out of college and confident that he foresees the future. His excitement at the prospect of political change in the emirates is genuine. At the same time, though, he has no difficulty acknowledging an adolescent appetite for sudden wealth. "That's like having a giant ATM machine on the lawn," he tells his wife. Nasir, a little older, shares Bryan's liberalism: Nasir boasts a PhD in economics from Georgetown. They both believe that social and economic engineering can transform the Middle East into a model of Western values. (Secretary of Defense from 2001 to 2005, Paul Wolfowitz effectively advocated this view.) The future can be bought with oil profits. Bryan's criticism means to alter the spending practices of the emirate.

Bryan and Nasir's ideological adversary is an articulate imam who proselytizes Pakistani teenagers. He chastises first left- and then right-leaning heathens. He does not think that the future is for sale. Economics is neither the cause of Muslim suffering, he argues, nor its cure.

> They will try to disguise the difference . . . to make Muslims who speak about religion appear to be fanatics or backward people. They will tell us the dispute is over economic resources or military domination. If we believe that, we play right into their hands with only ourselves to blame. It is not possible to bridge the divide between human nature and modern life through free trade. Impossible. The divine and the worldly are but a single concept and that concept is Koran. No separation of religion and state—Koran. Instead of kings legislating and slaves obeying—Koran. The pain of modern life cannot be cured by deregulation, privatization, and economic reform, or lower taxes. The pain of living in the modern world will never be solved by a liberal society. Liberal societies have failed. Christian theology has failed. The West has failed.

The imam understands that mind is all. He addresses the young and solicits conviction.

The film begins with a familiar aerial shot of the barracks-like sound stages at Warner Brothers studios in Burbank, but with a difference: the sound track is not "As Time Goes By" but a Muslim call to prayer. Then comes a gorgeous shot, again from up high, of an orange sun rising over a misty desert. One cannot see the particular landscape well; it will later be labeled "The Persian Gulf," as if nation-states were inconsequential there. The credits alternate with beautiful misty shots. Crowds of Pakistani

Syriana (2005)

laborers, who live in barracks, stand more or less in lines awaiting buses
to the gas fields. One watches, but cannot hear, a quarrel, as one white-
haired man is bullied away from the door to the bus by a labor boss who
must think him too old to work well. Then the faces of men wanting work
stare into the camera, as if asking a question one should recognize. The
film will get to the questions. In the meantime one knows only that a
question rises from a dreamy, Dantesque horizon. The individual characters who later emerge from the crowd of laborers will identify their dreams,
but not in forms of economic aspiration. The father speaks, evidently
often, of his childhood at the feet of snowy mountains in Pakistan. His
dream is more image than proposition. More particularly, father and son
are working toward a day they can bring their wife and mother to the Gulf.
The suicide bombers express their dreams on video cassettes to be played
posthumously at the mosque. The dreams of the laborers ultimately take
practical form in jihad. Mist on the desert, snowy peaks, wives and mothers of foreign workers all come together in the spirits of the oppressed, and
in a war on capitalist economy. The struggle of ideas is between these two
spokesmen—Bryan and the imam, capitalism/democracy versus Islam.

The war on terrorism is fought in defense of secularism and prosperity. The enemy has a considerable intellectual position. The imam more than holds his own against Bryan. Dean Whiting's law firm is a source of corruption and opportunism, but not of ideas. *Syriana*'s analysis is subtler than a materialist account of political power or economic need. In the end, the liberal Bryan surrenders the field and returns to his family. That is the film's darkness—"The West has failed."

By this is meant that Enlightenment values and prosperity are insufficient to arouse ardent conviction even in the most advanced capitalist nations. With one exception, the protagonists of all the special-agent films under discussion are motivated by secular considerations. Autonomy, not devotion, is the motor that drives noirs, and spy films too. In Cold War rivalry, the Soviet Union was commonly represented as a godless state bureaucracy, and the United States as a God-fearing nation. That has obviously changed. With the ideological support of Enlightenment secularism, the United States now faces jihadist Islam. However, secularism is controversial among US citizens. *Traitor* is exceptional because its protagonist, Samir (Don Cheadle), is a Muslim who is also an off-the-books FBI asset. The film begins with a very brief and teary representation of his last moments with his father. The point is that Samir's motivation is private—his father was a victim of jihadist assassins—and religious. He is more devout than patriotic. His wish is to defeat jihadists because they are Islam's worst enemies. The liberal view is that Muslims, like Christians and Jews, are obliged to worship, if they must, within a tolerant society. Those unwilling to conform to the protocols of pluralism should be controlled, especially by those of their own faith who recognize the need to preserve civil tolerance. Samir was born in Sudan, but raised in the housing projects of Chicago. He is intellectually and politically a pluralist who quotes both Martin Luther King Jr. and the Koran. Carter (Jeff Daniels), Samir's control agent, reminds him, "Remember who you answer to." Samir replies, "I answer to God. We all do." There is one standard for everyone, and it is not political. State authority is at best secondary to religious values. Agent Clayton (Guy Pearce) asks Dierdre Horn (Lorena Gale) whether she would describe her son as a devout Muslim. "You will never understand a man like Samir," she responds, "if you don't believe in God. . . . He's a Muslim. I don't believe there's a sliding scale. . . . Submission to God's will is absolute." All of these films push back against state power. This one is unusual in examining the consequences of a religious defense of a secular public sphere. Samir is the Muslim policeman of whom the liberal West dreams.

Traitor examines the contradiction between absolutist and consequentialist ethics. The former regard certain acts as inevitably blameworthy; the latter assess those acts in terms of their consequences.[11] Samir conceives of himself as an absolutist, though he is engaged in an operation justifiable only by its consequences. He knows that it is wrong to deceive others, and wrong to take life, regardless of the costly consequences of abstaining from doing so in some situations. Consequentialism can justify misdeeds, but it proposes no end to them. "If results were the only basis for public morality," Thomas Nagel says, "then it would be possible to justify anything, including torture and massacre, in the service of sufficiently large interests."[12] Samir cannot agree with Machiavelli that "when the act accuses [a prince], the result should excuse him." Nonetheless Samir resolves the plot by conniving to put thirty suicide bombers on a single bus, rather than on thirty passenger buses. He kills a few innocent bystanders—with definite foreknowledge—but reduces the jihadists' intended casualties dramatically. He chooses the lesser of two evils, as consequentialists do without hesitation. Absolutism is not only an alternative to consequentialism; it also sets limits to consequentialist calculations.

When Mussawi, in *Syriana*, says that Barnes lacks conviction, he does not mean that Barnes would as soon work for al-Qaeda as for the CIA. What is commonly alleged against US agents and citizens is that their convictions are insufficiently deep to compete with those of jihadists. Or more exactly: the secular justification of liberal convictions is insufficiently profound.[13] In *Traitor*, Samir admits that he sells arms promiscuously, without inquiry into the uses to which those weapons are put. In this, he says, he is like legitimate US arms dealers. FBI agent Max Archer (Neal McDonough) counters that US weapons are not used against innocent civilians. Samir contradicts him to say that the innocents injured by US arms are overlooked because they have brown skin. This exchange reveals the common dynamics of ideological contest in the United States. The United States has admirable ideals on which to base its policies—here, the protection of innocent civilians. However, those ideals are constantly undercut by a record of racist implementation. Samir's point is familiar and incontestable. The only open issue is the extent to which racist practice discredits the Bill of Rights. Agent Archer punches Samir, indicating that when confronted by the gap between ideals and practice, he has no more to say. His convictions have been bested. He no doubt retains those convictions, but they plainly lack adequate justification in the contest between secular democratic republics and jihadism.

The US failure to institute policies against racism counts against either the good faith of the government or the efficacy of the universalist principles of the Bill of Rights. This is the most compromising objection to those principles that has arisen from two centuries of historical experience. The allegorical significance of historical racism is understood to be a miserable distinction between policy and practice. The blackness of the protagonist of *Traitor* silently signifies the limits of the most idealist principles avowed by the US state. Yet he continues to serve the state and its policies. The valid charge of racism against the United States is insufficient to deter him from resistance to jihadism. The justification of his convictions—Islam itself—runs deeper than agent Archer's. However, the film is not concerned to say much about Islam or African American experience. The significance of this particular religion and racial group is abstract. Samir's belief is that a secular democratic republic presents an adequate context for his worship. He is convinced that, however much the United States has failed to overcome racism, it is capable of instituting religious tolerance. That proposition is at present more important than the failure to overcome racism. His convictions are both reasoned and ardent.

Traitor holds in focus the ambiguous concept of collective responsibility. For the terror strategist Nathir, this concept justifies bombing civilians. For Samir, there is no such thing as collective responsibility. His control says, "We set off a bomb" at the consulate in Nice. Samir corrects him: "No, *I* set off a bomb." How does state service affect individual agency? Are an official's acts comparable to those of any civilian? Or does state apparatus attenuate individual responsibility? If so, are collectives capable of bearing responsibility for the acts of their agents? Does a state diffuse responsibility evenly among its citizens, or only among its designated officials? *Traitor* comes at these questions from both ends of a spectrum of expected responses. Nathir claims exactly that all citizens of a democracy are equally responsible for all acts of the republic. This stringent viewpoint was articulated by Osama bin Laden in 2005: "America in its entirety is responsible for the atrocities that it is committing against Muslims."[14] Once Samir hears this proposition articulated, in a prayer, he is ready to execute Nathir and his lieutenant Fareed. Samir holds the counterposition that individuals, regardless of institutional affiliations, answer to God for all their acts. The acts that determine responsibility for Samir need not be intentional, though for many secularists awareness of consequences is a necessary condition of responsibility. Samir goes by an archaic sense of bloodguilt. His bombing of the US consulate in Nice

Traitor (2008)

causes two accidental deaths that were more or less foreseeable as collateral damage. Responsibility for those deaths brings him to despair. He hears what happened as he stands in the rain, and he cannot get clean. "We've got blood on our hands," he tells his control. "We've killed innocent people." "Yeah. And if we stop now," Carter replies, in the voice of modernity, "they'll have died for nothing. This is a war. You do what it takes to win." (Carter's variety of consequentialism discriminates quanta of pain rather than pleasure.) Samir retreats to his hotel room to wash his hands and pray for forgiveness. He is extreme in his resistance to affiliation with any collective other than Islam. In a political culture that increasingly adjudicates responsibility in collective terms, he insists on the discreteness of individual agency. He does not claim to be an American or a Sudanese; he is "from all over." The structure of the Nathir cell, on the contrary, is rigorously collective. "If you touch one of my brothers," Omar (Saïd Taghmaoui) tells a prison bully, "it will cost your life." The cell members conform to a military order that determines the outcome of all uncertainties. As a collective, they agree to eliminate all doubt—to act as if with one mind: no dissension, no debate. The contrary is the case within the US intelligence establishment. The FBI Special Task Force is represented as a deliberative organization with significant diversity, beginning with the two lead agents, Clayton and Archer, who disagree on most issues. They're FBI but they work outside their jurisdiction and collaborate with intelligence units that are not acknowledged to be governmental.

(Carter is apparently in this last category. He is an intelligence contractor somehow collaborating with the FBI.) No one collective here claims either preeminent authority or responsibility for operations.

Samir works outside all agencies. His ethical responsibility is consequently clear to him. He will not attribute his acts to an official role. "Office-holders or functionaries," Thomas Nagel observes, "are insulated in a puzzling way from what they do: insulated both in their own view and in the view of most observers. Even if one is in no doubt about the merits of the acts in question, the agents seem to have a slippery moral surface, produced by their roles or offices."[15] Within a public role, one may feel that one acts as a specialist, liberated from ordinary individual responsibility.[16] Omar is at peace with a collective responsibility to purge all liabilities from his cell, even when that entails execution of a seventeen-year-old boy. Samir concurs with Nagel that those who seek to elude personal responsibility by acting as special agents in fact encourage ruthlessness in public life.[17] Agent Clayton offers Samir his freedom in Yemen, an offer Clayton can make good because Samir holds a US passport. Never mind his role as an agent for the United States, Samir refuses even the comfort of citizenship, though the imminent alternative is indefinite imprisonment in Yemen. He is a loner to his bones. The ends realized by his acts are certainly bloody. A pox has fallen on many by the end of the film: two innocent workers at the Nice consulate, thirty bombers, three jihadist strategists, and a bus driver, plus Samir's control agent. Samir, however, accepts no absolution from a concept of collective responsibility. He is willing to execute the top two jihadist strategists—because they are hypocritical Muslims—but is unwilling to execute all jihadists. Omar is another sort of person: a murderous jihadist but a sincere Muslim. Samir would rather be shot by him than shoot his friend. Omar's participation in corrupt jihadist acts has not compromised his individual autonomy and rights, in Samir's judgment. Samir takes each jihadist as an individual. Collective affiliations, on his view, cannot establish mortal blameworthiness— neither for American citizens nor for jihadists.

Political philosophers have attended closely to the problem of dirty hands, of the difficult choice to do bad in order to do good. Samir sells munitions, makes bombs, lies to friends, and kills people; he is like other agents in spy films. It is easy enough to see the relevance of dirty hands. But politicians who calculate their acts and avowals on the basis of utility or expected consequences meet the issue of dirty hands still more commonly.[18] The literature on this problem begins with Machiavelli's definition of effective political leadership. Which political leaders better serve their constituents, those who do evil in order to achieve their objectives, or those who refuse to make such a deal? In the 1970s this problem engaged Michael Walzer and Bernard Williams, both of whom make peace with the idea that politicians should sometimes do evil in order to serve well. Walzer argued poignantly that a moral politician is a paradoxical figure who does evil reluctantly in order to meet an obligation to serve his constituency: "He is a guilty man. His willingness to acknowledge and bear (and perhaps to repent and do penance for) his guilt is evidence, and it is the only evidence he can offer us, both that he is not too good for politics and that he is good enough. Here is the moral politician: it is by his dirty hands that we know him. If he were a moral man and nothing else, his hands would not be dirty; if he were a politician and nothing else, he would pretend that they were clean."[19] Why should citizens of a democracy be moved by such a character? Walzer sees him as a character of mixed nature: a consequentialist certainly, in that he has his eye on results and will not forego achievement of his desired ends; but also an absolutist insofar as he is ashamed of his misdeeds. Walzer sees a need for criteria that transcend immediate consequences. But he apparently agrees with Weber, whom he cites: the fact that a ruling politician commands the state's access to violence changes everything.[20] The first obligation of a political leader is not truth-telling but the maintenance of security. Politicians must do what is necessary to protect their constituents. This is not to say, though, that politicians are justified in doing all that might possibly enhance the protection of their constituents. Security is the first but obviously not the only consideration for the state.

Jefferson's notion of citizen-leaders seems irrelevant. Walzer and Williams reach the conclusion that political leaders cannot be model citizens. Politicians are instead a special breed whose acts should, if not often then at crucial junctures, conflict with the principles avowed by the nation. A moral politician needs to know how to recognize an *exception* to absolute rules. He or she, Walzer argues, "will never be in a hurry to override the rules, but will wait until there is no choice, acting only to avoid consequences that are both imminent and almost certainly disastrous."[21] Writing a few years later, Bernard Williams seems to share the view that politicians must be willing to dirty their hands in order to achieve the moral ends of politics.[22] But he notes the hazard of exceptional calculations that override absolutist rules: because in public life the magnitude of gains and losses tends to be great, even a low probability of loss may seem to warrant a judgment that overrides rules. "Victims may find that their rights have been violated for the sake of an outside chance," as Williams eloquently puts it.[23]

One speaks abstractly of politicians doing evil as the problem that requires explanation, but Williams's warning suggests the importance of understanding the dynamics of particular evil deeds. Walzer observes that "the stock figure is the lying, not the murderous, politician—though the murderer lurks in the background."[24] The difference seems grave between these figures. That democratic politicians often lie is incontestable; that they often or ever murder is another matter altogether. Murder is diligently prosecuted in civil society; prevarication, even perjury, only rarely. Walzer suggests that the two violations are closely connected, because the normal business of politicians, as Weber said, is to wield violence on behalf of the state. *Body of Lies* and *Traitor* make clear that agents murder in order to sustain lies. Ferris executes a low-echelon jihadist in order to protect his own cover.[25] Samir plants a bomb in the Nice consulate in order to gain credibility with Nathir, and that bomb causes unintended but unsurprising collateral deaths. This is Williams's point put concretely. Some die for only an outside chance that a deception may produce a future benefit. So long as one is prepared to kill in order to preserve a deception, there is little distinction between lies and murder; in time, one produces the other.

CIA films are often general in their political analysis, even though they usually focus on the adventures of exceptional individuals.[26] One should understand that the noirs and their spy successors are postpolitical: they begin from a point at which political leadership is no longer interesting; they ask instead whether it is possible to construct an individual life in such a fashion that one can act effectively where others cannot. The problems these films address, as John Irwin observes, follow from the objective of working for oneself; spy films add to this objective a significant proviso: while serving the state. In the closing shot of the film, Samir is at worship in Chicago, and his eye is not on the political problems of the United States. He has chosen to live correctly rather than serve the state. Michael Walzer and Bernard Williams condone dirty hands because they cannot, as democratic political philosophers, propose that moral citizens resist the attractions and responsibilities of leadership. But that is what Samir chooses, because there is no alternative to dirty hands for one who labors for the state. The value of the film is that it looks squarely at the proposition that democratic citizens be ruled by those who make of their work the

Traitor (2008)

concealment of lies and murder. Samir sees the need to make a choice; he cannot remain a romantic figure torn by competing considerations. The twin notions that state service attenuates individual responsibility and that all citizens are alike responsible for the deeds of the state are contradicted by the narrative. Samir holds himself accountable, regardless of intentions or awareness, regardless of state service. The filmmaker advises audiences that the counsel of paradoxical intellectuals from Machiavelli to Michael Walzer and Bernard Williams is unsustainable in a democratic culture.

These spy films are all obviously skeptical about service to a state, but what alternative prospects do they envisage? The values left standing after the credits are particularly conservative. First is family. *Syriana* is held together not only by the logic of montage but also by the myth of the wounded family. Several sequences represent a failure of fathers to pass on to sons the authority of their own experience. More generally, *Syriana* and other films with plainly public subjects reveal the ways that political forces violate the integrity of private life. Repeatedly they show that no wall protects private from public life. The state reaches right into the heart of the family. Bryan Woodman comes to his senses after the assassination of Nasir and returns to his wounded family in the States. Bourne can remember no family to whom he might return, but family is nonetheless the value he affirms. His one failed mission—and his last for the CIA—was to assassinate Wombozi, an African leader in exile. He could not complete his task because the exile's young daughter was present, and Bourne could not kill her father in her presence. Jason's first assignment was the execution of a Russian politician and his wife. He made it appear that the wife killed her husband and then herself. Much later he travels to Moscow to inform their daughter that he assassinated her parents, and that he feels remorse. He must inform her that her mother did not kill her father, because the family is not just a collection of individuals; it has a moral structure. He regrets most of the murders he has committed, but he most regrets the destruction of families. That is the meaning of his refusal to kill the exile. Representations of the joys, hopes, and fulfillment of family life are modest in spy films; these benefits are assumed and prefigured more than represented. Family in the Bourne trilogy, in *Munich* and *Syriana* bears a particular relation to the state's claims on its guardians. The films begin from the notion that families are threatened by the state. The family is chiefly what *should be* protected in lieu of the state. Private life is proposed as a substitution for public life.

These films advocate retrenchment from imperial ambitions. Ultra-agents—Bourne, Ferris, Samir, Avner—want no more state service. The concept of devotion to an impersonal collective has been discredited. The relationships that count are conducted on a small scale, face to face, among people who treasure familiarity. This is not to say that CIA films recover the values that drove the noirs. Noir inquirers seek to construct exceptional relationships alongside the institutions of mass society. CIA films propose that recognizable pleasures are alternatives to the ambitions of empire—food, for instance, in *Munich* and *Body of Lies*. Avner cooks, as does the head of the private clandestine organization that provides his team with intelligence. When Avner first assembles his team, he serves them a brisket of beef, and the camera fondly shows their conviviality before setting out to kill. Much later in the film, the very large family of his intelligence merchant gathers for a bountiful outdoor banquet, and the dialogue makes an explicit case for family values. At the beginning and end of the film, Avner and his wife are making love. In between, they have produced a daughter. Avner wants more children, but his lovemaking at the end is troubled by recollected accounts of terrorism (not by his own memories of assassinations). In the duration represented by the film, he is unable to return to the eating, lovemaking, and reproduction he enjoyed before his mission. And his case officer Ephraim (Geoffrey Rush) pointedly refuses to break bread with him, as if Avner's deeds (or his expatriation) had polluted him. Avner was never a zealot. His chief values were all along more domestic than political. The film ends with some doubt about his ability to recover his values after his extralegal activities, but with no doubt about his renewed commitment to his wife and daughter.

Although the retrenchment envisaged by these films is frankly reactionary, they also propose a renewal of liberal tolerance and individual volition. Ultra-agents make genuine choices. They may prefer an accessible domestic order to the prestige of state authority and for that reason decline further service. That is a way out, in several cases, because a free press provides a buffer against retaliation by the state. CIA films are oriented on leadership cadres. Ordinary citizens are not directly affected by all the issues that engage ultra-agents. Whether agents retract their trust in the state, as most do, means little to ordinary folks, though the films nonetheless propose general lessons for a wide audience, because participation in state policies is an issue for many citizens. But what if one were asked to participate directly in the execution of state policies? What might one stand to lose in exchange for extreme individual potency? The comforting truth is that eating, sleeping, reproducing, worshipping—all that goes on still, among ordinary citizens, and Samir or Ferris or Avner can try to return there. The films focus on the failed ambitions of those who wish to lead the state. Bourne dives into the frigid Hudson to elude state agents. At the end of *Body of Lies* Ferris goes native. The satellite surveillance camera pulls out, and Hoffman says, "He's all by himself." Similarly Samir at the end of *Traitor* is a civilian in downtown Chicago. He says he is "going somewhere" and does not wish to talk with Clayton, nor to work for the FBI. Samir's last words are amusing—"And you should have started the conversation with that [As-salamu alaykum]"—but his point is that service to the state should be subordinate to the praise of God. That was always his express view, and the cause of his anxiety. He remains devout, but not in state service. The serious point is that Islam is there for him in a pluralist state that tolerates a private sphere. One recognizes American liberalism by contradistinction when one considers an Italian film, *The Stone Merchant* (2006). Alceo (Jordi Molla), a journalist-turned-professor, tells his editor that the west mistakenly thinks that it can look away from jihadists. The east has brought terror to the west. The war on terror is not optional, he argues. The climax of the plot is an explosion on a ferry from Calais as it enters the harbor at Dover. This sense of necessity driving the west into ever worse conflict with Islam is exactly what liberal US filmmakers resist. They retain hope that a retrenched state with more modest agents can adequately preserve a liberal society. *The Stone*

Merchant claims that no path leads to the status quo ante. Loving domesticity, the conviviality of friends, the peaceful streets of a pluralist society—these are treasured memories, but not objectives in the foreseeable future. A liberal society cannot defend itself against jihad without sacrificing its own values, as Golda Meir says at the outset of *Munich*. That familiar but severe claim is nudged from view by films that imply, as the Bourne films and *The Good Shepherd* do, that the republic's immediate need is for *reform* of the intelligence service.

CONCLUSION

I have crossed a lot of ground in the preceding chapters, some of it quickly. Back, then, to the shift from noirs (1941–1955) to spies (2000–2011). The aspirations of noir characters toward autonomous labor and commitment have been absorbed into those of the ultra-agents a half century later. Yet private detectives and spies are a contrastive pair, because the challenges to the state have changed. The older characters jealously and effectively guarded their autonomy, and the newer ones scramble for vestiges of autonomy. The two groups are poles apart with regard to agency; together they reveal the constriction of plausible individual action during these years. Films of both periods take for granted that skepticism and intelligence are largely the same. Noir inquirers typically doubt the veracity of what they hear, most of what is commonly thought to be known. Sam Spade tells Brigid O'Shaughnessy, "Of course, we didn't believe your story. We believed your $200." She entered his office a stranger. One may doubt all that is said by strangers, right down to their names. Sean Regan, Mr. Rutledge, Rollo Tomassi, the Maltese falcon—the noirs make a great deal of place-holders for absences or tolerable fakes. Geiger is not a bookseller. The Chinese Theatre, not Chinese. Lynn Bracken, not Veronica Lake; even Veronica Lake was Constance Frances Marie Ockelman. These names for what we pretend to know have only a faint referential function. What sort of agency is practicable where skepticism has vacated much of what one thought one knew? Both private eyes and spies pursue knowledge; they resolve difficulties by irregular, improvised means. Ultra-agents swear allegiance to a state so that they can act without concern about authorization. Their training in blank obedience is a prophylactic to skepticism and ignorance. Both sets of films push back against corrosive doubt.

Despite their skepticism, the strongest noir characters construct lives by making decisions. Weaker characters, yes, and even some strong ones, are blown about by circumstances, confused by misnomers, but the most memorable characters find paths through these minefields. This is not to say that strength of will effectively governs noirs: events themselves have causal power; the outcome of one decision becomes a cause of other events, and an occasion of new decisions. This dynamic lends support to Robert B. Pippin's claim that something like ancient fate governs noir lives. Yet the characters go on deciding, imagining life anew. They are drawn to quick changes, reversals of their past, shams—tomorrow a millionaire, freedom in Mexico, and so on. And for spies, it's not so different: an unlikely score, a forbidden peek. In the final episode of the BBC production of John le Carré's *A Perfect Spy* (1987), Magnus Pym's wife asks the double agent's control about her husband: "So what is he? Is he a communist? He can't be. It's too ridiculous." The Czech control replies: "He's a searcher. Isn't that enough? In our profession, I'm sure, we shouldn't ask for more. Can you imagine being married to an armchair ideologist?" Marlowe, Mike Hammer, Jeff Bailey, searchers all; malcontents too. They want to know what does not fit familiar categories. There are differences between spies and noir inquirers, but they are all looking for answers. Exactly that is their familiar charm.

The earlier films concentrate on the construction of trust between skeptical individuals. Heterosexual lovers whose essential features are self-discipline and stoical taciturnity configure trust in *The Big Sleep*. Their understanding derives from a male code: all lies in what is not said. Without that esteem of taciturnity, Marlowe would still be pestering Vivian to come clean. The imaginative project of noir—to conceive a new life on a basis of trust—is now lamentably gone. Recent films instead ask how far allegiance, rather than trust, can take one. Ultra-agents do not need to trust the state; they know that it will disavow them when they are most in need. They overcome their need of trust by swearing soldierly allegiance to the state, and are made miserable by doing so. Don Cheadle looks constantly pained, no matter what he does. The most prominent effort to establish meaningful trust in CIA films—between Hani and Ferris—comes to little, because state agents of an idealistic democracy (as not of a monarchy) must lie constantly. Spy films reckon the cost of surrendering trust along two lines of inquiry: First, is deception effective in the conduct of state affairs? *Body of Lies* claims that, on the contrary, US intelligence gathering in the Middle East is crippled by cynicism. And second, are the costs of deception in the personal lives of agents sustainable? No, because they ultimately render the state's activities insecure. These films, as distinct from the Bond films, assert that the affections of private life are necessary to a state agent's acts.[1] Edward's family is virtually destroyed. Ferris and Bob Barnes leave the CIA. Samir refuses any collaboration with the FBI. Avner quits Mossad. The noirs uphold a strictly personal ideal: deep trust between two friends or lovers. That trust requires self-restraint (in acknowledgment of others' autonomy), but not rigid conformity to a male code; Hani is more relenting than Joe Parkson in *Act of Violence*. *Body of Lies* asserts that even the conduct of state affairs might be enhanced by a variety of trust that the earlier films envisaged, or that deep trust might be a potent civic resource. Willed commitment alone is insufficient.

T. S. Eliot argued famously that the past "is altered by the present as much as the present is directed by the past."[2] Recent spy films reveal the political prescience of the noirs. I trace the contours of trust relations in order to establish that the noirs present an intellectually subtle account of deep trust in a context where civic action is constrained by the extensive reach and incompetence of the state. Noir inquirers are urged to concentrate their efforts on private life, where autonomy is practicable. When they go beyond cheating spouses and household homicides, they must be restrained—"Forget it, Jake. This is Chinatown." A half century after Mike Hammer, defeated, surrendered the locker key to federal authority, ultra-agents eagerly give their all to the state and are repeatedly let down. They snoop as shamefully as Mike did, but for the state. Their acts are publicly directed, even when the assignment is seduction or impersonation. They substitute compliance for autonomy, allegiance for trust, and these equations produce proficiency, but no joy, satisfaction, or hope. Ultra-agents see clearly, after their political adventures, that life's value lies in the construction of private lives. Faced with obstacles, they make no effort to switch allegiance to another state, as British spies of the Cold War era notoriously did. Their problem is with neither a particular state nor a particular ideology. The noirs presume that some past civic collaboration went bad before the films began. Some inquirers were former state agents, if only on a local level. Marlowe and Gittes were fired. Federal agents in *Kiss Me Deadly* make a point of humiliating Mike exactly because he is confined to the investigation of private matters as they are not. Confinement to a private sphere was, for noir inquirers, consolation for what they were forbidden to undertake. Samir returns to Chicago; Avner and Daphna maintain their Brooklyn exile. Noirs and spies tell a single tale of disappointed civic agency. Both sets of films, fifty years apart, arrive at the conclusion that civic activity is largely ignoble, and intimacy or family is the only site of hope.

Many film critics agree with Philip Green that "Hollywood is a force for social stability."[3] One easily imagines that an art dependent on mainstream institutions, large capital, and mass audiences tends inevitably toward legitimation of the economic and political status quo, but this is not entirely so. The budget of *The Bourne Ultimatum* is estimated to have been $110 million. Within just over three months from its release on August 5, 2007, it had grossed $227 million. *Green Zone* is a more narrowly topical film: it discredits President Bush's account of the causes of war with Iraq. It was less successful. Its budget is estimated to have been $100 million. It managed to gross only $35 million in its first two months—not enough, but a lot for political advocacy. These modest earnings are revealing concerning subject matter. The latter is a partisan attack on a very recent war president; the Bourne films criticize the US intelligence sector generally. This latter subject is the special property of neither Democrats nor Republicans. Both these films and many others too are sharply critical of government institutions—local police, the federal government generally, the FBI and CIA in particular—and, in *Syriana*, doubtful about state collaboration with industry. Hollywood has given audiences a critical analysis of the nation's economic and political objectives. It turns out that oppositional art, even of an explicitly political sort, is popular with US audiences, even with banks and underwriters. And apparently the more general and impersonal the critique, the better a film's chance at reaching audiences. I spoke of the didactic function of popular film in the introduction: Steven Spielberg said that "there are some very interesting lessons that emerge from the story" behind his *Munich*.[4] One lesson of these recent films is that the nation's political and economic activities are altogether dubious, but that its cultural expressions—even those pitched at mass audiences—have considerable ideological independence. We are accordingly not a nation determined by the state or the economy. We are movie people, negotiating ideals more than material facts, free to turn away from civic activity when it goes wrong. Or so mass audiences are pleased to believe.

Recent spy films deserve attention not just because they are frankly critical of the modern state, and of course the particular claims of some films concerning state abuses are more acute than those of others. If the state is a hydra, as in *Shooter* (2007), one can chop anywhere and not be wrong. Close discrimination is beside the point. These are libertarian films, with a small *l* as noirs were too, but now the volume has been turned up. Spies have to labor heroically just to be left alone by the state. Exactly because of this operatic element in recent spies, one appreciates the subtleness of the noirs. The task before political theorists is determining where the state oversteps reasonable authority and where it properly undertakes responsibility—such as defense—that only a state can effectively perform. The next question is where the state justly acquits its responsibilities in secret. That is, one wants to define carefully the boundaries around concepts of state authority so that communities can enjoy the benefits of collective action without undue sacrifice. The modern state is not a realistic enemy in the sense that a capable citizen might eliminate it or do well without it. Libertarian advocacy is a tonic against excess; it seeks to restrain state authority. The Bourne films do not advocate the elimination of the state, though they say nothing redeeming of the intelligence services. As the volume rises on critiques of the state, the concept of proper state action is obscured, and controversy about authority becomes blunt and unrealistic. The weaker films—*Shooter* is a considerable instance—are indifferent to the definition of proper state action.

Libertarianism is problematic. It has many faces, and it does not go away. Native individualism stands constantly ready to decry the failures of collective action; general resentment of the state has been deadly— Timothy McVeigh. The weaker films represent state activity as wrong from the start, hopeless. Subtler ones measure the malfunctions of one civil sector against the resources of another. *Three Days of the Condor* and *The Bourne Ultimatum* contrast the misdeeds of US intelligence agencies and the courage of an independent national press; these films reaffirm the Enlightenment ideal of transparency. Critical understanding requires that limitations of state power be assessed judiciously. One individual against a town or nation—this is a mythic topos in American letters, and it arrests political thought. A well-armed cowboy or Ranger is no remedy for government malfeasance. The possibilities of collective action are ill-served by films that pose the issue in this way. But the more or less annual suspension of approval of the federal budget in Congress shows that political capital is available to those who align themselves, however temporarily, with general libertarian skepticism. The enduring popular controversy is between expansive regulation and libertarianism. Efforts at social reform and state regulation founder on suspicion of the efficacy and integrity of public administration.

The spies send one back to the noirs to reconsider the work of the state.

New art does revise the past. The noirs present withdrawal from political activity as prudent. The state is more to be avoided than altered. Expect very little from the state, they seem to caution; seek self-reform, not social reform. But a rich private life as consolation for political inefficacy? Ours is an era of ambitious social reform. The private life is a hard sell, especially among intellectuals, after the successes of the civil rights and anti-war movements, but for just that reason some questioning of the promises of reform politics is timely. For the resolution of which problems should one turn to the resources of state action? Surely not for them all. The noirs and the spies consider (more than principles) the odds of political success, and they take for granted a vigorous individualism. One person is unlikely to alter the state, for it is large, forceful, and redundantly structured. Policy decisions are made by interested parties and then approved by committees, so that responsibility is dispersed, indefinite. Recent spy films indicate darkly that it is easier for the state to execute its enemies than to meet its citizens openly. This is a way of saying no, in narrative, to the challenges of reform politics. In the end these films return audiences to an earlier era's esteem for privacy, but with one difference: the noirs present a distinctive manner of private agency that rests on the autonomy of all parties—and a great deal of skepticism. That is what makes them necessary again, especially in intellectual culture, where their prestige, even in a reformist era, remains high.

David Webb, Samir, Avner, and Ferris all wanted civic engagement, consequential work. Who doesn't? Three of them trained to overcome all adversaries. Bourne and Samir are adept at hand-to-hand fighting; Ferris is an especially good shot. More than that, they are extraordinarily successful at eluding the reach of state power. Their unusual capacities indicate the range of their desires: they seek efficacy of a tangible sort, and do so strictly as individuals. Their mastery resolves a particular difficulty: feelings of inefficacy and vulnerability. One recognizes, though, the limitations of an agency designed for only such success, and the characters come to this recognition too. All four want a life, in the end, not greater technique. Their efforts to recover private lives look like a reduction of agency, a pursuit of only negative liberty. But they manage a victory over an inordinate hunger for civic effect, and that is something to consider in our own moment—particularly in intellectual circles. For the time being, they leave civic affairs to bureaucrats in order to recover a life with others that has an immediate future. But they do so within a familiar dialectic of private and public spheres. Raymond Geuss has argued that "it is a deep mistake to think that there is a single substantive distinction [between public and private spheres] . . . that can be made to do any real philosophical or political work."[5] Privacy may be plausibly constructed as access to meditation, to a life in letters, to a garden, and so on. The cases for these conceptions are familiar. Less familiar, as yet, is the conception of privacy as a feature of communication. The libertarian challenge now in the news focuses on surveillance, and the remedies proposed are encryption in private and transparency in public records.[6] But *The Good Shepherd, Munich,* and *Syriana* present privacy in terms of reproduction in order to test political regimes not for justice but for the capacity to engender a future one can love (as one loves one's children). And further movement in the dialectic between private and public spheres is neither foreclosed nor altogether obscured from view. The spies oscillate between public and private contraries; the pursuit of a mean is ongoing. I have described a recovered resistance to state power, but within sharp polarities of thought that doubtless continue to assert their attractiveness. One may regard this critically as a retreat from a possible future, but this judgment should be tempered by the fact that the noirs indicate that the private sphere is not a set form of life to which one withdraws. It is rather to be shaped to one's needs and aspirations; the noir trust project is not civic, but it is utopian. And it remains to be achieved. A private life is an imaginable future, not only in the land of Noir.

Great poets like Milton and Wordsworth, or Stevens and Pound, reach out with fresh imaginative and linguistic structures to master some recalcitrant feature of life. The films I have discussed share instead a defensive imaginative posture. Noir inquirers defend their autonomy against the powers of the state. Bogart could become a suspect or lose his license and thereby his livelihood. His defense is to employ strategic intelligence to solve the mysteries that are presented to him. The challenges he resolves ought to be resolved by the police. His superior capability protects him from the discipline that the state can employ. The trust he constructs with a single woman provides him a sense of hope and peace for them both. The later films, the spies, are still more defensive. Those inquirers are threatened by death. And the mortal powers of state agents are not to be taken lightly. Strategic intelligence again serves these agents well. But their hope is not for a relationship of unusual trust to enhance the quality of their lives. They hope instead for a private life, in particular a family, and then another generation.

NOTES

Introduction

1. Bill Harlow, quoted by Tricia Jenkins in her excellent study, *The CIA in Hollywood: How the Agency Shapes Film and Television* (Austin: University of Texas Press, 2012), 104.

2. Patrick McGilligan, "Hollywood Uncovers the CIA," *Jump Cut*, no. 10–11 (1976): 11–12. www.ejumpcut.org/archive/onlinessays/JC10-11folder/Pollack-McGilligan.html.

3. For a frank and knowledgeable account of the functional ambiguity of the term "film noir," see James Naremore, *More than Night: Film Noir in Its Contexts* (Berkeley: University of California Press, 1998), ch. 1.

4. William Park, *What Is Film Noir?* (Lewisburg, PA: Bucknell University Press, 2011), 27.

5. Ibid., 22.

6. Ibid., 133.

7. Ibid., 23.

8. Janey Place, "Women in Film Noir," in *Women in Film Noir*, 2nd ed., ed. E. Ann Kaplan (London: BFI, 1998), 51.

9. Robert B. Pippin, *Fatalism in American Film Noir: Some Cinematic Philosophy* (Charlottesville: University of Virginia Press, 2012), 18–19.

10. Stanley Cavell and Andrew Klevan, "What Becomes of Thinking on Film?" in *Film as Philosophy: Essays on Cinema after Wittgenstein and Cavell*, eds. Rupert Read and Jerry Goodenough (Hampshire, UK: Palgrave, 2005), 180.

11. Many scholars note that in Hollywood there was no awareness of noirs as constituting a genre during the peak years of their production; *film noir* is a term that has been used retrospectively, sometimes to characterize a cinematographic style, sometimes to refer to a thematic pattern. As to whether it is now helpful to think of noir as a genre, there is disagreement. On the difficulties of defining noir, see Raymond Borde and Etienne Chaumeton, *A Panorama of Film Noir, 1941–1953*, trans. Paul Hammond (San Francisco, CA: City Lights, 2002), 5–13;

Mark T. Conard, "Nietzsche and the Meaning and Definition of Noir," in *The Philosophy of Film Noir*, ed. Mark T. Conard (Lexington: University Press of Kentucky, 2006), 7–22; Ian Jarvie, "Knowledge, Morality, and Tragedy in *The Killers* and *Out of the Past*," in *The Philosophy of Film Noir*, 163–85. I employ the term *noir* capaciously. I rely upon family resemblances among films, some black-and-white and others in color. My sense is that the cinematographic techniques of early noirs became associated with particular thematic elements that were treated in subsequent films with other cinematographic styles. The distinction between noirs and neo-noirs after about 1955 is not particularly important to the argument of this book. (For distinctions between classic noir and neo-noir, see Jason Holt, "A Darker Shade: Realism in Neo Noir," in *The Philosophy of Neo-Noir*, ed. Mark T. Conard (Lexington: University Press of Kentucky, 2007), 23–40.

12. In the opening pages of *Political Psychology and American Myth: Violence and Order in Hollywood Westerns* (New Haven, CT: Yale University Press, 2010), Robert B. Pippin speaks of films as imaginings of political ideals or of "minimally acceptable" human lives. Even commercial Hollywood products, as he shows, are capable of representing compellingly fundamental human and specifically political conditions. His study of the Western has greatly influenced my sense of the exemplary quality of Hollywood films.

Chapter 1

1. Francis Fukuyama, *Trust: Social Virtues and the Creation of Prosperity* (New York: Free Press, 1995).

2. Danielle S. Allen, *The World of Prometheus: The Politics of Punishing in Democratic Athens* (Princeton, NJ: Princeton University Press, 2000), 3–5.

3. On the significance of self-employment, and more generally the relation of public and private spheres, see the excellent analysis of *The Big Sleep* in John T. Irwin, *Unless the Threat of Death Is Behind Them: Hard-Boiled Fiction and Film Noir* (Baltimore, MD: Johns Hopkins University Press, 2006), ch. 2.

4. For a fuller treatment of liberty and libertarianism in US film, see Paul A. Cantor, *The Invisible Hand in Popular Culture: Liberty vs. Authority in American Film and TV* (Lexington: University Press of Kentucky, 2012), esp. the preface and ch. 6.

5. Michael Walzer, "The Civil Society Argument," in *Theorizing Citizenship*, ed. Ronald Beiner (Albany: State University of New York Press, 1995), 166.

6. Samuel Johnson, *Lives of the English Poets*, ed. Arthur Waugh (London: Oxford University Press, 1964), I, 109.

7. There is disagreement among critics concerning Mike's motivation. I am largely in agreement with Jans B. Wager that Mike is an "homme fatal after money, and only money." Jans B. Wager, *Dames in the Driver's Seat: Rereading Film Noir* (Austin: University of Texas Press, 2005), 64. Some critics, however, understand

the plot to be driven by more abstract concerns, such as "the impossibility of communication." Andrew Dickos writes, "Motive without personal motive here is accompanied by a second strategy of creating a quest without reference." Andrew Dickos, *Street with No Name: A History of the Classic American Film Noir* (Lexington: University Press of Kentucky, 2002), 134. Alain Silver discusses the diversity of interpretations among critics of the film in "*Kiss Me Deadly*: Evidence of a Style," in *Film Noir Reader*, eds. Alain Silver and James Ursini (New York: Limelight, 2006), 209–35.

8. The political perspective I have elaborated is distinctive of the film version of *Kiss Me Deadly*. Mickey Spillane's novel of 1951, on which the film is loosely based, derives from a populist sense of national politics and an earlier moment too. The novel has Mike driven by hate and anger, not by any desire for monetary gain. His crusade is against the Mafia, corrupter of civic life, and the grail sought is a cache of contraband drugs, not nuclear fuel. James Naremore says that censorship concerning drugs in movies required the reference to nuclear fuel, but this revision of the novel effectively evokes an international political context that subordinates the populism of the novel (Naremore, *More than Night*, 153). Moreover Mike and Pat Murphy collaborate freely and effectively in the novel. The cold war critique of libertarian individualism that I discuss is the product of the 1955 film directed by Robert Aldrich. A. I. Bezzerides wrote the screenplay from Spillane's novel. For a penetrating stylistic analysis of *Kiss Me Deadly*, see Silver, "*Kiss Me Deadly*," 208–35.

9. Hannah Arendt, *The Human Condition*, 2nd ed. (Chicago, IL: University of Chicago Press, 1998), 60. Arendt made the point that the transformation of the public realm into an administrative form of government was underway in the nineteenth century and completed in the postwar era.

10. Pippin, *Fatalism*, 46. Pippin nicely analyzes Jeff's contradictory statements in the negotiations with Baylord at the Sterling Club. Jeff is an incoherent character in the sense that he behaves in a contradictory fashion in particularly important contexts.

11. Edward Dimendberg notes quite accurately: "Although the literature on film noir emphasizes a sense of narrative foreboding and inescapable fate as defining traits of the film cycle, the significance of chance . . . appears no less crucial, if often undervalued. Chance meetings, unexpected coincidences, and empty streets pervade film noir no less than the atmosphere of overdetermination that allegedly dominates its stories." Edward Dimendberg, *Film Noir and the Spaces of Modernity* (Cambridge, MA: Harvard University Press, 2004), 135–36.

12. I owe this observation to the novelist Tom Lutz.

13. Jeff fails to get to Meta before the police do. He is late getting back to Eels's apartment to help Eels elude those trying to murder him. His timing was off, as he tells the cabbie. Later he is late getting back to Eels's apartment again to retrieve Eels's corpse. The police get there first. He is late as well getting back to Whit's Tahoe home to close his final deal with Whit. Kathie has already

murdered Whit and is ready to testify against Jeff for this murder too. The
revealing observation that "Jeff is in no hurry" is Chris Fujiwara's in *Jacques
Tourneur: The Cinema of Nightfall* (Baltimore, MD: Johns Hopkins University
Press, 1998), 146.

14. Arendt, *Human Condition*, 179. My understanding of *Out of the Past* has benefited directly from conversations with my colleagues Kelly Austin and Robert B.
Pippin.

Chapter 2

1. Russell Hardin, *Trust* (Cambridge, UK: Polity, 2006), 17.
2. Ibid., 1.
3. Ibid., 26. Annette C. Baier, *Moral Prejudices: Essays on Ethics* (Cambridge, MA:
Harvard University Press, 1995), 101. Baier has a subtler sense of the triad: she
proposes that a truster trusts a trustee with that which might be lost in case of
betrayal.
4. J. Edgar Hoover objected to the film because he thought that it might weaken
the political authority of friendly Latin American regimes if it were known
widely that the FBI collaborated with governments in Latin America. Tim
Weiner explains that the FBI expanded its agent staff rapidly and significantly in
1940, when Hoover managed to create the Special Intelligence Service without
Congressional appropriation or even knowledge. The objective of this agency
was to undermine Soviet efforts to establish itself in Central and South America. See Tim Weiner, *Enemies: A History of the FBI* (New York: Random House,
2012), 94–104, 145. Hoover ordered agents out of Latin America and the Carib-
bean on July 8, 1946. *Notorious* was released two months later.
5. Ingrid Bergman would receive much more attention from Joseph I. Breen and
the Production Code Administration after she completed *Joan of Arc* (1948).
When she left her husband and daughter to be with Roberto Rossellini, she was
the target of strenuous ethical criticism and professional attack. See Thomas
Doherty, *Hollywood's Censor: Joseph I. Breen and the Production Code Administration* (New York: Columbia University Press, 2007), 283–91.
6. Alfred Hitchcock, in *Alfred Hitchcock: Interviews*, ed. Sidney Gottlieb (Jackson:
University of Mississippi Press, 2003), 207.
7. Tania Modleski, *The Women Who Knew Too Much: Hitchcock and Feminist
Theory* (New York: Routledge, 1988), 67–68.
8. Baier, *Moral Prejudices*, 110.
9. Ibid., 101.
10. The plot of *Black Angel* (1946) provides a good point of comparison. Martin
Blair (Dan Duryea) and Catherine Bennett (June Vincent) collaborate to find the
real killer of Mavis Marlowe (Constance Dowling), Blair's ex-wife. Catherine
Bennett's husband, who had been having an affair with Marlowe, has been convicted of the murder. His wife is convinced of her unfaithful husband's

innocence. In fact, Martin Blair killed his ex-wife, though this is not revealed until near the end of the film. Blair, however, has not assisted Catherine Bennett in bad faith, as Dixon did. Blair killed his ex-wife in a drunken stupor and then suffered alcoholic amnesia, the film explains. He discovers his own memories of the crime on the eve of the execution of Kirk Bennett (John Phillips) and informs the police and Mrs. Bennett as soon as he can, and Kirk Bennett is pardoned by the governor. The psychological diagnosis of alcoholic amnesia is necessary to prevent viewers from feeling about Martin Blair as they might about Mark Dixon. Bad faith is an especially unattractive offense in contrast to the unswerving loyalty of Catherine Bennett.

11. John Kleinig, "Loyalty," *Stanford Encyclopedia of Philosophy* (Summer 2013). http://plato.Stanford.edu/entries/loyalty/. A comment by Robert B. Pippin showed me that this film is specifically oriented on loyalty. I have benefitted too from John Kleinig's article on loyalty.

12. See Graham Greene, "The Virtue of Disloyalty," in *The Portable Graham Greene*, ed. Philip Stratford (Harmondsworth, UK: Penguin, 1973), 606–10.

13. The privacy of trust is complicated. Criminal law protects spouses from incriminating testimony by their partners. The law recognizes, that is, a need to make some form of trust entirely private. Children can indeed testify against parents or siblings. The legal wall around private trust is very tightly drawn around a single family member.

14. See Dana Polan's commentary on *The Third Man* on the Criterion DVD of the film.

Chapter 3

1. Ralph Waldo Emerson, *The Collected Works*, ed. Alfred R. Ferguson and Jean Ferguson Carr (Cambridge, MA: Harvard University Press, 1979), II, 28 and 51.

2. Gerald Dworkin, *The Theory and Practice of Autonomy* (Cambridge, UK: Cambridge University Press, 1988), 13; Marilyn Friedman, *Autonomy, Gender, Politics* (New York: Oxford University Press, 2003), 12.

3. Marina Oshana, "How Much Should We Value Autonomy," in *Autonomy*, ed. Ellen Frankel Paul, Fred D. Miller, Jr., and Jeffrey Paul (Cambridge, UK: Cambridge University Press, 2003), 100.

4. Harry G. Frankfurt, *The Importance of What We Care About* (Cambridge, UK: Cambridge University Press, 1988), 12.

5. David A. J. Richards, "Rights and Autonomy," in *The Inner Citadel: Essays on Individual Autonomy*, ed. John Christman (New York: Oxford University Press, 1989), 212.

6. Pippin, *Fatalism*, 99.

7. Ibid., 39.

8. Ibid., 41.

9. John T. Irwin sees noir detectives as more exclusively *private* agents than I do. He has a revealing chapter devoted to the importance of self-employment in noir fiction and film, particularly in *The Big Sleep* (chapter two). Marlowe "is a *private* detective, hired by individuals, not by the public, to investigate what are often confidential matters and to keep the results of those inquiries private, a paid agent who must, in deciding on a course of action, weigh the often conflicting demands of loyalty to a client against the moral and legal responsibilities of citizenship" (Irwin, *Unless the Threat of Death*, 53–54). Irwin observes that this fierce devotion to private employment effectively destroys what would commonly be called Marlowe's private life (ibid., 52). I want to account for the sensitivity of noir inquirers to the partial coincidence of their interests and those of the state.

10. Ernst Bloch, *The Utopian Function of Art and Literature: Selected Essays*, trans. Jack Zipes and Frank Mecklenburg (Cambridge, MA: MIT Press, 1988), 118.

11. Michael Wood, *America in the Movies* (New York: Columbia University Press, 1989), 65. For commentary focused on female agency in noir, see the essays collected by E. Ann Kaplan in *Women in Film Noir*, 2nd ed. (London: BFI Publishing, 1998); Wager, *Dames in the Driver's Seat*; Elizabeth Cowie, "*Film Noir* and Women," in *Shades of Noir*, ed. Joan Copjec (London: Verso, 1993).

12. S. I. Benn, "Freedom, Autonomy, and the Concept of a Person," *Proceedings of the Aristotelian Society*, n.s., vol. 76 (1975–1976): 113.

13. In Chandler's novel, Marlowe inadvertently disabled his car near Art Huck's. See Raymond Chandler, *The Big Sleep & Farewell, My Lovely* (New York: Modern Library, 1995), 182.

14. Benn, "Freedom, Autonomy, and the Concept of a Person," 109.

15. Friedman, *Autonomy, Gender, Politics*, 5.

16. Benn, "Freedom, Autonomy, and the Concept of a Person," 126.

17. Friedman, *Autonomy, Gender, Politics*, 15.

18. Immanuel Kant, *Groundwork for the Metaphysics of Morals*, as cited by Paul Guyer, in "Kant on the Theory and Practice of Autonomy," in *Autonomy*, ed. Frankel Paul et al., 88.

19. I owe this insight to the poet Susan Hahn.

20. The second of these scenes, which is crucial to my argument, is Hawks's interpretation of a quite different scene in Chandler's novel, which has Eddie Mars's wife (not Vivian Sternwood) free Marlowe at Art Huck's.

In the 1945 version of *The Big Sleep* there was one other pair of matched scenes of Bogart and Bacall: her visits to his office. But for the 1946 version of the film her second visit, with a veiled face, was deleted.

21. This crucial scene between Vivian and Marlowe after leaving Art Huck's is not part of Chandler's novel. This scene and others were added to the film, as John T. Irwin observes, to exploit the publicity concerning the romance between

Humphrey Bogart and Lauren Bacall (see Irwin, *Unless the Threat of Death*, 229–39). This is to say that the film is thematically richer, with regard to trust, than the novel, and for adventitious reasons.

22. In book two of the *Rhetoric*, Aristotle argues that one trusts an individual's ethical character and expects it not to change, though the trustee's choices may chart different practical courses.

23. Howard Hawks, in *Howard Hawks: Interviews*, ed. Scott Breivold (Jackson: University Press of Mississippi, 2006), 30.

24. Irwin, *Unless the Threat of Death*, 234. John T. Irwin argues for the possibility that Owen Taylor's death was suicide. His point is that Chandler wanted to write a detective mystery that did not tie up all its loose ends. My view is that Joe Brody admits to knocking Taylor unconscious and stealing the photos of Carmen somewhere in Beverly Hills. The way Brody measures out admissions and shifts positions to evade Marlowe's gaze make it is easy to imagine further inquiry getting to an admission that he finished off Taylor, even though Chandler does say that Brody is not the killer type (and Carroll Lundgren is just that).

Chapter 5

1. Cowie, "*Film Noir* and Women," 122.

2. Ibid., 135.

3. Janey Place, "Women in Film Noir," 47. William Park writes, "In a significant number of film noirs, the main character is a woman. It is she who investigates, she who makes the false step, she who becomes tarnished, and in general follows the same pattern as the male protagonists." Park, *What is Film Noir*, 119.

4. Sheri Chinen Biesen, *Blackout: World War II and the Origins of Film Noir* (Baltimore, MD: Johns Hopkins University Press, 2005), 116–23.

5. James M. Cain, *The Postman Always Rings Twice* [1934], in *Crime Novels: American Noir of the 1930s and 40s*, ed. Robert Polito (New York: Library of America, 1997), 95.

6. It is not entirely clear that they have made love at all. In the voice-over Walter says rather that they held each other for a while. Walter's pause for a cigarette as Phyllis prepares to leave is the conventional postcoital marker, but the film is a little ambiguous on this score. Richard Schickel says that the absence of explicit sex scenes in James M. Cain's original text was "a defect, incidentally, that Wilder and Chandler, still operating after all under Production Code rules, never quite compensated for in their adaptation." Richard Schickel, *Double Indemnity* (London: BFI Publishing, 1992), 22. *Double Indemnity*, the novel, apparently began with a sentence in Cain's *The Postman Always Rings Twice* (1934), but the earlier novel is bold and direct in asserting the lust that binds Frank Chambers and Cora Smith. Cain wanted something altogether different for the characters of *Double Indemnity*. My sense is rather that Cain, Chandler, and Wilder all understood that eros was not Walter's most powerful motive.

However, for a psychoanalytic interpretation of the film that regards the "love scene" as a genuine violation of patriarchal order, see Claire Johnston, "Double Indemnity," in *Women in Film Noir*, 2nd ed., ed. E. Ann Kaplan (London: British Film Institute, 1980), 89–98.

7. Moreover sarcasm about noir short guys is traditional. In *The Big Sleep*, Carmen Sternwood remarks to Phillip Marlowe that he isn't very tall; he replies cleverly that he tries to be. Later Vivian Rutledge tells him that he looks a mess, when he is sweaty from his conversation with General Sternwood in the solarium; he tells her: "I'm not very tall either. Next time, I'll come on stilts." He gets some revenge by remarking much later to Harry Jones (Elisha Cook Jr.) that Harry's girlfriend Agnes Lowzier (Sonia Darrin) is "too big for you." "That's a dirty crack," Jones responded, and Marlowe agrees.

8. James Naremore suggests that Wilder and Chandler mean to show that "under modernity, lovemaking is reified and mechanical." Naremore, *More than Night*, 89. My sense is that, even under modernity, lovemaking has redeeming qualities. The shallowness of Walter and Phyllis's love seems particular to these characters.

9. Billy Wilder spoke of the Walter-Keyes relationship as "the love story in the picture," and, as Richard Schickel observes, "he was not exaggerating." Schickel, *Double Indemnity*, 50.

10. Billy Wilder, in a 1978 interview with John Allyn, in *Billy Wilder: Interviews*, ed. Robert Horton (Jackson: University Press of Mississippi, 2001), 136.

11. Joan Copjec provides a wonderfully suggestive interpretation of the role of statistics in noirs: "The Phenomenal Nonphenomenal: Private Space in *Film Noir*," in *Shades of Noir*, ed. Joan Copjec (London: Verso, 1993), 167–97.

12. "Spade agreed in a tone that was utterly meaningless" (18); "His face was stupid in its calmness" (23); "His face was expressionless" (28); "His yellow-gray eyes were hard and implacable" (42); "His eyes, holding no particular expression . . ." (47); "Spade, wooden of face" (71); "Spade's face was blank" (84); "The sight of his bloody hand brought not the least nor briefest of changes to Spade's face" (161); "'Sure,' he said absent-mindedly" (165); "his dispassionate glance" (189). Page numbers refer to Dashiell Hammett, *The Maltese Falcon* (New York: Everyman, 2000).

13. Hammett is explicit about this contradiction. Just after he learns of Miles's death, Sam tells Effie: "I think we've got a future. I always had an idea that if Miles would go off and die somewhere we'd stand a better chance of thriving. Will you take care of sending flowers for me?" (ibid., 44). At the very end, he tells Brigid that Miles "was a son of a bitch. I found that out the first week we were in business together and I meant to kick him out as soon as the year was up. You didn't do me a damned bit of harm by killing him" (ibid., 221).

14. Hammett has Sam tell Brigid, "Miles hadn't many brains" (ibid., 216; cf. 12).

15. At this point in the film, Brigid leans back, horizontal, and Sam bends down to kiss her. In the novel, this is their last exchange before they go to bed (ibid., 92).

16. Onora O'Neill, *A Question of Trust* (Cambridge, UK: Cambridge University Press, 2002), 70.

17. Ibid., 97.

18. Irwin, *Unless the Threat of Death*, 222–29. John T. Irwin gives a fine and comprehensive account of the threatricality of the entire film; my point concerns only the felt difference between Gutman's entourage and the other characters.

19. This is the richest speech in all the noirs. Bogart essentially gave it again (as Rip Murdock) in *Dead Reckoning*, but with a straightforwardly misogynistic point. He had already told Dusty (Lizabeth Scott), "I forgot to tell you: I don't trust anyone, especially women." (When he ends his speech in *Dead Reckoning*, Lizabeth Scott shoots him.) The misogyny of *Dead Reckoning* is always present in these films about women who cannot be trusted. Johnny Farrell in *Gilda* says that Ballin's cane knife is feminine rather than masculine because it appears to be a cane but is in fact a knife. That is apparently what noir men have against noir women: that they may appear to be what they are not, whereas men tend to be what they appear to be, as *The Narrow Margin* proposes.

20. Irwin, *Unless the Threat of Death*, 228.

21. Ibid., 2.

Chapter 6

1. T. S. Eliot, *The Complete Poems and Plays, 1909–1950* (New York: Harcourt, Brace & World, 1962), 49.

2. By 1954, if not sooner, severe punishment of male fantasies characterized a recognized subgenre of crime films. In *Black Widow* the accused murderer Peter Denver (Van Heflin) says that he was at a movie theater, watching *Girl in the Window*, at the time of the murder in question. Nunnally Johnson wrote the screenplays for *Woman in the Window* and *Black Widow*.

3. Ralph Waldo Emerson, "Self-Reliance," in *Collected Works*, ed. Joseph Slater (Cambridge, MA: Belknap, 1979), II, 35. There is a sense in which noirs appeal to the vestiges of Judeo-Christianity in the secular context of the 1940s and 1950s. The strict economy of violation and punishment has an enduring appeal. Robert B. Pippin observes that the fatalism so central to the noirs "is strange because we would normally assume that this concept of fate or destiny is relevant only on the assumption of certain religious views, as is especially clear in the context of ancient Greek epics and tragedies." Pippin, *Fatalism*, 16.

4. William Carlos Williams, "Asphodel, That Greeny Flower" in *The Collected Poems*, ed. Christopher MacGowan (New York: New Directions, 1988), II, 325.

5. Russell Hardin describes the encapsulated interest model in brief: "the right intentions on your part as a person we might trust are to want to take our interests (or possibly our welfare), as *our* interests, into account in your actions. You and we could have coincidental interests, so that, while acting in your own interests you happen also to serve ours." Hardin, *Trust*, 17.

6. Nicholas Ray's film is far superior to Hughes's novel of 1947. Edmund H. North, who adapted the novel, took great liberties with his source, as the plot's screenwriter Dix Steele takes creative liberties in adapting a weak novel to the film medium. Hughes's novel has Dix Steele as a serial killer. Its plot portrays primarily the efforts of police to solve these murders, and only secondarily on Dix's intense effort to make Laurel Gray the center of a new life after he spent one night with her.

7. Wallace Stevens, "Lebensweisheitspielerei," in *Collected Poems* (New York: Knopf, 1954), 504.

8. Ernst Bloch, "Can Hope Be Disappointed?" in *Literary Essays*, trans. Andrew Joron et al. (Stanford, CA: Stanford University Press, 1998), 344.

Chapter 7

1. Irwin, *Unless the Threat of Death*, 39, 52, 58.

2. Quoted in Philip Agee, *Inside the Company: CIA Diary* (New York: Stonehill, 1975), 9.

3. Robert Baer, *See No Evil: The True Story of a Ground Soldier in the CIA's War on Terrorism* (New York: Three Rivers, 2002), 26.

4. T. S. Eliot, quoted in Frank Kermode, *The Classic: Literary Images of Permanence and Change* (New York: Viking, 1975), 15.

5. See the CIA website, under Vision, Mission, Ethos, and Challenges: https:// www.cia.gov/about-cia/cia-vision-mission-values.

6. Catherine Seelye, ed., *Charles Olson and Ezra Pound: An Encounter at St. Elizabeth's* (New York: Grossman, 1975), 24.

7. For an instance of the counter notion—intelligence agents as team players—see the BBC series *MI-5*.

8. The suicide letter from Thomas Wilson, Edward's father, addressed to his "dear family," is handwritten on personal stationery with the name of the father at the top. Or, rather, almost at the top: over the name is a little clipper ship.

9. Tom Mangold discusses Angleton's family life but with far less particularity than the film does; see his *Cold Warrior: The CIA's Master Spy Hunter* (New York: Simon and Schuster, 1991).

10. Ibid., 299.

11. Bernard Williams, *Truth and Truthfulness: An Essay in Genealogy* (Princeton, NJ: Princeton University Press, 2002), 6.

12. The Guatemalan coup of 1954 is represented as originating much earlier, in 1947; the actual timeline of the events is inessential to the film as fable. For instance, in the summer of 1960, a few months before the inauguration of John Kennedy, Eisenhower gave an order to the CIA to eliminate Patrice Lumumba from three decades of rule in the Congo. The film makes no direct reference to this CIA adventure that was being planned at the same time as the Bay of Pigs invasion (which *is* a crucial part of the plot of the film). Nonetheless Lumumba

is symbolically present insofar as Junior is in Leopoldville, Congo, when he betrays his father's confidence concerning the timing and location of the Bay of Pigs adventure. Edward and Ulysses meet in the love nest, but why was Junior, the aspiring CIA agent, in the Congo? Because the CIA was there to overthrow Lumumba.

13. The CIA was recently sued for noncompliance with the Freedom of Information Act. The agency compiled a five-volume history of the Bay of Pigs Invasion but has released only one of the five. *Los Angeles Times*, April 14, 2011.

14. James C. Scott, *Seeing Like a State: How Certain Schemes to Improve the Human Condition Have Failed* (New Haven, CT: Yale University Press, 1998), 22. Scott writes, "No administrative system is capable of representing *any* existing social community except through a heroic and greatly schematized process of abstraction and simplification."

15. Robert Bly, "The Teeth Mother Naked at Last," in *Sleepers Joining Hands* (New York: Harper and Row, 1973), 21.

16. Mearsheimer, quoted in Martin Jay, *The Virtues of Mendacity: On Lying in Politics* (Charlottesville: University of Virginia Press, 2010), 140. Bernard Williams asserts the same starting point: "No one can expect a government to make full disclosure about everything, and often it is unclear anyway what full disclosure would be. It is equally undesirable that they should be able to get away with anything they like in order to deceive the public" (*Truth and Truthfulness*, 109).

17. Jay, *The Virtues of Mendacity*, 172. Sissela Bok observes that "some experienced public officials . . . argue that vital objectives in the national interest require a measure of deception to succeed in the face of powerful obstacles. Negotiations must be carried on that are best left hidden from public view; bargains must be struck that simply cannot be comprehended by a politically unsophisticated electorate." Sissela Bok, *Lying: Moral Choice in Public and Private Life* (New York: Random House, 1978), 168–69. The pragmatic justification of political mendacity is asserted not only by public officials. Political scientists, historians, and philosophers do not have a clear account of where in political discourse candor is properly to be expected.

18. Jay, *The Virtues of Mendacity*, 173.

19. Bernard Williams says that "One relationship that by its nature excludes deceit is agency, in the sense of an agent's doing things on behalf of or in place of a principal, things that the principal is poorly placed, for instance, or too occupied to do for himself." Williams, *Truth and Truthfulness*, 210.

20. Tim Weiner, *Legacy of Ashes: The History of the CIA* (New York: Anchor, 2008), 158.

21. Max Weber, *Political Writings*, eds. Peter Lassman and Ronald Speirs (Cambridge, UK: Cambridge University Press, 1994), 311.

22. Robert Hass, *Time and Materials: Poems 1997–2005* (New York: HarperCollins, 2007), 66.

23. Tim Weiner reports that CIA director George Tenet was reluctant to approve an

assassination attempt on Osama bin Laden very shortly before September 11, 2001 (*Legacy of Ashes*, 554).

24. Robert Bly, *Sleepers Joining Hands* (New York: Harper and Row, 1973), 21.

25. Kai Bird, *The Good Spy: The Life and Death of Robert Ames* (New York: Crown, 2014), esp. 192–94. This excellent study of the life and work of CIA agent Robert Ames makes it difficult to generalize about what the CIA neglects. Ames maintained his commitment to those who provided him information, even when contact with them was explicitly forbidden by the agency. He worked closely with Ali Hassan Salameh (and consulted with Yasir Arafat) when contact with the PLO was strenuously forbidden by the Carter administration. Ames too was the CIA and would have understood well the appeal of the character Ferris.

Chapter 8

1. Quoted in Garry Wills, *John Wayne's America* (New York: Simon and Schuster, 1997), 59.

2. Weiner, *Legacy of Ashes*, 275, 377.

3. Tim Weiner's history of the CIA is entitled *A Legacy of Ashes* because the agency's positive achievements have been so meager.

4. Robert Baer, *See No Evil*, 4, 41.

5. Ibid., 267.

6. Ezra Pound, *The Cantos* (New York: New Directions, 1970), 59.

7. Cited as an epigraph by Tim Weiner, *Legacy of Ashes*.

8. See Mark Mazzetti, *The Way of the Knife* (New York: Penguin, 2013) on recent US covert interventions.

9. On the failure of civilian oversight of the CIA, Tim Weiner cites the 9/11 Commission (2004) but in a larger context: "The commission correctly described congressional oversight of intelligence as 'dysfunctional.' . . . For years, there had been next to no engagement on the life-and-death issues that confronted the CIA by House and Senate intelligence committees. . . . A quarter of a century of congressional oversight had produced little of lasting value. The intelligence committees and their staffs had applied an occasional public whipping and a patchwork of quick fixes for ever-present problems." Weiner, *Legacy of Ashes*, 578.

10. Georg Lukács, *The Historical Novel*, trans. Hannah and Stanley Mitchell (Boston, MA: Beacon, 1963), 33.

11. Walter Sinnott-Armstrong offers this definition: "*Act consequentialism* is the claim that an act is morally right if and only if that act maximizes the good, that is, if and only if the total amount of good for all minus the total amount of bad for all is greater than this net amount for any incompatible act available to the agent on that occasion. . . . *Hedonism* then claims that pleasure is the only intrinsic good and that pain is the only intrinsic bad. Together these

claims imply that an act is morally right if and only if that act causes 'the greatest happiness for the greatest number,' as the common slogan says." "Consequentialism," in *Stanford Encyclopedia of Philosophy*, Spring 2014 edition, accessed April 23, 2015. http://plato.stanford.edu/archives/spr2014/entries/consequentialism/.

12. Thomas Nagel, "Ruthlessness in Public Life," in *Mortal Questions* (Cambridge, UK: Cambridge University Press, 1991), 89.

13. For a clear distinction of the function of explanation from that of justification, see Christine M. Korsgaard, et al., *The Sources of Normativity*, ed. Onora O'Neill (Cambridge: Cambridge University Press, 1996), 10–18. I am extending her analysis to ideological contest.

14. Cited by Igor Primoratz in "Terrorism," *Stanford Encyclopedia of Philosophy*, Spring 2015 edition, accessed April 23, 2015. http://plato.stanford.edu/archives/spr2015/entries/terrorism/.

15. Nagel, "Ruthlessness in Public Life," 75.

16. Ibid., 77, 80.

17. Ibid., 82.

18. Michael Walzer, "Political Action: The Problem of Dirty Hands," in *War and Moral Responsibility: A Philosophy and Public Affairs Reader*, ed. Marshall Cohen (Princeton, NJ: Princeton University Press, 1974), 64.

19. Ibid., 69–70.

20. Ibid., 65–66.

21. Ibid., 72.

22. Bernard Williams, *Moral Luck* (Cambridge, UK: Cambridge University Press, 1981), 60.

23. Ibid., 62.

24. Walzer, "Political Action," 65.

25. In *Body of Lies*, Ferris executes a low-level jihadist on a crowded street in Amman, Jordan. Three years later Raymond Davis, then a CIA employee, shot two young Pakistani men on a crowded street in Lahore, Pakistan. Davis may have been trying to protect the confidentiality of his own activities, though his motives are not known with any certainty. For accounts of this notorious case, see Mazzetti, *The Way of the Knife*, 1–6, 257–77; and Jeremy Scahill, *Dirty Wars*: The World Is a Battlefield (New York: Nation Books, 2013), 403–7, 414–29. Scahill remarks: "Whatever Davis was doing and for whom he was doing it . . . what happened that day was straight out of a spy movie" (418).

26. Michael Walzer observes that the problem of dirty hands is not exclusively political, though it is especially clear for politicians: "No doubt we can get our hands dirty in private life also. . . . But the issue is posed most dramatically in politics for the three reasons that make political life the kind of life it is, because we claim to act for others but also serve ourselves, rule over others, and use violence against them." Walzer, "Political Action," 76.

Conclusion

1. Michael Denning provides an insightful account of the public/private distinction in *Cover Stories: Narrative and Ideology in the British Spy Thriller* (London: Routledge and Kegan Paul, 1987), 130–34.
2. T. S. Eliot, *Selected Essays* (New York: Harcourt, Brace and World, 1960), 5.
3. Philip Green, *Cracks in the Pedestal: Ideology and Gender in Hollywood* (Amherst: University of Massachusetts Press, 1998), 6; cited approvingly by Wager, *Dames in the Driver's Seat*, 1, 3. Wager goes on to say that "the capitalist patriarchy—even the white supremacist capitalist patriarchy—determines all film form" (6).
4. Steven Spielberg, introduction to *Munich* on the DVD.
5. Raymond Geuss, *Public Goods, Private Goods* (Princeton, NJ: Princeton University Press, 2001), 106. He goes on to ask "*Why* exactly do we want to distinguish private and public? . . . The reason we will use will be a contextually located human power, not some abstract faculty of reading off the moral demands of the universe from the facts of the case" (113).
6. See Julian Assange, *Cypherpunks: Freedom and the Future of the Internet* (New York: OR Books, 2012), 5.

INDEX